Hawai'i Legal Research

Daniel Han

CAROLINA ACADEMIC PRESS
LEGAL RESEARCH SERIES

Tenielle Fordyce-Ruff, Series Editor
Suzanne E. Rowe, Series Editor Emerita

❧

Arizona, Fourth Edition — Tamara S. Herrera
Arkansas, Second Edition — Coleen M. Barger, Cheryl L. Reinhart & Cathy L. Underwood
California, Fourth Edition — Aimee Dudovitz, Sarah Laubach & Suzanne E. Rowe
Colorado, Second Edition — Robert Michael Linz
Connecticut — Jessica G. Hynes
Federal, Second Edition — Mary Garvey Algero, Spencer L. Simons, Suzanne E. Rowe, Scott Childs & Sarah E. Ricks
Florida, Fifth Edition — Barbara J. Busharis, Anne E. Mullins & Suzanne E. Rowe
Georgia — Nancy P. Johnson, Elizabeth G. Adelman & Nancy J. Adams
Hawai'i — Victoria Szymczak, Cory Lenz & Roberta Woods
Idaho, Third Edition — Tenielle Fordyce-Ruff
Illinois, Second Edition — Mark E. Wojcik
Iowa, Second Edition — John D. Edwards, Karen L. Wallace & Melissa H. Weresh
Kansas — Joseph A. Custer & Christopher L. Steadham
Kentucky, Second Edition — William A. Hilyerd, Kurt X. Metzmeier & David J. Ensign
Louisiana, Fourth Edition — Mary Garvey Algero
Massachusetts, Second Edition — E. Joan Blum & Shaun B. Spencer
Michigan, Fourth Edition — Cristina D. Lockwood
Minnesota — Suzanne Thorpe
Mississippi — Kristy L. Gilliland
Missouri, Fourth Edition — Wanda M. Temm & Julie M. Cheslik
New York, Fourth Edition — Elizabeth G. Adelman, Courtney L. Selby, Brian Detweiler & Kathleen Darvil
North Carolina, Third Edition — Brenda D. Gibson, Julie L. Kimbrough, Laura P. Graham & Nichelle J. Perry
North Dakota — Anne E. Mullins & Tammy Pettinato Oltz
Ohio, Second Edition — Sara Sampson, Katherine L. Hall & Carolyn Broering-Jacobs
Oklahoma — Darin K. Fox, Darla W. Jackson & Courtney L. Selby
Oregon, Fourth Edition, Revised Printing — Suzanne E. Rowe & Megan Austin
Pennsylvania, Second Edition — Barbara J. Busharis, Catherine M. Dunn, Bonny L. Tavares & Carla P. Wale
Tennessee, Second Edition — Scott Childs, Sibyl Marshall & Carol McCrehan Parker
Texas, Second Edition — Spencer L. Simons
Washington, Second Edition — Julie A. Heintz-Cho, Tom Cobb & Mary A. Hotchkiss
West Virginia, Second Edition — Hollee Schwartz Temple
Wisconsin — Patricia Cervenka & Leslie Behroozi
Wyoming, Second Edition — Debora A. Person & Tawnya K. Plumb

❧

Hawai'i Legal Research

Victoria Szymczak
Cory Lenz
Roberta Woods

Tenielle Fordyce-Ruff, Series Editor
Suzanne E. Rowe, Series Editor Emerita

Carolina Academic Press
Durham, North Carolina

Copyright © 2022
Carolina Academic Press, LLC
All Rights Reserved.

Library of Congress Cataloging-in-Publication Data

Names: Szymczak, Victoria, author. | Lenz, Cory, author. | Woods, Roberta, author.
Title: Hawaii legal research / Victoria Szymczak, Cory Lenz, Roberta Woods.
Description: Durham, North Carolina : Carolina Academic Press, 2021. | Series: Legal research series
Identifiers: LCCN 2021018357 (print) | LCCN 2021018358 (ebook) | ISBN 9781531017149 (paperback) | ISBN 9781531019402 (ebook)
Subjects: LCSH: Legal research—Hawaii.
Classification: LCC KFH75 .S99 2021 (print) | LCC KFH75 (ebook) | DDC 340.72/0969—dc23
LC record available at https://lccn.loc.gov/2021018357
LC ebook record available at https://lccn.loc.gov/2021018358

Carolina Academic Press
700 Kent Street
Durham, North Carolina 27701
(919) 489-7486
www.cap-press.com

Printed in the United States of America.

Summary of Contents

List of Tables and Figures	xiii
Preface	xix
Series Note	xxi
Chapter 1 · Research Process and Strategies	3
Chapter 2 · Overview of the Hawaiian Legal System and Its Origins	19
Chapter 3 · The Constitution	29
Chapter 4 · Researching Kānaka Maoli (Native Hawaiian) Custom and Law	55
Chapter 5 · Secondary Sources	61
Chapter 6 · The Judiciary and Case Reporters	85
Chapter 7 · Using and Finding Cases	99
Chapter 8 · Statutes	131
Chapter 9 · Hawaiʻi Legislative History	159
Chapter 10 · Administrative Law	183
Chapter 11 · Legal Citation	207
Appendix 1: Sample Research Plan	237
Appendix 2: Common Boolean Search Connectors	241
Appendix 3: Citator Symbols	245
Index	247

Contents

List of Tables and Figures	xiii
Preface	xix
Series Note	xxi
Chapter 1 · Research Process and Strategies	**3**
I. Introduction	3
II. Creating a Research Plan	5
A. Checklist for Developing a Research Plan and Log	5
B. Develop Search Terms and Create Search Phrases	6
C. Building a Research Plan and Log	11
1. Identify Secondary Authorities	12
2. Identify Primary Authorities—Statutes and Legislation	12
3. Identify Primary Authorities—Cases	13
4. Identify Primary Authorities —Regulations	13
D. Using a Citator to Update and Verify the Law	13
E. Become Familiar with the West Digest Topic and Key Number System or Topics on Lexis	15
F. How to Use This Book	18
Chapter 2 · Overview of the Hawaiian Legal System and Its Origins	**19**
I. Introduction	19
II. Approaching Your Research for the Different Eras of Governance	24
A. Territorial Era Research (July 7, 1898–Aug. 20, 1959)	25
B. Martial Law (Dec. 7, 1941–Oct. 24, 1944)	26
C. Statehood Research (Aug. 21, 1959–present)	27

Chapter 3 · The Constitution — 29
  I. Introduction — 29
  II. History of the Hawai'i Constitution — 30
   A. Kingdom of Hawai'i — 30
   B. Republic and Territory — 34
   C. Statehood — 35
  III. Finding and Searching Within the Hawai'i Constitutions — 37
   A. Using a Checklist as a Roadmap for Researching Constitutional Law — 37
   B. Finding Relevant Constitutional Provisions in the Print and Electronic Platforms — 39
   C. Using the Annotations in the Print and Electronic Platforms — 43
  IV. Updating the Constitution of the State of Hawai'i — 50
  V. Interpreting the Constitution of the State of Hawai'i — 51

Chapter 4 · Researching *Kānaka Maoli* (Native Hawaiian) Custom and Law — 55
  I. Introduction — 55
  II. Checklist for Researching Native Hawaiian Custom and Law — 55
  III. Native Hawaiian Law, a Treatise — 56

Chapter 5 · Secondary Sources — 61
  I. Introduction — 61
  II. What Are Secondary Sources? — 61
  III. Features of and Tips for Finding Secondary Sources Online — 62
  IV. Types of Secondary Sources — 63
   A. Finding Aids — 63
    1. Legal Encyclopedias — 64
    2. *American Law Reports* (A.L.R.s) — 69
   B. Highly Persuasive Secondary Authorities — 71
    1. Law Review and Law Journal Articles — 71
    2. Dictionaries — 72
    3. Treatises — 74
    4. Restatements and Principles of the Law — 75
     a. Restatements — 75
     b. Principles of the Law — 77

	C. Practitioner Aids	77
	1. Hawaiʻi Specific Practitioner Aids published by the Hawaiʻi State Bar Association	77
	2. Pattern Jury Instructions: Hawaiʻi and Ninth Circuit	78
	3. General Practice Aids	79
	a. Am Jur Proof of Facts (POF)	79
	b. Am Jur Trials	80
	c. Causes of Action	80
	d. Federal Practice and Procedure (Wright and Miller)	80
	e. Moore's Federal Practice	81
	f. Weinstein's Federal Evidence (Weinstein's)	81
	4. Current Awareness Resources	81
	V. Using Subject Oriented Approaches on Bloomberg Law, Lexis, and Westlaw	82
	VI. Locating Additional Secondary Sources	83
	VII. Updating Secondary Sources	83

Chapter 6 · The Judiciary and Case Reporters — 85

	I. The Hawaiʻi Courts	85
	A. Introduction	85
	B. The Appellate Courts of the State of Hawaiʻi	86
	C. The Trial Level Courts of the State of Hawaiʻi	87
	D. The Specialized Courts of the State of Hawaiʻi	87
	II. The Federal Courts	89
	III. Case Reporters	90
	A. Reported v. Unreported Opinions	90
	B. State Case Reporters	92
	1. Official Reporters	92
	2. Unofficial Regional Reporters	95
	3. *Hawaiʻi Legal Reporter*	96
	C. Federal Case Reporters	97
	D. Updates to Case Reporters	98

Chapter 7 · Using and Finding Cases — 99

	I. Introduction	99
	II. The Structure of a Judicial Opinion	99
	A. Parts of a Judicial Opinion	100

III. Weight of Case Law Authority	105
A. Similarity of Cases	105
B. Binding and Persuasive Authority	105
C. State Law in Federal Court	106
IV. Case Finding	106
A. West Digests Topic and Key Numbers	107
1. Print Research Using the West Digest Topic and Key Number System	107
B. Online Methods for Finding Relevant Cases	111
1. Finding Case Law on Westlaw	111
C. Keyword Searching in Case Law Databases	112
D. Chasing Headnotes	117
V. Using Citators to Update, Verify, and Find More Authorities	120
A. Is It Still "Good Law"?	120
B. Citators for Cases	121
1. Shepard's Citator Service	122
2. KeyCite	126
3. B-Cite	128
Chapter 8 · Statutes	**131**
I. Introduction	131
II. Hawai'i State Statutes	131
A. Hawai'i Revised Statutes Online	136
III. Understanding the Statute — Anatomy of a Statute and the Statutory Scheme	138
A. Search Strategies for Hawai'i Statutes	140
1. Citation Method	140
2. Index Method	140
3. Definition Method	143
4. Popular Name Method	143
5. Topical or Analytic Method	144
6. Keyword Method	144
B. Finding Relevant Cases and Secondary Authorities Discussing a Statute	144
C. Temporary Laws	146
D. Federal Statutes	148

E. Using Citators in Your Statutory Research	152
1. Validating Statutes	152
2. Using a Citator to Update Your Research	156

Chapter 9 · Hawai'i Legislative History   159

- I. Introduction   159
  - A. Legislative Journals   161
- II. The Four Steps to Determine Legislative Intent   161
  - A. Step 1 — Get the statute's history in the *Hawai'i Revised Statutes*   162
  - B. Step 2 — Find the bill number and committee report numbers in the session laws   163
  - C. Step 3 H & S — Locate Committee Reports (House and Senate Journals)   167
  - D. Step 4 H & S — Check for debates or additional information spoken in chamber in the journals   170
- III. Keeping Track of Your Research   179
- IV. Conducting Earlier Legislative History Research (Pre-1984)   180
- V. Directory of Images for Hawai'i Legislative History   180

Chapter 10 · Administrative Law   183

- I. Introduction   183
- II. Hawai'i Administrative Law Research   184
  - A. Identify the Enabling Act and Implicating Acts   184
  - B. Finding Hawai'i Agency Rules   185
    - 1. Access the Lt. Governor's Website and Review the Agency Website   186
    - 2. Search in the Hawai'i Administrative Code with Lexis and Westlaw   189
    - 3. Use the Hawai'i Government Register   191
  - C. Finding Hawai'i Agency Decisions and Attorney General Opinions   193
- III. Federal Administrative Law Research   197
  - A. Finding Federal Agency Regulations   197
  - B. Updating with the Federal Register   202
  - C. Finding Federal Agency Decisions and Attorney General Opinions   205

Chapter 11 · Legal Citation	207
I. Introduction to the *Bluebook*	207
II. *Bluebook* and Local Rules for Citing Hawai'i Legal Authority in Legal Documents	209
A. Constitutional Law	214
B. Statutory Law	215
1. Print Statutory Compilations	215
2. *Id.* and Modified Short Forms	217
3. Online and Electronic Statutory Compilations	219
4. Hawai'i Distinctions	220
C. Administrative Law	221
D. Case Law	222
1. Individuals	223
2. Businesses	224
3. Government Agencies	224
4. Geographic Location as the Named Party	225
5. Court Location and Year Parenthetical	226
6. *Id.* and Modified Short Forms	227
7. Procedural Phrases	228
8. Parentheticals and Subsequent History	229
9. Citing Other State Cases and Federal Cases	229
E. Secondary Sources	230
III. Citing Hawai'i Legal Authority in Scholarship	232
Appendix 1: Sample Research Plan	237
Appendix 2: Common Boolean Search Connectors	241
Appendix 3: Citator Symbols	245
Index	247

List of Tables and Figures

Table 1-1. Developing Search Terms Example	6
Table 1-2. Using Root Expanders Example	7
Table 1-3. Understanding Proximity Connectors	8
Table 1-4. Using Proximity Connectors	9
Table 1-5. Adding Jurisdictions to Search Terms	10
Table 1-6. Adding a 'Why' to Search Terms	11
Table 2-1. Historical Compilation of Codes and Statutes	20
Table 2-2. Index Volumes for the Hawai'i Revised Statutes	28
Table 3-1. Checklist for Constitutional Law Research	37
Table 4-1. Example of Research Log for Native Hawaiian Topic	57
Table 5-1. Preliminary Research Plan for Attractive Nuisance	65
Table 5-2. Developed Research Plan with Secondary Sources	68
Table 5-3. Dictionaries	73
Table 6-1. Chart of Hawai'i Judiciary	86
Table 6-2. Timeline of Case Reporting for Different Eras of Governance	94
Table 6-3. West's Regional Reporters	96
Table 8-1. Features of the Hawai'i Revised Statutes Online	135
Table 8-2. Index Volumes to the Hawai'i Revised Statutes	142
Table 9-1. Post 1984 Hawai'i Legislative History Checklist	159
Table 9-2. Source Note Abbreviations	163
Table 9-3. 1986 Hawai'i Legislative History Aloha Spirit Law HRS 5-7.5	179
Table 9-4. Directory of Figures 9-1 to 9-24 with Steps and Resource	180
Table 10-1. Coverage of Hawai'i Administrative Decisions on Westlaw and Lexis	195

Table 11-1. Typeface and Capitalization Requirements for
    Non-Academic and Academic Citations 208
Table 11-2. Types of Citations 211
Table 11-3. Signal Order 213
Table 11-4. Short Citation Form, Constitutions 214
Table 11-5. Statutory Supplements in a Full Citation 217
Table 11-6. Short Citation Forms, Hawaiʻi Statutory Law 218
Table 11-7. Full Citation and Modified Short Forms,
    Hawaiʻi Administrative Rules 221
Table 11-8. Court Location for Pre-Statehood Hawaiʻi Case
    Law Citations 226
Table 11-9. Full Citation and Short Forms, Outside States
    and Federal Case Law 229
Table 11-10. Full Citation and Short Forms, Secondary Sources 231
Table 11-11. Non-Academic Versus Academic Citations 233

Figure 1-1. Showing a Link to a Topic Summary on Lexis from a Case 17
Figure 1-2. Lexis Topic Summary Report Example 17
Figure 1-3. Westlaw—Search Tips 18
Figure 3-1. Constitutional Convention Journals 42
Figure 3-2. Citing References for Article XII, Section 7 of the Hawaiʻi
    Constitution 45
Figure 3-3. Filtering by Relevant Key Numbers to Narrow Results 47
Figure 3-4. Searching Within the Citing References 49
Figure 5-1. Am Jur 2d Section 295 66
Figure 5-2. Am Jur 2d Cross References to Other Resources 67
Figure 5-3. Example of an A.L.R. Article 70
Figure 5-4. Example of a Rule in the Restatement (Second) of
    Torts Displayed on Westlaw 76
Figure 6-1. Example from Volume 1 Hawaiʻi Reports 93
Figure 7-1. Example of a Case from the Hawaiʻi Reports 100
Figure 7-2. Example of Digest Topics in Print 108
Figure 7-3. Example of Key Numbers in Print Digest 108
Figure 7-4. Example of a Case Annotation in a Print Digest 109
Figure 7-5. Entry in the Descriptive Word Index for Mistake 110
Figure 7-6. Example of Key Number Search Results with Filters 111
Figure 7-7. Example of Key Numbers on Westlaw 112

Figure 7-8. Searching for Key Numbers on Westlaw	113
Figure 7-9. Search Results from Key Number Search on Westlaw	113
Figure 7-10. Lexis Filters for Case Law	116
Figure 7-11. Westlaw Filters for Case Law	116
Figure 7-12. Example of Headnotes on Westlaw with Key Numbers	118
Figure 7-13. Example of Headnotes on Lexis	119
Figure 7-14. Example of Points of Law on Bloomberg Law	120
Figure 7-15. Case on Lexis with Shepard's Signals	123
Figure 7-16. Shepard's Report	124
Figure 7-17. Shepard's Grid View for Headnotes	125
Figure 7-18. Example of Direct History of a Case in Shepard's	126
Figure 7-19. KeyCite Ribbon	126
Figure 7-20. Graphical View of Direct History in KeyCite	127
Figure 7-21. Example of B-Cite on Bloomberg Law	129
Figure 8-1. Hawai'i Revised Statutes (Official)	133
Figure 8-2. Bloomberg Law Editorial Enhancements	134
Figure 8-3. Lexis Editorial Enhancements	134
Figure 8-4. Westlaw Editorial Enhancements	135
Figure 8-5. Bloomberg Law Example of Statutory Scheme	136
Figure 8-6. Lexis Example of Statutory Scheme	137
Figure 8-7. Westlaw Example of Statutory Scheme	137
Figure 8-8. 6D Statutory Scheme	138
Figure 8-9. Lexis Statutory Example	140
Figure 8-10. Official Index	142
Figure 8-11. Westlaw Index	143
Figure 8-12. Hawai'i Revised Statutes (Official) Example of a Case Annotation	145
Figure 8-13. Hawai'i Revised Statutes (Westlaw) Example of a Case Annotation	146
Figure 8-14. Hawai'i Revised Statutes (Lexis) Example of a Case Annotation	146
Figure 8-15. Tables of Disposition	147
Figure 8-16. Table of Disposition Showing Omitted Section	148
Figure 8-17. Identifying Parts of a Federal Statute	151
Figure 8-18. Shepard's Flag	153
Figure 8-19. Shepard's Report	153
Figure 8-20. KeyCite Flag	154

Figure 8-21. KeyCite Report	154
Figure 8-22. Shepard's Comprehensive Report for Statutes	155
Figure 8-23. KeyCite Filters for Statutes	156
Figure 9-1. Hawaiʻi State Legislature Website	164
Figure 9-2. Link to Finding Committee Reports Table	164
Figure 9-3. Committee Reports Table Headers	165
Figure 9-4. Act 202 Committee Reports	165
Figure 9-5. Showing Act 202 of the 1986 Session Laws of Hawaiʻi	166
Figure 9-6. Link to Senate Pages	167
Figure 9-7. Link to Senate Journals by Year	168
Figure 9-8. Link to Committee Reports (Senate Journal) & Showing Legislative Day and Date	168
Figure 9-9. Senate Standing Committee Report 833-86	170
Figure 9-10. Link to History of Bills (Senate Journal)	171
Figure 9-11. 1986 Senate Journal, Page 377	171
Figure 9-12. History of HB 2569-86 Also Called the Index	172
Figure 9-13. 1986 Senate Journal, Page 392	172
Figure 9-14. 1986 Senate Journal, Page 519	173
Figure 9-15. 1986 Senate Journal, Page 545	173
Figure 9-16. Link to House of Representatives Site	174
Figure 9-17. Link to House Journals by Year	174
Figure 9-18. Link to House Journal Committee Reports & Front Section	175
Figure 9-19. House Standing Committee Report 399-86	175
Figure 9-20. Link to History of House Bills	176
Figure 9-21. History of HB 2569-86 in House Journal — These Are Page Numbers in the Journal Section	176
Figure 9-22. House Journal, Page 293 with Report and Legislative Day	177
Figure 9-23. Finding the Date for the Legislative Day	177
Figure 9-24. House Journal, Page 334 — Beginning of Discussion and Debate	178
Figure 10-1. Regulations Citing the Relevant Enabling and Implicating Statutes	185
Figure 10-2. Locating the Enabling and Implicating Statutes via the Relevant Rule	188

Figure 10-3. Searching the Hawaiʻi Administrative Rules on Lexis	190
Figure 10-4. Searching Proposed and Final Rules	192
Figure 10-5. Searching and Browsing the CFR Online	199
Figure 10-6. Parallel Table of Authorities	200
Figure 10-7. Authority and Federal Register Source for CFR Title 14, Part 77 (showing various sections)	201
Figure 10-8. CFR Sections Affected	203
Figure 10-9. CFR Parts Affected in the Federal Register	204
Figure 11-1. Anatomy of a Full Citation to the Hawaiʻi Constitution	214
Figure 11-2. Anatomy of a Full Citation to Hawaiʻi Statutory Law	215
Figure 11-3. Anatomy of a Full Citation to Hawaiʻi Statutory Law from an Electronic Database	219
Figure 11-4. Anatomy of a Full Citation to Hawaiʻi Case Law	223

Preface

The target audience for this book is law students who are learning about the legal authorities in Hawaiʻi and how to research legal issues. Others who are researching the law in this jurisdiction, or need to understand how legal information is arranged in Hawaiʻi, will also benefit from this publication. Throughout this book, we provide suggestions on how to research legal issues and identify specific resources where you can locate the information needed to form a legal analysis. We also offer suggestions on how to plan and keep track of your research as you learn more about the legal issues that you research. The significance of Hawaiʻi's unique legal history plays an important role in this jurisdiction. Where appropriate we provide an overview of how that history interfaces with researchers today.

Writing a book like this is a collaborative effort. In deciding how to approach the organization of the book, we chose to focus chapters on specific types of resources while attempting to illustrate how these resources integrate with each other when conducting a research project. Many of the tables and recommendations we make are a direct result of teaching a course on legal research collaboratively at the William S. Richardson School of Law, University of Hawaiʻi at Mānoa. There are many aspects of legal research that are unique to the State of Hawaiʻi. This is the first attempt at capturing and explaining legal research in this jurisdiction with specificity.

While writing this book, we all took primary responsibility for specific chapters and as our editor, Tenielle Fordyce-Ruff, guided us through the process, some of our chapters merged into others or resulted in new chapters. We are grateful for her expertise and patience as we proceeded. Vicki Szymczak spearheaded the project and is responsible for the chapters on Secondary Sources, The Judiciary and Case Reporters, Using and Finding

Cases as well as the material in the Appendices which are used in her legal research classes. She also contributed to the first chapter on Research Process and Strategies; however, Roberta Woods's steady hand maintained principal responsibility for that chapter. Roberta Woods's expertise in Hawaiian law is reflected in the Overview of the Hawaiian Legal System, Researching Kānaka Maoli (Native Hawaiian) Custom and Law, Hawaiʻi State Statutes and Hawaiʻi Legislative History. Cory Lenz took responsibility for writing the chapter on the Hawaiʻi Constitution, Administrative Law, and Legal Citation. In particular, the chapters on the Overview, Kānaka Maoli Custom and Law, the Constitution, and Finding Case Law should be read together when researching problems that have their solutions rooted in pre-statehood authorities.

In the native Hawaiian language, the phrase "many hands working together" is expressed by the word laulima. Without all of us working together, this project would not benefit from our collective experiences.

Series Note

The Legal Research Series published by Carolina Academic Press includes an increasing number of titles from states around the country. The goal of each book is to provide law students, practitioners, paralegals, college students, and laypeople with the essential elements of legal research in each state. Unlike more bibliographic texts, the Legal Research Series books seek to explain concisely both the sources of state law research and the process for conducting legal research effectively.

Hawaiʻi Legal Research

Chapter 1

Research Process and Strategies

I. Introduction

Legal research uses resources particular to finding and understanding the law. The goal of legal research is to find binding or mandatory authority that controls the legal situation being researched. The legal researcher must first understand the sources of law and primary authority.

Primary authority is the law itself as created by each of the three branches of government: legislative, executive, or judiciary. The constitution is the foundational legal document for all laws. Statutes originate in the legislative branch while the executive branch, tasked with enforcing statutes, generates regulations. The judiciary interprets and applies the law to specific factual issues brought before the courts.

The task of finding binding or mandatory authority that a court must follow for specific factual issues involves consulting various resources known as finding aids. Finding aids are secondary authorities that include indexes, annotations, restatements, legal encyclopedias, legal treatises, and legal dictionaries. Typically, the modern legal researcher relies on legal research platforms made available online; however, research in print is still common in Hawai'i. As you work through this book print resources will also be introduced.

This book begins with recommendations for starting, continuing, and completing a research project under Hawai'i law. Researchers should be able to start their research from a variety of different vantage points depending on the information you have at different stages in your research. For example, if you are researching a common law issue, secondary sources (e.g., treatises and articles) and case law will be most relevant. You might start your research with a known treatise that will explain the law and point you to important cases, or you might already know a good case and use that case to find important secondary authority. Similarly, an area of law that is regulated by statute or agency rules might put you in a different starting gate. Using a statutory citation, you can then find your secondary authority and case law by following the recommendations outlined in the following chapters. Each chapter should give you enough information to start your research using that type of resource.

Throughout this book, we refer to several open access resources and proprietary databases. The five most common databases we point you to for resources are listed below. Of these five, we focus heavily on Lexis and Westlaw as they are often accessible at court, academic, and private law firm libraries. You will need log on credentials to access these databases. Consult with your local law library to determine if you have access to them. Alternatively, you may be able to conduct your research on the open access resources or using print material at your local law library. We will provide direct URLs where it is appropriate, otherwise, the URL will be to the generic website with the correct path to find the cited resource. Each of these databases provide training videos and FAQs on how to use their product.

- Bloomberg Law, http://news.bloomberglaw.com
- HeinOnline, https://home.heinonline.org/
- LLMC Digital (This not-for-profit maintains an open access portal and a subscription portal), http://llmc.com
- Lexis, http://www.lexis.com
- Westlaw, http://www.westlaw.com

Before getting into the details of your research, it is important to be aware of the history of the Hawai'i legal system and the development of the state constitution because Hawai'i existed as a sovereign Kingdom before it was annexed to the United States. Pre-statehood laws are still valid, and cases decided during this period are still precedential. Chapters 2–4 review this historical period and recommend research methods when completing research during the pre-statehood eras. The resource specific chapters following the historical narrative are focused mainly on the current legal system. We begin with the basics of efficient legal research.

II. Creating a Research Plan

Research efficiency for a legal researcher is paramount. It is the reason, for instance, that you will research in an annotated code rather than an unannotated code. It will also guide your decisions when purchasing access to a legal research platform.

What follows is a suggested checklist of the entire process of legal research. A brief explanation follows, but more detailed information will be found in the chapters for each resource. The checklist is a reminder. It is important to be flexible and use common sense as you research your legal issues. An example of how to organize this information into a Research Plan is found in Appendix 1—Sample Research Plan. Remember: You are searching first and foremost for *binding legal authority*, which is the authority that a court is bound to follow according to the rules of precedent. A research plan and research log is your roadmap to that goal.

A. Checklist for Developing a Research Plan and Log

- Develop Search Terms and Search Phrases.
    - Who, What, When, Where, Why?
        - Remember to go from specific to generalized terms.
    - Put the terms together & create search phrases.
        - Include root expanders: *, !
        - Include proximity connectors: e.g. /p, /s, w/3, etc.
        - Include Boolean connectors: And, Or, Not (And Not or But Not)[1]
        - Add parentheses to group similar words
- Identify jurisdiction (Use a separate plan for each jurisdiction).
- Use search terms or a search phrase to identify secondary authorities.
    - Read or scan looking for primary authorities—Note citations.
- Identify area(s) of law to research—Is there a treatise?
- Identify primary authorities & determine binding and non-binding authority.
    - Statutes & Legislation.

---

1. Lexis uses AND NOT while Westlaw uses BUT NOT. Bloomberg uses either.

- Determine the statutory scheme. Does it fall under the area of law for your facts?
- Look for definitions, exemptions, limitations.
- Check citing references.
- New or pending legislation? Check the Legislature website.
- For state jurisdictions, is it a Uniform or Model Act? Check uniformlaws.org to find other states that adopted the same law for case citations.
- Is it still "good law"? Validate with a citator.
   o Cases
- Check citing references in your jurisdiction.
- Use headnotes or similar to find more cases.
- Is the case still "good law"? Validate with a citator.
- Is the case binding authority? If not, is it persuasive?
   o Regulations
- Look for definitions, exemptions, limitations.
- Identify the agency in charge.
- Update the research plan as your research progresses
- Update primary authorities

B. Develop Search Terms and Create Search Phrases

Before beginning to search anything, assess your own knowledge on the subject. To begin developing search terms and phrases, identify interrogative pronouns: Who? What? When? Where? Why? Move from a specific word or name to a more generalized one. For example, Who? might mean Jacob, but Jacob could be an accountant who works in an accounting firm and that could also make him either an employee or owner. Jacob could also be a plaintiff or a defendant. Thus, if Jacob is bringing suit as an employee against his employer a list of terms for Who would be:

Table 1-1. Developing Search Terms Example

Who:	accountant	employee	plaintiff
Where he works:	accounting firm	employer	business entity

Table: Roberta F. Woods.

From this list see if you have similar words with different endings that would make using a root expander possible. A root expander takes the root of a word that would have different endings and ignores all but the root when searching. Here, accountant and accounting have the root word *account*. For now, use an exclamation point to indicate a root expander. Therefore the search term would become *account!*.

Searching just for employee or employer would be too limiting since the entire employment situation needs to be considered. Understanding the legal relationship between the employee and employer is vital. So, add *employ!* to the list because it will catch all possible endings including employee, employer, and employment.

Table 1-2. Using Root Expanders Example

Who: Jacob	accountant	employee	plaintiff
Who: Where he works	accounting firm	employer	business entity
Root Expanded Who	account!	employ!	

Table: Roberta F. Woods.

Another Who? could be Jacob's employer or supervisor. Identify all possible Who[s]? and focus on how each one relates to the others. For example, if Jacob reports to Kalani then Kalani in this fact pattern could be a supervisor or manager or administrator depending on how the accounting firm is set up. Use a thesaurus to develop more terms.

Do this for each of the interrogative pronouns Who, What, When, Where, and Why. Not every category will likely have a unique search term, but do not worry about that at this point. Remember to go from a specific term to a generalized one and focus on relationships.

As your research unfolds and develops, return to this brainstorming process again and again adding or refining search terms and phrases until the facts begin to build a legal framework for analysis. However, do not stop too soon because it is sometimes one fact that separates a particular legal analysis from another, and that "smoking gun" is found in the text of a law or a secondary authority.

For example, continuing our employment situation facts of Jacob and Kalani, Jacob is a male Filipino born in Hawai'i of Filipino parents. Jacob believes he was discriminated against by Kalani because he is a Filipino. Kalani has some Native Hawaiian ancestry. These facts help us clarify Who?

Update the Who? section of our search terms and add some proximity connectors. How close together do the terms need to be in a document to be relevant? Given the facts it might be relevant to have the word "discrimination" in the same paragraph with Filipino or race or "national origin." Using the paragraph proximity connector /p we can create a search phrase to use: discrim! /p (Filipino or race or "national origin"). It may not be enough to narrow the results into a manageable set though. Sometimes your search returns too many results for you to read and carefully evaluate. In that case you could try using closer proximity connectors instead of the same paragraph, try the same sentence. Alternately, identify all of the "ORs" in your search and rerun the search with each term rather than "OR-ing" them to determine which term returns the most relevant results. Also consider adding another AND term because ANDs limit the results while ORs expand them. Conversely, if you get too few results, remove some of the terms with ANDs or change them to ORs, and you could also expand the space between words with proximity connectors instead of within the same sentence, try within the same paragraph.

Table 1-3. Understanding Proximity Connectors

Search terms can come anywhere in a document. One could come at the beginning of the document and the other at the end of it. It does not mean that the two concepts are closely related. Proximity Connectors help by connecting search terms more closely. If two search terms are in the same sentence, the document is probably a better match for our facts than if they came at different ends of the document. Most platforms have unique ways to search their databases that are not common to the other platforms. Search the help section of the platform you are using to learn how it resolves Boolean search arguments and proximity connectors. Appendix 2 lists and compares the Boolean operators for these three databases.

Table: Victoria Szymczak.

Explore What? Although there could be a gender-based discrimination, Jacob has not alleged that it was. Therefore, our facts could lead us to this search argument though there are others: (*work! /s discrim!*) /p (*Filipino or race or "national origin"*). Using parenthetical groups tells the database to evaluate these terms together. In plain language this search expression is looking for any word beginning with *work* in the same sentence as any word beginning with the word *discrim* coming in the same paragraph as the words Filipino, race, or the exact phrase "*national origin.*" The proximity connectors make the results more relevant.

Table 1-4. Using Proximity Connectors

Who: Jacob	male	Filipino	born in Hawai'i
	gender	sex	race	national origin	not Native Hawaiian
Who: Kalani	female	Native Hawaiian	???
What:	workplace discrimination	civil rights	employment
Root Expanded:	work! discrim!		work!	employ!
Connectors:	work! /s discrim!	Filipino or race or "national origin"	

Table: Roberta F. Woods.

When? When gives us the time framework. The incident must be within the statute of limitations for our laws. The law in force at the time the incident occurred is the only one that matters. Making a timeline of the incident and the laws in effect can help. For the sake of filling out our search terms table, say the incident happened earlier this year in May.

Where? Answering this question provides the necessary jurisdiction. The offices where Jacob and Kalani work are in Honolulu, Hawai'i, USA. This means that we might use Hawai'i state or U.S. federal laws to resolve this incident. It also informs the legal researcher in what databases to search.

Table 1-5. Adding Jurisdictions to Search Terms

Who: Jacob	male	Filipino	born in Hawai'i
	gender	sex	race	national origin	not Native Hawaiian
Who: Kalani	female	Native Hawaiian	???
What?	workplace discrimination	civil rights	employment
When?	May 2020		
Where?	Honolulu, Hawai'i, USA	Juris: Hawai'i	US	
Root Expanded:	work! discrim!		work!	employ!
Connectors:	work! /s discrim!	Filipino or race or "national origin"	

Table: Roberta F. Woods.

Why? can often be difficult to discern in the beginning. Assume for our facts that Kalani promoted a non-Filipino woman born in California who had only been on the job for a year while Jacob has been on the job for five years. They both held the same positions. Now update our interrogative pronoun table and create terms and connectors search arguments.[2] Notably here there is not a unique search term to aid our research, but reading some online summaries will likely expose more terms that are more targeted to the fact specific legal issue being researched.

---

2. This is a search argument for our facts: (work! /s discrim!) /p promot! /p (Filipino or race or "national origin").

Table 1-6. Adding a "Why" to Search Terms

Who: Jacob	male	Filipino	Born in Hawaiʻi
	gender | sex	race | national origin	not Native Hawaiian
Who: Kalani	female	Native Hawaiian	???
	supervisor or owner?		
Who: other worker	female	non-Filipino	Born in California
What?	workplace discrimination	civil rights	employment
	promotion		
When?	May 2020		
Where?	Honolulu, Hawaiʻi, USA	Juris: Hawaiʻi | US	
Why?	Jacob passed over for promotion	Favored new worker (1 yr) over 5-yr Jacob	
Root Expanded:	work! discrim! promot!		work! | employ!
Connectors:	(work! /s discrim!)	(Filipino or race or "national origin")	promot!

Table: Roberta F. Woods.

After thoroughly examining the interrogative pronouns and creating a search argument with terms and connectors, consider the database to conduct the search in given that it could be a state or federal issue. The result list could be lengthy so learn how to filter your results by type of authority (primary or secondary) and jurisdiction (state or federal).

C. Building a Research Plan and Log

A research plan shows the order that you will consult resources to complete a thorough research product. Referring to the Checklist for Developing a Research Plan, on pages 5 and 6 of this book, begin with search terms developed by brainstorming the interrogative pronouns and the search arguments put together with terms and connectors. Leave plenty of room to add to this list. Record this information and date it; if additional facts come later the date will serve as a reference point.

Once the research terms and phrases have been identified, it is time to begin researching in online platforms or books. Before doing so, create a research log where the steps followed are captured along with results. We will recommend different strategies for keeping a research plan and log; however, everyone will develop their own way to keep these notes that makes sense for their own reference. The important thing is that you actually track your research intelligently. Remember to create a separate log for federal or state jurisdiction if researching more than one jurisdiction. If you have multiple issues, it is wise to create a log that tracks each issue. At the validation stage, the date/status can be updated to ensure that your law is still "good law."

1. Identify Secondary Authorities

Reading broad, general secondary authorities can be a good place to start especially if you lack experience in an area of law. Finding a treatise, a book about law written by a legal authority, is the best place to read about the law being researched. Typically, law students are not familiar with legal authorities or treatises. Consult a law librarian for guidance. Once found, remember to use the table of contents to find relevant passages. During this phase refine search terms to create targeted search results. Document everything in your Research Logs. Chapter 5 provides additional guidance on how to find treatises and other secondary sources.

2. Identify Primary Authorities—Statutes and Legislation

Filtering the results in a broad online database is a method to locate binding statutory authority especially with a refined and targeted search argument. Secondary authorities should have led to a reference to a statute if one exists. Check the statutory scheme to get the big picture of the law. Look for definitions, exemptions, or other limitations. Then check the citing references for case law. Often in Hawai'i you will not find many cases interpreting the law. However, if your statute was created from a uniform or model law, check other jurisdictions that have adopted the exact same uniform or model law section for case law. Case law from another jurisdiction in such a situation would be persuasive to the court. Search the Uniform Law Commission website to identify other states with the same uniform or model laws.[3] In

---

3. https://www.uniformlaws.org.

addition, the American Law Institute also created model laws that could be in effect in Hawaiʻi.[4]

Lastly, check a citator—Is it still "good law"? If the Legislature is in session it is possible that proposed legislation could be lurking out there that will pass and become law that could impact your research. Chapter 8 provides more guidance on how to research statutory issues.

3. Identify Primary Authorities—Cases

Check for cases either as citing references or notes of decisions. Use a citator to expand and validate the cases. If possible, cases that are binding authority are preferable to persuasive or non-binding authority. Document the headnotes within the case that are relevant in your Research Log. Chapter 7 provides more guidance on how to research case law.

4. Identify Primary Authorities —Regulations

Depending on the resource you use you may not find state regulations linked from the statute. Researching in a Hawaiʻi Regulatory database is, therefore, essential to complete the legal research on the issue(s). Every regulation must have authorizing legislation from the legislature. Even if you find nothing, document it in your research plan and log. Chapter 10 provides more guidance on how to research regulatory law.

D. Using a Citator to Update and Verify the Law

A citator is used to update the case, statute, or regulation which you rely upon for your analysis. The basic function of a citator is to provide citations to authorities that cite back to your case, statute, or regulation. Sometimes, you can also use a citator to see where secondary authority has been cited.[5]

A citator has two main purposes for attorneys. First, it tells you what subsequent primary and secondary authorities have referred to a case, statute, or regulation. Second, it advises you if that subsequent treatment was positive or negative in relation to the source that you are updating. For example, when updating a case, a researcher may find that ten other cases cited the one you are researching. The citator may indicate that eight cases followed the

---

4. These are available on proprietary resources including Westlaw, LEXIS, and HeinOnline.

5. For example, an important secondary authority is the Restatement (Second) of Torts. If you want to see where a particular rule has been cited in the Hawaiʻi Supreme Court, you can use a citator to make that determination.

reasoning of your case, but two of them did not. This is important because you will need to analyze how that negative treatment affects your reliance on that case.

When updating a statute or a regulation, a citator will inform you if it has been amended, and it will lead you to cases that interpret that statute or regulation. In all cases, citators will also lead you to commentary in the form of secondary sources to help you contextualize the application of the law you are researching. Citator services use a combination of words and symbols to convey meaning about the citing resources. The current listing of symbols and terminology for citators appears in Appendix 3. For these reasons, citators are used both during your research process as a method to find additional commentary and primary law, and at the completion of your assignment to make sure that none of your cases have been overruled or any of your statutes or regulations have been repealed or held unconstitutional.

There are three online citator tools to learn about: B-Cite (Bloomberg Law), Shepard's (Lexis), and KeyCite (Westlaw). Of the three, Shepard's has been around the longest and also exists in print.[6] Over the years, attorneys have come to call the process of updating the law as "shepardizing," due to the long-standing presence of Shepard's Citators in legal practice.[7]

Citators are particularly useful in the context of statutory and case law research, although Bloomberg Law's B-Cite is only available for case law

---

6. *Shepard's Citations* began with a legal service provided by Frank Shepard (1848–1902). It was initially called *Shepard's Adhesive Annotations* because the citing sources were printed on little gummed pieces of paper and inserted into case reporters where the cited case was published. This service evolved into the Frank Shepard Company and the stickers were replaced with bound volumes listing the cases citing each reported case, and referencing the headnotes being referenced in those cases. The company is now owned in part by Reed Elsevier, Lexis's parent company and has branched out to cover statutes, cases, regulations, and secondary authorities.

7. In Hawaiʻi, researchers will need to use the print version to get a complete report on a statute. This is because the different revisions of the *Hawaiʻi Revised Statutes* are not always reflected in the statutory history of a statute. It prevents the algorithms that power the online citators from picking up all the cases that are citing to a statute in its various stages throughout the history of the state, territory, and kingdom of Hawaiʻi. Additionally, because not all acts of the legislature appear in the *Hawaiʻi Revised Statutes*, the print version of Shepard's is the only way to determine case interpretation of those unconsolidated laws.

research. A section on how and when to use citators is included in the chapters devoted to those resources.

E. Become Familiar with the West Digest Topic and Key Number System or Topics on Lexis

Proprietary resources like Westlaw and Lexis include many value-added features to aid the legal researcher in locating binding legal authority and in forming an analysis of the law once found. Regardless of which resource you use, learn how to make the most of the features it contains. The West Digest System is the oldest and also exists in print form while Topics in Lexis is a more recent addition. To further distinguish these two platforms, West employs editors to distill complex legal issues into its Digest System while Lexis takes the language from the case itself to create case headnotes within Topics.

The West Digest Topic and Key Number System Key Number System is a classification system of U.S. law organized under approximately 400 legal topics called digest topics. Each digest topic is assigned a number. For example, *adjoining land owners* is a digest topic and it is assigned number 15. Each Digest Topic is further divided into legal issues related to the Digest Topic. Each legal issue is also assigned a number called a Key Number. For example, within the Digest Topic of *adjoining land owners*, Key Number 10 represents the "right to and obstruction of light, air, or view." The Digest Topic together with the Key Number are collectively and redundantly called—a Key Number. In this example, the complete Key Number can be represented numerically as: 15k10.

Another example is the Digest Topic of *negligence*. It is assigned number 272. Each legal issue within *negligence* is further divided into sub-categories such as "III. Standard of Care," which has Key Numbers 230 to 239 represented by k230-k239. Key number 230 is "Standard of Care, In General." The complete Key Number would be 272k230.

West products tag the content with Key Numbers, including cases in the case reporters that they publish. The convenience of knowing the Key Number representing your legal issue is particularly useful when looking for secondary sources and case law on your topic. Because West products all follow this system, you can easily identify secondary sources and case law since they are all tagged in the same way. When using West's online platform, Westlaw, you can simply type in the Key Number in the search box—such as,

15k10—and retrieve all of the West secondary sources and case law that include that Key Number tag.

The Digest Topic and Key Number System was originally developed to help find cases, but it has evolved to become the powerful engine behind KeyCite, Westlaw's citator. The System essentially forms a web of research for a legal issue. And, it is an elastic System meaning it can expand or contract as the law evolves. That also means that the System is ripe for change and in print or online you may encounter a redirection to a revised numbering scheme.[8] In the chapters that follow, we discuss how to identify the appropriate key numbers for the issues that you research and how to use them in your research process.

Lexis offers Topics on its platform that are used to create case headnotes. Topics are broad areas of law and the headnotes are free of editorial content because the language is lifted directly from the case opinion for the headnote. Secondary sources are not included in Lexis Topics nor are other categories of primary authority like statutes or regulations unless you find a case that includes a topic summary in the About this Document panel on the right-hand side. For example, *Ryan v. Stavros*, 348 Mass. 251, 203 N.E.2d 85 (1964) includes a topic summary about property descriptions. In the summary are links to statutes and rules as well as secondary sources and seminal cases on the issue. See Figures 1-1 and 1-2 for an example of a Topic Summary.

---

8. West Publishing recognized the need for an index or digest soon after it published the Northwestern Reporter, the first unofficial reporter originally called "The Syllabi" in 1876. The aim of the Digest System has not changed much over the years. It functions much like an index to cases that are filed chronologically and reported by appellate courts. John B. West, *Multiplicity of Reports*, 2 Law Libr. J. 4 (1909); Robert B. Jarvis, *John B. West: Founder of West Publishing Company*, L (50) THE AMERICAN J. OF LEGAL HISTORY 1, 6–8 (2008–2010). Jarvis writes that West announced his ambitious plan to index and digest case law in 1887 with the creation of The American Digest Classification Scheme. The evolution of digests is revealed in a copyright case involving *West Publishing Co. v. Edward Thompson Co.*, 169 F. 833, 849 (E.D.N.Y. 1909).

Figure 1-1. Showing a Link to a Topic Summary on Lexis from a Case

Business & Corporate Compliance > ... > Discrimination ▾ > Labor & Employment Law ▾ > Discrimination ▾

Labor & Employment Law > ... > 🗐Racial Discrimination ▾ > Employment Practices ▾ > Demotions & Promotions ▾

View more legal topics

HN3 ⬇ **Labor & Employment, Discrimination**

29 C.F.R. § 29.30(1) states that this part sets forth policies and procedures to promote equality of opportunity in apprenticeship programs registered with the U.S. Department of Labor and in state apprenticeship programs registered with recognized state apprenticeship agencies. These policies and procedures apply to the recruitment and selection of apprentices, and to all conditions of employment and training during apprenticeship. The procedures established provide for review of apprenticeship programs, for registering apprenticeship

Source: Lexis, used by permission.

Figure 1-2. Lexis Topic Summary Report Example

The information in this article applies to the following LexisNexis® products and services: Lexis+™, Lexis®, Practical Guidance

When you use Boolean search logic, such as *violat! w/5 rico and corn and wheat or soy w/10 crop or industry*, the service runs a **terms & connectors** search. With a terms & connectors search, you can control which terms appear in all results and the proximity of those terms to one another. An algorithm analyzes your search terms and retrieves results based on the relevance of your terms.

The following information helps explain what happens when the service runs your search as a terms & connectors search:
- The service counts and searches all terms. None of your search terms are ignored in a terms & connectors search.
- The Lexis service treats any text between two connectors as a single phrase. For example, the search *national football league and collective bargaining agreement and players* retrieves documents with **collective bargaining agreement** as a phrase but does not return a document based on **bargaining agreement** or **collective agreement**.
- If you enter a connector as part of a recognized legal phrase, the service does not treat it as a connector and searches as part of the entire phrase. For example, recognized phrases include **search and seizure**, **act or omission**, **cease and desist order**, or **clear and convincing evidence**.

You can use the following **connectors** when constructing your terms & connectors search:

- **and** – finds all terms
- **or** – finds any or all terms
- **w/n** or **near/n** – finds terms in proximity to each other
- **pre/n** or **onear/n** – finds terms in ordered proximity
- **w/sent** or **w/s** – finds terms approximately in the same sentence
- **w/para** or **w/p** – finds terms approximately in the same paragraph
- **w/seg** – finds terms approximately in the same document segment
- **and not** – excludes terms from your results
- **not w/n**, **not pre/n**, **not w/s**, or **not w/p** – finds terms not in proximity to other terms

For more information about each connector, see **Search Connectors**. When using proximity connectors, you may want to use parentheses to group your terms the way you want the search to run. For more information, see **Using Parentheses in a Terms & Connectors Search**.

Source: Lexis, used by permission.

Figure 1-3. Westlaw — Search Tips

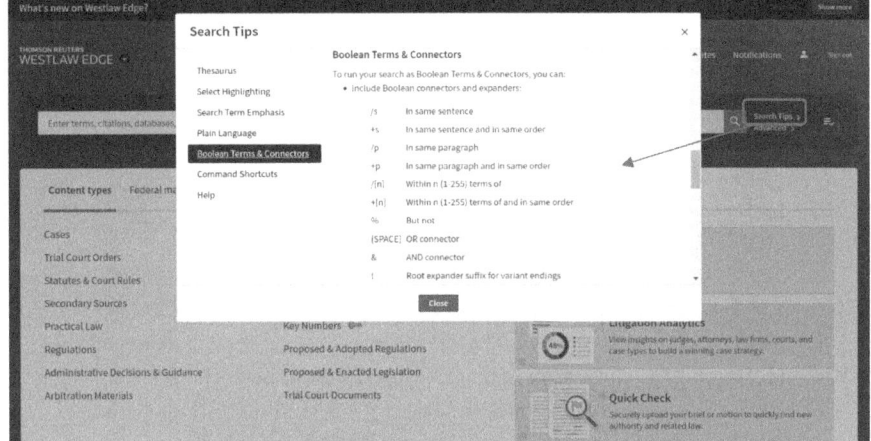

Source: Westlaw, by permission.

Often one headnote includes several topics. Just make sure the Topic you are following conforms to the law you are researching. Lexis Topics are tied into Shepard's citator making it convenient to find other cases on the same point of law.

F. How to Use This Book

Use this book to become an efficient legal researcher. Read the information on creating a research plan and set up a system to log your research before you begin researching a legal issue. Use the plan you develop to guide you in the steps to take to ensure the thoroughness of your research. Systematically documenting your research saves you time in the long run. Use the checklist to review the path you have taken in your research.

As you read through the examples, follow along in your own research platform or in print. It is not necessary to use this book in the order it is laid out. Every legal issue does not have every primary authority associated with it. For example, there are statutes without regulations or cases. And there are cases without statutes or regulations.

Chapter 2

Overview of the Hawaiian Legal System and Its Origins

I. Introduction

Researching law in Hawaiʻi requires a basic understanding of Hawaiʻi's history because you must research in the appropriate jurisdictional authorities that were in control for the era. For example, Hawaiʻi was once an independent nation and certain rights relating to property law that began in the Kingdom era have been preserved and are precedent in the State of Hawaiʻi. Consider also that when Hawaiʻi became a Territory, U.S. federal law governed and during World War II, under martial law, the U.S. military governed. Table 2-1 summarizes the historical periods for legal research.[1] Some of the earlier historic materials are available online, but not comprehensively in one platform as are current legal authorities.

Legal pluralism prevailed in the early Kingdom Era. The foreign population, including representatives of foreign governments, merchants, and sailors, made use of the criminal system[2] prior to 1840, but merchants settled

---

1. *The Fundamental Law of Hawaiʻi*, Honolulu: *Hawaiian Gazette*, (Lorrin A. Thurston, ed. 1902), *available at* https://books.google.com/books/about/The_Fundamental_Law_of_Hawaiʻi.html?id=vW9LAQAAIAAJ.

2. *The Cow Proclamation* (Oct. 7, 1829) put the foreign population on notice that they would be held accountable under Hawaiian laws including customary laws for their actions after an incident involving the British Consul, Richard Charlton. Prior to the proclamation, foreign residents claimed that Hawaiian laws applied only to the native population while the laws of their home country applied to them.

civil disputes by their own system of arbitration.[3] A recurring legal issue in Hawai'i is the role of customary law and how it is applied.

What began in 1782 as an absolute monarchy under Kamehameha I that promulgated its laws orally evolved into a constitutional monarchy under Kamehameha III with the first constitution in 1840. Laws were agreed upon by the House of Nobles and the representatives to the Legislature. It was constitutionally mandated that a record of those meetings be preserved.[4] Session laws began publication in 1841, but compilations and codes have been irregularly published. The table below shows the compilations and codes for Hawai'i statutes.

Table 2-1. Historical Compilation of Codes and Statutes

Authorizing Legislation	Era	Published	Code or Compilation?
	Kamehameha III	1834	Compilation
	Kamehameha III	1841 (Haw.) 1842 (Eng.)	Compilation
Joint Resolution, June 24, 1845; Joint Res. April 27, 1846	Kamehameha III	1846 Statute Laws (vol. 1)[5] 1847 Statute Laws (vol. 2)[6]	(John Ricord)
Legislative Council, Resolution Sept. 27, 1847	Kamehameha III	1850 Penal Code Ka Elele (Haw.) & Polynesian (Eng.)	Code (William Little Lee)
Joint Resolution, June 30, 1856 (p. 60)	Kamehameha IV	1859 Civil Code[7]	Code (May 17, 1859)

---

3. A thorough examination of legal pluralism in Hawai'i prior to 1840 can be found in Wendie Ellen Schneider, *Contentious Business: Merchants and the Creation of a Westernized Judiciary in Hawai'i*, 108 YALE L.J. 1389 (1999); and Sally Engle Merry, *Legal Pluralism*, 22 LAW & SOC'Y REV. 869 (1988).

4. Many of the early Journals are freely available online through LLMC's Open Access collection: http://www.llmc.com/OpenAccess/search.aspx.

5. Freely available online: https://books.google.com/books?id=AXUDAAAAQAAJ.

6. Freely available online: http://www.llmc.com/OpenAccess/docDisplay5.aspx?textid=55679507.

7. Freely available online: https://books.google.com/books?id=CB04AAAAIAAJ.

Act, June 22, 1868; L. 1870, Act 1 (July 7, 1870)	Kamehameha V	1869 Penal Laws	Became Code (1870)
L. 1880, Act 32, Aug. 13, 1880	Kalakaua	1884 Compiled Laws[8] (incl. penal laws)	Compilation (McCully)
Art. 92 § 2 Const. of the Republic	Republic	1897 Civil Laws	Compilation (Ballou)
L. 1892, Act 57 § 10	Republic	1897 Penal Laws	Compilation (Ballou)
L. 1903, Act 45, April 25, 1903	Territory	1905 Revised Laws[9]	Compilation
L. 1913, Act 11, March 11, 1913	Territory	1915 Revised Laws[10]	Compilation
L. 1923, Act 17, March 29, 1923	Territory	1925 Revised Laws	Compilation
L. 1933, Act 178, May 31, 1933	Territory	1935 Revised Laws	Compilation
L. 1943, Act 8, March 12, 1943	Territory	1945 Revised Laws[11]	Compilation
L. 1953, Act 179, June 4, 1953	Territory	1955 Revised Laws	Compilation
L. 1966, Act 29; (HB 16) L. 1967, Act 38; (HB 498) L. 1968, Act 16 (SB 24)	State	1968 Hawaiʻi Revised Statutes	Compilation
L. 1976, Act 173 § 4	State	1976 Replacement Hawaiʻi Revised Statutes	Compilation

---

8. Freely available online: https://books.google.com/books?id=qBtKAQAAIAAJ.
9. Freely available online: https://books.google.com/books?id=gyFFAAAAYAAJ.
10. Freely available online: https://books.google.com/books?id=-B1KAQAAIAAJ.
11. Freely available online: https://books.google.com/books?id=wiJKAQAAIAAJ.

L. 1977, 1st Sp. Sess., Act 8 § 1; L. 1984, Act 90 § 1 (HRS § 23G-15)	State	1985 Hawai'i Revised Statutes	Compilation
L. 1993, Act 285	State	1993 Hawai'i Revised Statutes	Compilation
After 1993, HRS §§ 23G-20, 23G-16 allow continuous revision & pub. of replacement vols. L. Sp. 1977, 1st, Act 8, pt. of §1	State	1996 Replacement Hawai'i Revised Statutes	Compilation

Table: Roberta F. Woods.

Without the courts embracing the common law as England and the United States did, there was not a need to report the cases since precedent was not the rule.[12] Courts evolved from this informal system of island governors and chiefs settling disputes at a local level to a more western system with courts of record that created and relied on previous case precedent in 1847 when an American trained lawyer wrote *An Act to Organize the Judiciary Department*.[13] The Supreme Court, the Superior Court of Law and Equity, and Circuit Courts were courts of record.[14] The Police Courts and District Courts were trial level courts that did not create legal precedent.[15]

---

12. The first constitution in 1840 created tax and island judges and a Supreme Court headed by King Kamehameha III to hear appeals, yet a record of these decisions was not required to be reported.

13. John Ricord was the first Attorney General of Hawai'i. He trained in law under his uncle in Buffalo, New York, and became a member of the New York Bar.

14. Act to Organize the Judiciary Department, Chapter I, Sec. XV, Principles and Rules Relating to the Courts in General, STATUTE LAWS OF HIS MAJESTY KAMEHAMEHA III, KING OF THE HAWAIIAN ISLANDS; PASSES BY THE HOUSE OF NOBLES AND REPRESENTATIVES, DURING THE TWENTY-SECOND YEAR OF HIS REIGN, AND THE FIFTH YEAR OF HIS PUBLIC RECOGNITION, vol. II, 1847, p. 8 *available at* http://www.llmc.com/OpenAccess/docDisplay5.aspx?textid=55679507. Chapter III of this Act lays out National Courts of Record, p. 26.

15. Trial courts were, however, required to keep Minute books of their decisions.

Decisions of the courts of record[16] beginning in 1847 were published in volume one of *Hawai'i* or *Hawaiian Reports*.[17] The cases in volume one spanned 10 years (1847–1856), but they are not of the full court on appeal meaning they are not necessarily precedent. And some of the decisions consisted of charges to juries typically only found at a trial level court. But that was in the early days of the constitutional monarchy in Hawai'i. It took time to get things completely sorted out. Volume two included the shortened title of *Hawaiian Reports, vol. II*. Each volume thereafter until volume twenty carried this name. Volume twenty changed to *Hawai'i Reports* as it continued until 1994 when West Publishing took over its publication and named it *West's Hawai'i Reports*.

Statehood in 1959 brought about a change in court reporting for Hawai'i. After Hawai'i became the fiftieth state, Supreme Court decisions were also reported in West's regional reporter for the Pacific region.

The Intermediate Court of Appeals (ICA) was created in 1979[18] to implement Article VI of the Constitution of the State of Hawai'i following the Constitutional Convention of 1978. Beginning in 1980, ICA opinions were reported in a separate reporter called *Hawai'i Appellate Reports* and in West's regional reporter for the Pacific region (beginning with 611 P.2d). When West Publishing took over the printing of Hawai'i's reporters in 1994 the *Hawai'i Appellate Reports* was discontinued. Since then, ICA opinions have been included in *West's Hawai'i Reports* and in the *Pacific Reporter*.

---

16. Black's Law Dictionary defines court of record. A court that is required to keep a record of its proceedings. The court's records are presumed accurate and cannot be collaterally impeached. Court, Black's Law Dictionary (11th ed. 2019).

17. The title of volume one: REPORTS OF SOME OF THE JUDGMENTS AND DECISIONS OF THE COURTS OF RECORD OF THE HAWAIIAN ISLANDS FOR THE YEARS ENDING WITH 1856 by George M. Robertson. Robertson was an associate justice of the Supreme Court. Hawaiian and Hawai'i Reports volumes 1–27 (1847–1924) are freely available online at http://www.llmc.com/OpenAccess/Volumes.aspx?set=77101. The early reporters have some anomalies. For a complete list see Wade Warren Thayer, Preface, A DIGEST OF THE DECISIONS OF THE SUPREME COURT OF HAWAI'I, 1916, freely available online at https://books.google.com/books/about/A_Digest_of_the_Decisions_of_the_Supreme.html?id=zuoDAAAAYAAJ.

18. L. 1979, Act 111, An Act Relating to the Judiciary. H.B. 92. Approved May 25, 1979.

II. Approaching Your Research for the Different Eras of Governance

In the previous section a broad history of Hawaiʻi and its eras of governance were introduced. How do they impact one's ability to do thorough legal research? Each era relied on different sources for legal authority. For example, Kingdom Era legal material may be available online, but much of it is still only available in print at libraries and in archival collections at the University of Hawaiʻi Law Library,[19] Hamilton Library at the University of Hawaiʻi,[20] the Hawaiʻi State Archives,[21] the Hawaiʻi Supreme Court Law Library,[22] the Legislative Reference Bureau,[23] the Bishop Museum Library,[24] the Hawaiian Mission Houses Library,[25] the Hawaiian Historical Society Library,[26] or the Judiciary History Center.[27] Become familiar with the protocols archival repositories require and follow them. Additionally, the Revised Laws of 1905–1955 reprinted many of the older documents in their volumes.

Under the 1840 Constitution, the Legislature met annually beginning in April. This continued until 1856 when the 1854 Constitution was amended, and the Legislature met biennially.[28] Civil laws and criminal (penal) laws were published separately until 1905 when the Territory of Hawaiʻi combined them into one set of laws covering both civil and criminal situations.

The Superior Court of Law and Equity established in 1847 was the appellate court of record for Hawaiʻi.[29] By the 1852 Constitution that court was

---

19. UH Law Library: https://library.law.hawaii.edu/.
20. UH Hamilton Library: https://manoa.hawaii.edu/library/.
21. Hawaiʻi State Archives: https://ags.hawaii.gov/archives/about-us/archives-research/.
22. Hawaiʻi Supreme Court Law Library: https://histatelawlibrary.com/.
23. Legislative Reference Bureau, Public Access Room: https://lrb.hawaii.gov/par/.
24. Bishop Museum Library: https://www.bishopmuseum.org/library-and-archives/.
25. Hawaiʻi Mission Houses Library: https://hmha.missionhouses.org/.
26. Hawaiian Historical Society Library: https://www.Hawaiian history.org/research/library/.
27. Judiciary History Center: https://www.jhchawaii.net/.
28. Art. 6, Act of Apr. 18, 1856, amending art. 61 of the 1854 Constitution. See Chapter 3 for a more complete history of the Constitution and how to research constitutional issues in Hawaiʻi.
29. W.F. Frear, The Evolution of the Hawaiian Judiciary, Papers of the Hawaiian Historical Society, No. 7, Honolulu, 1894, 21. The name change happened in 1852.

renamed as the Supreme Court. Although the King was originally the Chief Justice of the Supreme Court, after the 1852 Constitution, the King in Privy Council did not sit on a court. Instead, he appointed the judges in all courts of record.[30] Those cases are found in *Hawaiian Reports* or *Hawaiʻi Reports* depending on the year.

A. Territorial Era Research (July 7, 1898–Aug. 20, 1959)

Governance of Hawaiʻi passed to the United States on April 30, 1900, when the U.S. Congress passed the Organic Act.[31] This act created the territorial government in Hawaiʻi. During this era, the Territorial Legislature of Hawaiʻi met during odd-numbered years except for special sessions. In addition, the U.S. government also passed laws concerning Hawaiʻi that are found in the Statutes at Large and the United States Code.[32] Researching older legislative materials (pre-1980) including committee reports may require you to familiarize yourself with either books, microfiche, or a proprietary[33] online resource that indexes the U.S. Congressional Serial Set like Heinonline (use the link to Heinonline Serial Set), Newsbank Readex (listed as U.S. Congressional Serial Set), or ProQuest Congressional.[34] To limit your results, search for "Hawaii Territory" without the ʻokina (ʻ) in Hawaiʻi.

Generally, a working knowledge of researching federal materials including the United States Code, Statutes at Large, the Code of Federal Regulations,

---

The King, the Premier, and four chiefs that comprised the original Supreme Court continued to sit with the three judge Supreme Court that had originally been the Superior Court of Law and Equity until 1869 when the original members found it inconvenient to continue to sit with the panel.

30. Articles 81–93 "Of the Judiciary," in FUNDAMENTAL LAWS OF HAWAIʻI at 13.
31. Pub. L. 56-339, 31 Stat. 141.
32. The Statutes at Large are the session laws for the U.S. (federal) government.
33. The copyright laws increase the difficulty of finding freely available resources online for the period between 1924 and today. Even if a resource is not protected by copyright laws, the cost of digitizing thousands of pages and making them available can be staggering. Information vendors take on the cost and sell access to the content to libraries who make it available exclusively to their patrons.
34. The University of Hawaiʻi School of Law Library has microfiche of many of the early legislative materials. Newsbank Readex is maintained by Hamilton Library. Heinonline and ProQuest Congressional are maintained by the Law Library. All are proprietary databases available to the William S. Richardson School of Law through links on the Law Library's website and are common resources at most law school libraries.

and the Federal Register will aid you when researching laws in the Territorial Era. While many more recent materials are available online on .gov sites, older materials may be difficult to find. A search for .edu sites that may provide research guides with links can offer guidance. Or speak to a reference librarian who likely has more familiarity with print and microform materials.

Cases from the Federal District Court for the District of Hawai'i during the Territorial Period were published in the four volumes of *Estes Reports* covering 1903–1917. The decisions in these volumes do not appear in the *Federal Reporter* covering the same time frame. The *Federal Supplement*, a West Publishing created reporter of decisions of the federal district courts, began in 1933. Prior to 1933, federal district court decisions appeared in the *Federal Reporter*.[35]

B. Martial Law (Dec. 7, 1941–Oct. 24, 1944)

On December 7, 1941, following the Japanese attack on Pearl Harbor martial law was imposed on Hawai'i by Governor Joseph Poindexter under section 67 of the Hawaiian Organic Act, and by proclamation he suspended the privilege of the writ of habeas corpus. On December 9, 1941, President Franklin Roosevelt sent the governor a telegram approving it under U.S.C. title 48, section 432. Martial law placed Hawai'i under military governance. Military officers moved into Iolani Palace and assumed all legislative, executive, and judicial powers.[36] The commanding general of the army in Hawai'i governed by issuing general orders during this era that were legal mandates to the people. Locating general orders from this era will likely involve some familiarity

---

35. The so-called "Estee's Reports," named for Judge Morris March Estee was an early case reporter in the Hawaiian Territory. Only four volumes of decisions of the United States District Court (USDC) for the Territory of Hawai'i were ever printed. They span the years 1903–1917. Roberta Freeland Woods, *History of the Four Volumes of Decisions of the United States District Court for the Territory of Hawai'i 1903–1917*, June 27, 2016, *available at* https://papers.ssrn.com/sol3/papers.cfm?abstract_id=3411194.

36. Iolani Palace was the home of Hawai'i's last reigning monarchs and served as the official royal residence. https://www.iolanipalace.org/.

with researching in the National Archives.[37] Martial law ended October 24, 1944, by Presidential Proclamation 2627.[38]

Lieutenant Colonel Thomas H. Green became executive to the military governor and was responsible for countless daily operations of the American military government. His personal papers are available at the Library of Congress site as a .pdf file and offer insight into this era.[39]

C. Statehood Research (Aug. 21, 1959–present)

Hawai'i became a state by The Admission Act, Pub. L. 86-3, 73 Stat. 4 (March 18, 1959). In 1949, the Territorial Legislature of Hawai'i approved "An Act to provide for a constitutional convention, the adoption of a State constitution, and the forwarding of the same to the Congress of the United States, and appropriating money therefor."[40] It was then adopted by a vote of the people of Hawai'i in the election held on November 7, 1950.

The first compiled statutes after statehood, the *Hawai'i Revised Statutes*, were published in 1968. The publication of the indexes lags behind the statutory sets. For example, the 1993 *Hawai'i Revised Statutes Replacement Volumes* did not have an index published until 1996. Until then the 1987 index and its supplement were used. This does make the print sets somewhat difficult to use since the index may not be shelved with the appropriate set. The table below indicates the index volumes of the *Hawai'i Revised Statutes*.

---

37. https://www.archives.gov/research.
38. Pres. Proclamation 2627, *Termination of Martial Law in the Territory of Hawai'i*, 9 Fed. Reg. 12831, Thurs. Oct. 26, 1944. The proclamation ending martial law was effective Oct. 24, 1944, but not published until Oct. 26.
39. https://www.loc.gov/rr/frd/Military_Law/pdf/Martial-Law_Green.pdf
40. L. 1949, c. 334 (May 20, 1949).

Table 2-2. Index Volumes for the Hawai'i Revised Statutes

Authorizing Legislation	Published	Volumes
L. 1966, Act 29; (HB 16) L. 1967, Act 38; (HB 498) L. 1968, Act 16 (SB 24)	1968 Hawai'i Revised Statutes	Vol. 8 includes index
L. 1976, Act 173 § 4	1976 Replacement Hawai'i Revised Statutes	Vols. 8 + 3a, 5a, & 7a vol. 8 is 1969 Index
L. 1977, 1st Sp. Sess., Act 8 § 1; L. 1984, Act 90 § 1 [HRS § 23G-15]	1985 Replacement Hawai'i Revised Statutes	Vol. 12 plus index vol. 1982 Replacement
L. 1993, Act 285	1993 Replacement Hawai'i Revised Statutes	Vol. 14 plus index vol. 1987 Replacement
After 1993, HRS §§ 23G-20, 23G-16 allow continuous statutory revision & pub. of replacement volumes	Various depending on individual volume yyyy Replacement Hawai'i Revised Statutes	Index vol. 1996 Replacement

Table: Roberta F. Woods.

When doing research in state statutes in Hawai'i after 1959 or even earlier, pay particular attention to the history given in the statute. If the first or oldest law listed is a recodification rather than a session law (beginning with the letter L), then historical research will require going into the session laws prior to the recodification to find the original law.[41] Often the history is also missing the location of a statute in a recodification and you will need to look the statute up in each iteration of the code. Case annotations are not comprehensive in the official *Hawai'i Revised Statutes*. Refer to Chapter 8 for more information on statutory research and interpretation.

---

41. See Table 2-1, Historical compilation and codes.

Chapter 3

The Constitution

I. Introduction

The Constitution of the State of Hawai'i, like other state constitutions, is the highest authority of the state. As the highest authority, when a client's issue arises under the constitution, it controls even if other legal authorities address the same issue. For a practitioner, understanding this hierarchy is significant because it sets the roadmap for the research strategy. A constitutional law issue requires research within secondary sources that discuss and analyze these issues and annotated constitutions to locate the relevant cases that interpret and apply the governing provision. From this research, the practitioner demonstrates the hierarchy and application of the relevant law to the client's facts in clear and concise court filings. Further a state constitution cannot provide lesser protections than the United States Constitution, but it can provide more, and the Hawai'i Constitution does provide greater protections for its environment, culture, and citizens. Identifying these greater protections on behalf of a client or cause elevates the importance of devising a research strategy that includes resources discussing and interpreting the Constitution.

Hawai'i has a unique history among the other states as the only sovereign nation to be overthrown and annexed into the union. The uniqueness of this history continues to play out in the governance of the state and the protections of its resources and culture, but this history—with all its dramatic arcs and exertions of power—are preserved and mirrored in the state's constitutions, both before and after the overthrow of Queen Lili'uokalani in 1893. Thus, researchers of Hawaiian law need to make themselves familiar with the state's history and its many constitutions. This chapter begins with that history and then illustrates how to research a Hawai'i constitutional law issue.

II. History of the Hawai'i Constitution

A. Kingdom of Hawai'i

Since the Kingdom, Hawai'i has operated under nine constitutions. There were four constitutions during the constitutional monarchy, one for the Republic of Hawai'i, one while Hawai'i was a territory, and a statehood constitution that was amended and revised by two constitutional conventions (the 1968 Constitution and the 1978 Constitution).

The first two constitutions, in 1840 and 1852, were adopted during the rule of Kamehameha III (1825–1854). The prior kings—Kamehameha I (1782–1819) and Kamehameha II (1819–1824)—had ruled as absolute monarchs, but Western foreigners and missionaries living in Hawai'i, or *haoles* as they were called, saw a written constitution as essential to giving "the government a measure of fixity and tangibility" and their influence on Hawai'i's rulers and people grew.[1] Kamehameha III and his chiefs drafted the constitution during the summer and fall of 1840, and the King and his Kuhina Nui, or Regent, signed it on October 8, 1840. It subsumed the Declaration of Rights of 1839, commonly referred to as the Hawaiian Magna Charta; put forth a process for constitutional amendment; created a bicameral legislative branch of the House of Nobles (the King, Kuhina Nui, and fourteen other chiefs) and House of Representatives; and established the Supreme Court (the King, Kuhina Nui, and four appointees of the House of Representatives).[2]

The Constitution of 1840 remained the law for twelve years without additional amendments. But events during those years as Kamehameha III looked to contain and, at the same time, accommodate the growing influence of foreigners—namely, official recognition of Hawai'i as an independent nation by England and France in 1843, *The Great Mahele* in 1848,[3] and soon after the

---

1. Ralph S. Kuykendall, *Constitutions of the Hawaiian Kingdom: A Brief History and Analysis* 7 (Papers of the Hawaiian Hist. Soc'y No. 21, 1940).
2. *Id.* at 13.
3. *The Great Mahele*, or Great Division, of 1848 introduced a Western land tenure system to the Hawai'i Kingdom, thereby replacing—peacefully—the ancient system of land tenure where all lands in Hawai'i were the personal property of the king and were distributed to his principal supporters and their dependents at the inauguration of each monarchy. This landmark reformation of the land system in Hawai'i set aside 1.5 million acres of land for the chiefs and konohikis (headmen of the ahupua'a, a subdivision of land under the ancient system); 1 million acres of land for Kamehameha III as *Crown Lands*; and 1.5 million acres for the government and the people.

Kuleana Act of 1850,[4] where the monarchy allowed private ownership of land in fee for the first time—revealed the inadequacies of the constitution and the need for a revision.[5] A three-member commission appointed by the Legislature drafted an entirely new constitution. The Legislature adopted it on June 14, 1852, and Kamehameha III later signed it. The Constitution of 1852 granted suffrage to all adult males for the first time, irrespective of any property qualification; changed the house of nobles from a hereditary body to lifetime appointments by the king; and further defined the separation of powers of the government's three branches.[6]

See Minutes of the Privy Council of the Hawaiian Kingdom, 250–308 (1847–48), http://llmc.com/OpenAccess/search.aspx (open the "Hawaii" dropdown, select "1845-92, Privy Council Minutes, Typed" from the list of titles and then "1847-48-English"); *Buke Kakau Paa no ka mahele aina i Hooholoia iwaena o Kamehameha III a me Na Lii a me Na Konohiki ana Hale Alii* ("The Mahele Book") (1848) (translation on file with author), http://llmc.com/OpenAccess/search.aspx (open the "Hawaii" dropdown and then select "1848, Hawaii Public Lands, The Mahele Book" from the middle of the list of titles); Jon J. Chinen, *The Great Mahele: Hawai'i's Land Division of 1848,* 31 (1958), http://llmc.com/OpenAccess/search.aspx (open the "Hawaii" dropdown and then select the respective title from the list of titles).

4. Kuleana Act, 1850 Kingdom of Haw. Sess. Laws 202, http://llmc.com/OpenAccess/search.aspx (open the "Hawaii" dropdown and then select "1850 Penal Code, Eng." from the bottom of the list of titles) (confirming "certain resolutions of the King and Privy Council . . . granting to the common people allodial titles for their own lands and house lots"), *amended by* 1851 Kingdom of Haw. Sess. Laws 98, http://llmc.com/OpenAccess/search.aspx (open the "Hawaii" dropdown, select "Hawaii Session Laws, Eng., 1841–date" from the list of titles and then select "1851 April-June" from the middle of the list of non-sequential dates) (removing some language that seemed to allow konohikis to prohibit tenants' full rights to the awarded land); *see also* Chinen, *supra* note 3 (indicating that while the Land Commission responsible for distributing the lands during *The Great Mahele* awarded about 30,000 acres of land to thousands of native tenants who occupied and improved any portion of the Crown, Government, or Konohiki Lands, many thousands of native tenants also relinquished their claims to these *Kuleana Lands* by failing to file with and/or appear before the Land Commission); Melody Kapilialoha MacKenzie, *Historical Background, in* Native Hawaiian Law: A Treatise 15 (Melody Kapilialoha MacKenzie et al. eds., 2015) (providing numerous reasons why the native tenants did not secure more kuleana parcels, and noting native tenants received another 167,000 acres through other provisions of the Kuleana Act and other laws allowing the sale of Government Lands).

5. Kuykendall, *supra* note 1, at 15.

6. *Kingdom of Haw. Const. of 1852*, arts. XIX, XXIII, LXXII, *reprinted in The Fundamental Law of Hawai'i 157-66* (Lorrin A. Thurston ed. 1904), http://llmc.com/OpenAccess/search.aspx (open the "Hawaii" dropdown, scroll to the bottom of the list of titles and select "1840-1900, Fundamental Law, Thurston"*);* Anne Feder Lee, *The Hawai'i State Constitution 6 (2011).*

During the rule of King Kamehameha IV (1855–1863), the House of Nobles and House of Representatives engaged in a tug-of-war to amend the constitution to better "meet the necessities of the people, [and] the wants of the country" as each saw fit.[7] The King and his advisors wanted a constitution firmly entrenched in the principles of a constitutional monarchy, so they pushed through a constitutional amendment to weaken the Kuhina Nui's, House of Representatives', and Privy Council's power to restrain and control the king's actions.[8] The House of Representatives, however, looked to solidify its power and refused to approve the House of Nobles' commission to revise the constitution.[9] King Kamehameha V (1863–1872) ultimately pushed aside the constitutional process that his brother had negotiated, refused to take the oath to uphold the Constitution of 1852, and arbitrarily repealed it.[10] He took this action believing that it was a sovereign right reserved for him by Kamehameha III who, according to the letters of his advisors, had observed the right to abrogate the Constitution of 1852.[11] The King and his advisors then drafted Hawai'i's third constitution, which came into effect on August 20, 1864. The Constitution of 1864 placed literacy and property qualifications on voting and restored royal power by, for instance, stipulating that the monarch did not have to seek advice and counsel from the nobles, forming the cabinet as directly subject to the king, and making the appointment of all judges the exclusive prerogative of the king.[12]

The Constitution of 1864 remained the law for 23 years, revised by only a single insignificant amendment.[13] After Kamehameha V's death in 1872, with no successor to the throne named, King Lunalilo (1873–1874) became the first elected monarch.[14] He was not a fan of the Constitution of 1864 and

---

7. Kuykendall, *supra* note 1, at 26.

8. *Id.* at 21.

9. *Id.* at 27.

10. Lee, *supra* note 6.

11. Kuykendall, *supra* note 1, at 27–30, 35–36.

12. Lee, *supra* note 6, at 7.

13. *Kingdom of Haw. Const. of 1864,* art. LVI (1868), *reprinted in The Fundamental Law of Hawai'i* 176 (Lorrin A. Thurston ed. 1904), http://llmc.com/OpenAccess/search.aspx (open the "Hawaii" dropdown, scroll to the bottom of the list of titles and select "1840-1900, Fundamental Law, Thurston") (increasing the compensation of the Representatives from one hundred and fifty to "two hundred and fifty dollars for each session.").

14. *Kamehameha V*, HawaiiHistory.org, www.hawaiihistory.org (last visited July 11, 2021) (click on the "Library" tab, scroll down to the "Monarchs" section and then select "Kamehameha V") (explaining that after his sister Victoria Kamamalu's death

instead of abrogating it, sought to make it more democratic through amendment.[15] He restored suffrage to all adult males without restriction but would not see all of his amendments go up for final action: he died of tuberculosis a year into his reign, and the people then elected King Kalakaua (1874–1891) to succeed him.[16]

Only a single amendment removing the property qualification of voters, out of the thirty democratic amendments that had been proposed by Lunalilo, was adopted by the 1874 Legislature[17] and this cycle of failed legislation continued throughout the rule of Kalakaua, not least of all because corruption and abuses of power during his reign left him unpopular.[18] He was particularly unpopular with a politically powerful group of *haoles* called the Hawaiian League, and with his own troops, so when the group led a bloodless revolt against Kalakaua demanding significant curtailments of the monarch's powers, he had no choice but to give into their demands.[19] The fulfillment of one such demand became the Constitution of 1887, commonly referred to as the *Bayonet Constitution of 1887*,[20] which rolled back royal powers by, for example, making the House of Nobles, like the House of Representatives, an elected rather than an appointed body; allowing legislative override of the king's veto; and requiring legislative approval for removal of cabinet members.[21] Throughout the remainder of Kalakaua's rule, a series of movements developed to

---

in 1866, Kamehameha V did not name another heir, but then an "hour before his death in 1872, he asked Bernice Pauahi Bishop, a great-granddaughter of Kamehameha I, to take the throne but she declined.").

15. Kuykendall, *supra* note 1, at 42.
16. Lee, *supra* note 6, at 7.
17. *Kingdom of Haw. Const. of 1864*, art. LXII (1874), *reprinted in The Fundamental Law of Hawai'i* 177 (Lorrin A. Thurston ed. 1904), http://llmc.com/OpenAccess/search.aspx (open the "Hawaii" dropdown, scroll to the bottom of the list of titles and select "1840–1900, Fundamental Law, Thurston").
18. Kuykendall, *supra* note 1, at 43.
19. Lee, *supra* note 6, at 7. The Hawaiian League members, which included Lorrin A. Thurston and Sanford B. Dole, were Western and American businessmen, lawyers, missionaries, and plantation owners with strong imperialist interests. *See, e.g.*, P. Kalawai'a Moore, *American Hegemonic Discourse in Hawai'i: Rhetorical Strategies in Support of American Control over Hawai'i*, 3 Haw. J.L. & Pol. 73, 77 (2021).
20. *The Constitution Signed*, Daily Herald, July 7, 1887, https://chroniclingamerica.loc.gov (filter by Hawai'i and then conduct an advanced search with the words *bayonet constitution*) (describing the signing as being "held under guard of two hundred rifles and bayonets, with ammunition in goodly supply.").
21. Lee, *supra* note 6, at 7.

replace the Constitution of 1887. Native Hawaiians objected to the voting restrictions that diminished their role in the political life of the country, while elevating the political power of *haoles*, and loyalists demanded a return of the sovereign's powers akin to the Constitution of 1864.[22]

B. Republic and Territory

Upon Kalakaua's death in 1891, his sister, born Lydia Kamakaeha, took the name Liliʻuokalani upon becoming Queen (1891–1893). She quickly proposed a new constitution to restore the power of the monarchy and the rights of the disenfranchised Native Hawaiians, but this only ignited the annexationist sentiment of her all-ready powerful *haole* opponents. They staged a bloodless revolution, deposing her on January 17, 1893, and established a provisional government under martial law of the United States government. The United States did not rapidly move to annex the islands,[23] so the provisional government adopted a constitution—by decree, without popular vote—for the Republic of Hawaiʻi on July 4, 1894. Aside from ending the monarchy and recognizing the American separation of powers, the Constitution of the Republic of Hawaiʻi consolidated the power of Western foreigners by establishing stringent voting requirements that effectively disqualified Native Hawaiians and other groups from the Pacific Rim countries that had begun coming to the islands in the mid-1800's to work the sugar plantations.[24]

In 1898, the United States formally annexed Hawaiʻi. The new constitution for the Territory of Hawaiʻi, the *Act to Provide a Government for the Territory of Hawaiʻi*, referred to as the Organic Act, became law on June 14, 1900. The Organic Act consisted of six chapters—General Provisions, The Legislature, The Executive, The Judiciary, United States Officers, and Miscellaneous—and created structures like those of the other united states. However, there were

---

22. Kuykendall, *supra* note 1, at 50; *see also* Moore, *supra* note 19, at 82 (stating the "1887 constitution effectively disenfranchised over eighty percent of the aboriginal Hawaiian population").

23. *The 1897 Petition Against the Annexation of Hawaiʻi*, National Archives, https://www.archives.gov/education/lessons/hawaii-petition (last updated Aug. 15, 2016) (explaining that while President Benjamin Harrison had signed a treaty of annexation with the provisional government, Grover Cleveland replaced Harrison as president before the Senate could ratify it and subsequently withdrew the treaty and sought to restore Queen Liliʻuokalani to power, which the provisional government blocked, successfully arguing the U.S. had no right to interfere in Hawaiʻi's internal affairs).

24. Lee, *supra* note 6, at 8.

notable differences: 1) while members of the territorial house of representatives and senate were popularly elected, the governor and territorial court justices were appointed by the U.S. president, and 2) ultimate power and control remained with Congress so that it could specifically legislate for Hawai'i, nullify legislation passed by the territorial legislature, and alone could amend the Organic Act.[25] The Organic Act also removed the stringent voting requirements and made all persons—including Native Hawaiians, though excluding Asian immigrants—who were citizens of the Republic as of August 12, 1898, citizens of the United States and of the Territory of Hawai'i.[26]

C. Statehood

On June 17, 1959, an overwhelming number of voters in Hawai'i elected for statehood and affirmed two amendments to the *hope chest* constitution, which had been prepared and overwhelmingly adopted by voters almost a decade earlier "to demonstrate how thoroughly the people of the islands were imbued with American political and cultural traditions."[27] Shortly thereafter, on August 21, 1959, Hawai'i officially became the fiftieth state of the Union, and the *hope chest* constitution became the Statehood Constitution. Although the Statehood Constitution looks like other states' constitutions, it is different in many ways, namely that it: 1) explicitly prohibits segregation in any state military organization; 2) fixed the state voting age at twenty, while most states had set it at twenty-one; 3) establishes a single centralized school system for the state; 4) centralizes responsibility for public health, public assistance, slum clearance, low-income housing, and conservation of the land; and 5) calls for voter consideration, as a ballot initiative, at least once every ten years, as to whether the constitution should be reviewed by a constitutional convention.[28]

The 1968 Constitution came about after the Hawai'i State Supreme Court held that article III, section 2 of the State Constitution was invalid because it did not correctly apportion the state senators per senatorial district on the one

---

25. *Id.* at 9.
26. *Id.*
27. Norman Meller, *With an Understanding Heart: Constitution Making in Hawai'i*, 84 (New York: National Municipal League 1971).
28. Lee, *supra* note 6, at 12–13. In 1970, an extension of the Voting Rights Act of 1965 lowered the voting age to 18 in all federal, state, and local elections. Voting Rights Act Amendments of 1970, Pub. L. No. 91-285, § 301, 84 Stat. 318 (1970).

person-one vote principle set out in *Reynolds v. Sims*, 377 U.S. 533 (1964).[29] In response, two thirds of voters gave their approval for a constitutional convention. The 1968 Constitutional Convention incorporated provisions for future senate apportionments in the 1968 Constitution that had been left out of the Statehood Constitution. The 1968 Constitution also accomplished the following: 1) included a requirement for minimum representation for each county and *fractional votes* for legislators elected from neighbor islands to protect them from being overwhelmed by Oahu, where eighty percent of the state's population lived; 2) adopted annual sixty-day legislative sessions, ending the alternation of sixty-day legislative sessions with thirty-day budget sessions; 3) removed the requirement of the ability to read and write English or Hawaiian as a qualification for voting; 4) enabled collective bargaining for public employees; 5) added provisions protecting against invasion of privacy; and 6) guaranteed appointment of counsel for indigent defendants.[30]

Several additions to the 1978 Constitution affected voters of Hawaiian ancestry, including new sections concerning conservation, marine and water resources, and a guarantee to each person of the right to a clean and healthful environment.[31] The 1978 Constitutional Convention also made the following changes to the Constitution's bill of rights: 1) incorporated a right to privacy; 2) required twelve-person juries in criminal trials; and 3) created an independent counsel for grand juries.[32] The 1978 Constitution also accomplished the following: 1) created a new intermediate court of appeals; 2) gave local governments power over real property taxation; 3) created the Office of Hawaiian Affairs; 4) enhanced the Hawaiian Home Lands rehabilitation program; 5) required teaching Hawaiian culture in public schools; 6) established Hawaiian as an official language; 7) protected traditional and customary rights; 8) limited the use of adverse possession for acquiring title to land; and 9) granted constitutional status to the state motto, written in Hawaiian, as well as to the edict of King Kamehameha, called the *Law of the Splintered Paddle*.[33]

---

29. *Guntert v. Richardson*, 47 Haw. 662, 666, 394 P.2d 444, 447 (1964); *see also Holt v. Richardson* (Holt I), 238 F. Supp. 468, 478 (1965) (concurring with the Supreme Court of Hawai'i in *Guntert* that any change in the representation from any senatorial district must be by constitutional amendment).

30. Lee, *supra* note 6, at 17–18.

31. Haw. Const. art. XI, §§ 1, 9.

32. Lee, *supra* note 6, at 22–23.

33. *Id.*

III. Finding and Searching Within the Hawai'i Constitutions

The current Hawai'i Constitution is located within the state's official and unofficial print codes and online via Lexis, Westlaw, and the Hawai'i State Legislature website. The historical state constitutions are available in print and online at the Hawai'i State Archives Digital Collections, and the pre-statehood constitutions are available in print and online at LLMC Digital and Google Books. Using a checklist can significantly advance the research intended to locate a relevant constitutional provision within these resources.

A. Using a Checklist as a Roadmap for Researching Constitutional Law

Similar to using a checklist to guide an overall research strategy, a researcher might also consider creating and following a checklist to guide the research within specific resources likely to yield relevant authority governing an issue. Table 3-1 provides a sample checklist for conducting research to identify relevant constitutional law provisions.

Table 3-1. Checklist for Constitutional Law Research

A Checklist for Constitutional Law Research
If you already know your governing provision, locate it in a print or electronic annotated code.
Use the finding tools to understand how the courts have interpreted and applied the governing provision.
Consult relevant notes of decisions.
Consult relevant citing references to case law.
Use the finding tools to gather more background information and context about the governing provision.
Consult relevant citing references or research references to secondary sources.
If you do not know your governing provision and need to locate it in a print or electronic annotated code.

Locate relevant key terms in the indices of appropriate secondary sources (print or electronic).	
	Treatises
	Law reviews and journals
	American Law Reports
	Encyclopedias
Use relevant key terms or search strings to search within appropriate secondary sources on Westlaw or Lexis.	
	Treatises
	Law reviews and journals
	American Law Reports
	Encyclopedias
Locate relevant key terms in the index of the appropriate annotated code (print or electronic).	
Use relevant key terms or search strings to browse or search within the appropriate annotated code on Westlaw or Lexis.	
	Search from the universal search box on the home page, using as one of your search terms pr("constitution of the state of X").
	Drill down in the annotated code to locate the constitution and then browse the table of contents to locate the governing provision.
	Drill down in the annotated code to locate the constitution and then search within using relevant key terms or search strings to locate the governing provision.
Once the relevant provision is located, use the finding tools discussed at the top of this checklist to further your knowledge of the provision's background, interpretation, and application.	
Hawai'i Distinction: Use simple and relevant key terms to search the Statehood Constitution and the 1968 and 1978 Constitutions and Constitutional Convention documents (open access available at the Hawai'i State Archives Digital Collections).	
Hawai'i Distinction: Use simple and relevant key terms to search the pre-statehood constitutions (open access available at LLMC Digital and Google Books).	

Table: Cory Lenz

The discussion in the next section illustrates strategies from the checklist.

B. Finding Relevant Constitutional Provisions in the Print and Electronic Platforms

Researching the Hawai'i Constitution in print or electronically often starts in secondary sources to guide the researcher towards the applicable constitutional sections that the issue triggers. For instance, suppose your clients are seeking to stop the Department of Land and Natural Resources (DLNR) from air dropping a poison on the Big Island of Hawai'i to eradicate the black rat, a predator of native birds that along with the mongoose, feral cats, mosquitos, and other invasive species of European contact has caused the extinction of more than half the 68 native bird species that existed on the islands in 1893.[34] Your clients, who are of Native Hawaiian descent, hunt wild pigs. They consider this a traditional and customary practice being threatened by DLNR because the poison will harm their dogs and make the pig meat too toxic to eat. Consulting the print indexes of various secondary sources with the key terms describing your clients' issue or formulating a search string with the same terms in Westlaw or Lexis might lead to a governing authority. Searching with the search string, *(boar OR pig OR game) /3 hunt! & (tradition! OR custom!)*, in the secondary sources on the Hawai'i page in either Westlaw or Lexis yields several helpful law review articles that point to the first mention of article XII, section 7 of the Hawai'i Constitution, which protects Native Hawaiian traditional and customary practices.[35] You would capture this information in your research plan, along with any mention of cases interpreting and applying section 7.

---

34. Sharon Levy, *Getting the Drop on Hawai'i Invasives*, 53 BioScience 695 (Aug. 2003).

35. *See, e.g.*, Gina M. Watumull, *Pele Defense Fund v. Paty: Exacerbating the Inherent Conflict Between Hawaiian Native Tenant Access and Gathering Rights and Western Property Rights*, 16 U. Haw. L. Rev. 207, 208 (1994) (stating that "[i]n the 1992 case of *Pele Defense Fund v. Paty*, the Hawai'i Supreme Court rendered a landmark decision which broadly held that native Hawaiian rights protected by article XII, section 7 of the Hawai'i Constitution 'may extend beyond the ahupua'a in which a native Hawaiian resides where such rights have been customarily and traditionally exercised in this manner.'").

Were this strategy not fruitful, there are others to help you find the governing law. Relevant sections from the Constitution of the State of Hawai'i, published by the state of Hawai'i, LexisNexis, and Thomson Reuters, can be located using the table of contents at the beginning of each statutory volume or the general index located at the end of each statutory set. Notably, Lexis does not provide electronic access to the index, while Westlaw and the state of Hawai'i do. None of the key terms from your clients' issue when brought into the index of the *Hawai'i Revised Statutes* leads to anything relevant. Though in Westlaw, cross references within the index lead us along the following path:

Pigs > *Hogs*, as a cross reference > *Fish and Game*, as a cross reference > *Natives, Subsistence Hunting and Fishing*: HI Const Art. 12, § 7.

Searching within secondary sources and finding aids, such as indexes, have helped you find the constitutional law governing your clients' issue. Were these strategies not successful, there are still more strategies to try, such as searching within the Constitution. Lexis and Westlaw feature the Constitution of the State of Hawai'i—with extensive annotations—the Organic Act, and Admission Act on the Hawai'i page, which is accessible from the home page via the *State* tab. On Lexis, the Constitution has its own hyperlink under *Statutes & Legislation* separate from the other legislative documents. Lexis does, however, drop the Organic Act and Admission Act in a *Hawai'i Historical Documents* folder under *Michie's Hawai'i Revised Statutes Annotated*.

Similarly, on Westlaw, the Constitution and historical documents can be located by following the hyperlink to *Hawai'i Statutes & Court Rules*. To search the Constitution in both databases, you can either 1) search the entire *Hawai'i Statutes & Court Rules* from the universal search box on the home page, using as one of your search terms *pr("constitution of the state of Hawai'i")*, which will find only documents with *Constitution of the State of Hawai'i* in the preliminary field; 2) drill down and browse the Constitution's table of contents; or 3) drill down and search within the Constitution using plain language or Boolean connectors and expanders. For instance, you might try searching your clients' issue in the Constitution with the same search string used to search the secondary sources. Doing so yields zero results, thus you might modify the search string accordingly: *"Native Hawaiians" & (tradition! OR custom!)*. This strategy also leads us to article XII, section 7 as a top result in both Westlaw and Lexis; surprisingly, so does searching the *Hawai'i Revised Statutes* on the Hawai'i State Legislature website with either the phrase *traditional customary rights* or *Native Hawaiians*.

With the governing constitutional provision in hand, you would want to research the historical constitutions to gather more background information about the relevant provision that you might use to persuasively argue on behalf of your clients. Of course, the historical constitutions from the Kingdom to that of 1978 are unannotated but, nevertheless, tracking the relevant provision back through its amendments to the Kingdom is important to understanding the provision's purpose and historical significance. Afterall, many of the Kingdom laws have application to Hawai'i's modern jurisprudence. Locating relevant provisions within the historical state constitutions and pre-statehood constitutions is only hindered by the simplicity of the platform's search function. The *Hope Chest* Constitution; Statehood Constitution; 1968 Constitution, along with its Constitutional Convention documents and journals; and 1978 Constitution, along with its Constitutional Convention documents and journals are available for free electronically at the Hawai'i State Archives Digital Collections (Figure 3-1).[36] Searching the collections has the limitation of allowing only a search within PDF, so the process of finding relevant sections within historical state constitutions since the 1950 Constitutional Convention requires a bit more patience. For instance, in using key terms (e.g., *customary rights*) to search within the State Archives Digital Collections, you learn more about your clients' issue from a debate at the 1978 Constitutional Convention about the significance of protecting the traditional and customary rights of Native Hawaiians. At that convention, article XII, section 7 governing your clients' issue was renumbered, which is important for you to know to track the history of its amendments.

Simple and relevant key terms also work best when researching within open access resources for relevant provisions from the pre-statehood constitutions. The four constitutions that governed the Kingdom of Hawai'i, the Constitution of the Republic of Hawai'i, and the Organic Act that governed

---

36. Available at https://digitalcollections.hawaii.gov/greenstone3/library. These same documents, along with the journals of the 1950 Hawai'i Constitutional Convention, are available in print at the William S. Richardson School of Law Library and electronically on LLMC Digital by subscription. The Statehood Constitution can also be found in the *First State Legislature 1959* folder, in the Session Laws Library on HeinOnline. Studies pertaining to the issues addressed at the 1978 Constitutional Convention are available for free electronically at the Hawai'i Legislative Reference Bureau (LRB) (http://lrbhawaii.org/reports/1978concon.html). The current state Constitution, without annotations, is also available electronically at the LRB (http://lrbhawaii.org/con/), and with annotations via a PDF of the Hawai'i Revised Statutes, on the Hawai'i State Legislature website (https://www.capitol.hawaii.gov/docs/HRS_Index.pdf).

Figure 3-1. Constitutional Convention Journals

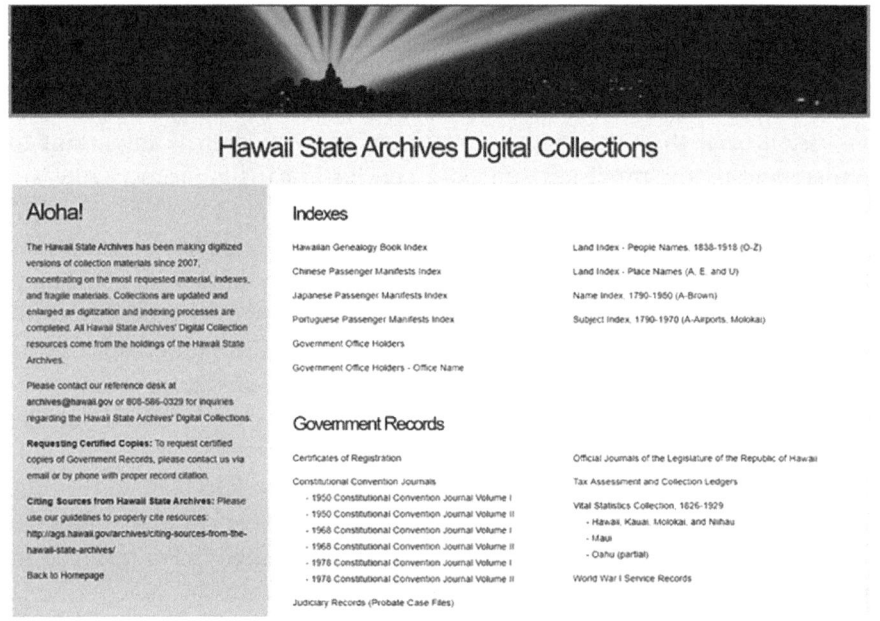

Source: Hawai'i State Archives.

the Territory were edited and indexed by Lorrin A. Thurston in *The Fundamental Law of Hawai'i* (Honolulu: Hawaiian Gazette Co., 1904). This resource is freely available on LLMC Digital[37] and Google Books.[38] Searching the pre-statehood constitutions within either of these open access resources requires only simple search terms unbounded by connectors and expanders. For instance, in researching your clients' issue in LLMC Digital, you discover the Kingdom laws make no mention or implication that pig hunting or the

---

37. Available at http://llmc.com/OpenAccess/search.aspx (open the "Hawaii" dropdown, scroll to the bottom of the list of titles and select "1840-1900, Fundamental Law, Thurston") (includes the following constitutions: 1st, by Kamehameha III, Oct. 8, 1840, at 1–9 & 291–94; 2nd, by Kamehameha III, June 14, 1852, at 155–68 & 325–36; 3rd, by Kamehameha V, Aug. 20, 1864, at 169–80 & 337–48; and 4th, by Kalakaua, July 6, 1887, at 181–94 & 349–62; Constitution of the Republic of Hawai'i, July 4, 1894, at 201–42 & 368–90; Organic Act, June 14, 1900, at 257–90 & 395–428). Additionally, the 1894 Constitution and related documents are available online at the Hawai'i State Archives, https://ags.hawaii.gov/archives/online-exhibitions/1894-constitutional-convention/.

38. Available at books.google.com (search with the terms *fundamental law thurston* and select the respective title).

hunting of game generally was a traditional or customary practice, though the laws do say this about fishing, a fact that might be extrapolated in arguing for your clients.³⁹

C. Using the Annotations in the Print and Electronic Platforms⁴⁰

In print, the current annotated Constitution of the State of Hawai'i is published officially by the state of Hawai'i in volume 1 of the *Hawai'i Revised Statutes*; unofficially by LexisNexis, in volume 15 of *Michie's Hawai'i Revised Statutes Annotated*; and unofficially by Thomson Reuters, in volume 1 of *West's Hawai'i Revised Statutes Annotated*. These resources also include significant documents from the Territory of Hawai'i, namely the Organic Act

---

39. Laws of 1942, ch. 11, § 1, *reprinted in The Fundamental Law of Hawai'i* 51, 54, 58 (Lorrin A. Thurston ed. 1904), http://llmc.com/OpenAccess/search.aspx (open the "Hawaii" dropdown, scroll to the bottom of the list of titles and select "1840-1900, Fundamental Law, Thurston") (explicitly protecting fishing rights). The eminent Hawaiian ethnographer Kepā Maly conducted an extensive review of historical records from 1840–1910 and found that pua'a or pigs were only referenced in the context of being raised, not hunted, and that the term "hunting" was rarely ever used, only in reference to the traditional collection of native birds for food or their feathers. *Pele Def. Fund v. Dep't of Land & Nat. Res.*, NO. CAAP-14-0001033, 2018 Haw. App. LEXIS 12, at *5–6. In the early 1800's, hunting was a more common practice for Native Hawaiians, but they were primarily hunting bullocks, goats, and other introduced grazers, and mainly at the request of landlords and ranchers. *Id.* at *6.

Interestingly, the earliest mentions of game or pig hunting in the archival newspaper databases describe the practice as sport among foreigners on the Islands, not as a tradition or custom among Native Hawaiians. *See, e.g., Memorandum of a Trip Around Mauna Kea*, Polynesian, Nov. 20, 1847, https://chroniclingamerica.loc.gov (filter by Hawai'i and then conduct an advanced search with any of the words *boar* OR *cattle* OR *game* OR *swine* OR *pig* OR *bull* and all the words *hunt**) (stating that "[t]his morning, I set out, accompanied by Mr. French, Mr. Parker, a guide and five natives, loaded with our provisions, for a tour around Mauna Kea...[and] geese hunting..."); *Hunting Sketches on Hawai'i*, Hawaiian Gazette, Nov. 26, 1884 (stating that "[w]ild cattle or pig hunting in Hawai'i may afford tame sport as compared to the thrilling adventures of the chase in India or Africa, but exciting enough have been some of the incidents connected with various hunting expeditions on the slopes of our larger mountains.").

40. In this section, we refer to secondary sources and methods of statutory and case law interpretation that are more fully explained in the relevant chapters. For example, specific secondary sources identified in this research example are more completely discussed in Chapter 5, Secondary Sources. The use of citators for case law and statutory materials are covered in Chapters 7 and 8 respectively.

and the Hawaiian Homes Commission Act, 1920; the Admission Act; and the Constitution of the United States. Annotations to other primary and secondary sources accompany each of these documents to help a researcher understand its historical significance or the court's interpretation and application of its provisions. The annotations that follow each amendment, article, or section within the official and unofficial Hawai'i constitutions include citations to attorney general opinions, case notes, law reviews and journals, and cross references to other Hawai'i statutes and administrative regulations that interpret or provide greater context to the respective provision. While the law reviews and journals only include the citation so that you can locate the resource, the attorney general opinions and case notes (or notes of decisions) include the citation along with a brief summary of the relevant constitutional issue addressed by the referenced source. Of course, you cannot judge the relevance of the source by its short summary; rather, you would want to critically read the text of the source to determine its relevance.

The Hawai'i Constitution in the unofficial annotated statutory codes, published by LexisNexis and Thomson Reuters, offers more annotation types and a greater number of annotations within each type than the Constitution in the official code. They include additional references in the historical notes and other annotations to secondary sources beyond law reviews and journals that include *American Law Reports*. There are also many more case notes or notes of decisions interpreting and applying the relevant constitutional law. If there are many case notes for an amendment, article, or section, the editors aid their navigation by grouping the court opinions topically as to their analysis and interpretation of the specific law. In print, this topical organization appears as a table of contents before the case notes start, and on the electronic platforms, as a filter in the notes of decisions.

Lexis and Westlaw offer the same annotations as their print equivalents, plus hyperlinks for ease of navigation within the annotations. The electronic platforms also have the advantage over the print of offering the more current Constitution, not only as to the text but the annotations as well. The variety of annotation types between the electronic platforms is not the same, however. Westlaw offers a greater variety of annotations to the Hawai'i Constitution than Lexis, including trial court orders and trial and appellate court documents that cite or discuss an amendment, article, or section of the Constitution; encyclopedias, treatises, and practice forms and guides that give more context or analysis; and cross references to related United States Code sections (Figure 3-2). Lexis does not include these additional resources. Its archive of the Constitution, though, goes back to 1991, compared to 2007 on Westlaw.

Figure 3-2. Citing References for Article XII, Section 7 of the Hawai'i Constitution

Source: Westlaw, reprinted with permission from Thomson Reuters.

At this point in your research, various strategies have identified article XII, section 7 of the Hawai'i Constitution as the governing law for your clients' issue. To gather more background and context about this section, in Westlaw you might consider the secondary sources under the *Citing References* and *Context & Analysis* tabs and in Lexis, those listed under *Research References & Practice Aids* at the bottom of the main page or under *Other Citing Sources* at the top of the page. Bolstering an argument with analogies or distinctions between the instant facts and those from relevant precedent cases that analyze, interpret, and apply the specific constitutional or statutory section is a vital and best practice in legal writing. Consulting the cases in the *Notes of (to) Decisions* and *Citing References (Decisions)* will help locate additional case law relevant to your clients' issue to both expand your research and bolster your clients' argument with good law.[41]

On Westlaw, the *Notes of Decisions* tab collects the headnotes from cases that significantly interpreted or applied the specific constitutional or statutory section; while the same cases also appear in the *Citing References*, they sometimes duplicate across the *Notes of Decisions* because multiple headnotes within the case will summarize the legal significance of the same constitutional or statutory section. The Westlaw editors write the headnotes, while those on Lexis adopt the actual language from the court opinion that succinctly states the legal principle. The table of contents and filters by date, jurisdiction, and key number on Westlaw will narrow the results and help you locate relevant cases for your clients' issue. For instance, the table of contents in the *Notes of Decisions* topically filters for those cases that analyze and interpret fishing and gathering rights as traditional and customary practices under article XII, section 7, but not hunting rights. Nevertheless, since the activities are similar, you would strategically skim those cases for relevance, using the headnotes to navigate to the relevant parts in the opinion, and note any in your research plan. You might filter out the federal cases since their interpretation and application of article XII, section 7 of the Hawai'i Constitution would not be binding, but you also might choose otherwise were you to need persuasive authority because of a lack of binding authority.

Searching or narrowing results by relevant Key Numbers is always a good research strategy in Westlaw. Here, filtering by the relevant Key Number, *209X Hunting, fishing, and similar rights (17)*, narrows the case notes from about 80 cases to 17 cases that specifically discuss the constitutionally protected customary or traditional Native Hawaiian practices (Figure 3-3).[42] After a strategic skim of the cases, you would note the relevant ones in your research plan, especially if in your research the case has been often cited across multiple resources and finding aids (e.g., secondary sources, notes of decisions, citing references, custom digest). You would also want to note in

---

41. In Westlaw, the *Notes of Decisions* are organized topically in a separate tab and the cases can be filtered by topic. Whereas in Lexis, the *Notes to Decisions* are organized topically on the main page below the constitutional law but cannot be filtered by topic or any other criteria. Additionally, in Westlaw the *Citing References* are in a separate tab, while in Lexis, the *Citing Decisions* are linked at the top of the page.

42. See Chapters 1 and 7 for a more complete discussion of the West Digest Topic and Key Number System.

Figure 3-3. Filtering by Relevant Key Numbers to Narrow Results

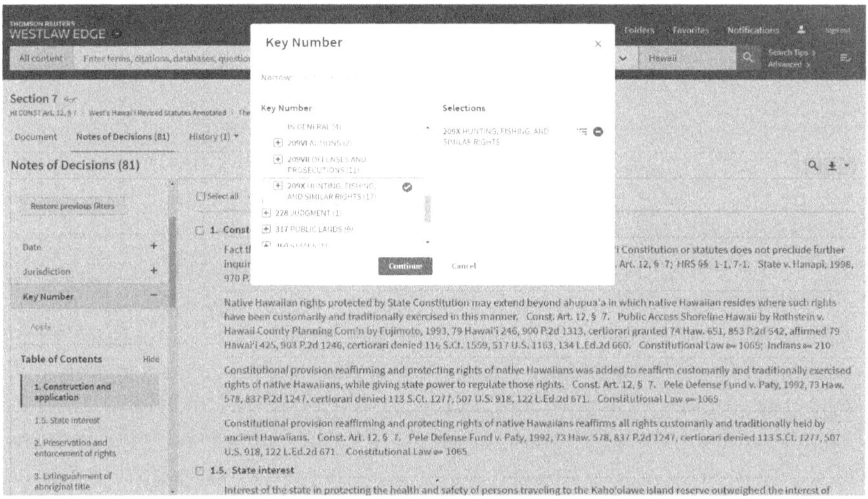

Source: Westlaw, reprinted with permission from Thomson Reuters.

your research plan any case or resource that raises questions needing additional research; for example, here you would note *State v. Pratt* because it introduces a new concept, the three-factor *Hanapi* test,[43] which establishes conduct that is protected under article XII, section 7 of the Hawai'i Constitution as a Native Hawaiian right, and a balancing test of the constitutionally protected practice and the State's interests.[44] Finally, you can also isolate the most relevant case notes by searching within the results using key terms and Boolean connectors or expanders.

---

43. *State v. Hanapi*, 89 Hawai'i 177, 185–86, 970 P.2d 485, 493–94 (1998) (identifying that conduct is constitutionally protected as a Native Hawaiian right when the party: 1) qualifies as a Native Hawaiian within the guidelines set out in *Pub. Access Shoreline Haw. v. Haw. Cnty. Plan. Comm'n (PASH)*, 79 Hawai'i 425, 903 P.2d 1246 (1995); 2) establishes that the claimed right is constitutionally protected as a customary or traditional Native Hawaiian practice; and 3) proves that the exercise of the right occurred on undeveloped or less than fully developed property).

44. *State v. Pratt*, 124 Hawai'i 329, 355, 243 P.3d 289, 315 (Ct. App. 2010) (holding that the "consideration of a balancing of interests was necessary to the court's legal determination of whether, under the circumstances before the court, the exercise of customary and traditional native Hawaiian practices was constitutionally protected.").

Consulting both Westlaw and Lexis during the research process is important because the platforms have different case notes and annotations, and not doing so could negatively impact a client. Your clients' issue is a perfect example. The Westlaw case notes do not discuss hunting as a traditional or customary right; however, on Lexis the *Notes to Decisions* include two cases under topics related to hunting: *Pele Defense Fund v. DLNR* and *State v. Palama*. Were you to have researched only in Westlaw, you possibly would have excluded these cases from your court filing, making you vulnerable to attorney misconduct claims. Though the decisions are unpublished and, thus, persuasive authority,[45] you would include both in your research plan, noting the unique challenge each presents: 1) *Pele Defense Fund* would need to be distinguished because the court held against the pig hunters for failing the *Hanapi* test and implicitly suggested the State's preservation interests would outweigh the hunters' practice were it constitutionally protected[46] and 2) while *Palama* held for the pig hunter for satisfying the *Hanapi* test, the hunting occurred on private property, not on public lands as in your clients' case, and the State offered no evidence to controvert the hunter's experts' and kama'aina witnesses' testimony that pig hunting is "an established native Hawaiian custom or tradition practiced prior to 1892."[47]

The *Citing References* in Westlaw and *Citing Decisions* in Lexis are tools to determine the treatment of the law and to locate relevant cases that analyzed, interpreted, and applied the specific constitutional, statutory, or regulatory section.[48] Generally, the citing references in both research platforms include cases, statutes, court rules, regulations, administrative decisions, secondary sources, and court documents, across jurisdictions (e.g., federal, state, tribal

---

45. Haw. R. App. P. 35, https://www.courts.state.hi.us/docs/court_rules/rules/hrap.pdf (stating that "unpublished dispositional orders are not precedent, but may be cited for persuasive value").

46. *Pele Def. Fund v. Dep't of Land & Nat. Res.*, NO. CAAP-14-0001033, 2018 Haw. App. LEXIS 12, at *31, *38, *40 (Jan. 22, 2018) (acknowledging the uncertainty on whether or not hunting for pigs is considered a traditional cultural practice, but finding the hunters did not "provide a foundational basis for assertion of a traditional or customary native Hawaiian practice, for instance in the form of an asserted specialized knowledge or kama'aina witness testimony, as it relates to pig hunting in the Ka'ū Forest Reserve ... [and] that some regulation was necessary to preserve the native ecosystem and watershed").

47. *State v. Palama*, NO. CAAP-12-0000434, 2015 Haw. App. LEXIS 587, at *19–20 (Dec. 11, 2015).

48. See Chapters 7 and 8 for an understanding of how these tools are used generally.

law). For article XII, section 7 of the Hawaiʻi Constitution, Westlaw includes all these citing references, whereas Lexis only includes case law and a few law reviews and journals. In both research platforms, there are over sixty cases citing the governing law of your clients' issue and various filters to help narrow the results (e.g., date, jurisdiction). In Lexis, there are additional *Analysis* or treatment filters and on Westlaw, *Reported Status* and *Notes of Decisions Topics* filters. You can also narrow the results by using key terms from your clients' issue to search within the citing references. For instance, with synonyms of the key terms and connectors or expanders, you might use the following search string to identify the relevant cases (Figure 3-4):

(pig OR swine OR boar OR bull OR cattle) & (hunt! OR stalk! OR trap!)

On Westlaw, this search identifies the *Palama* and *Pele Defense Fund* cases that searching and filtering within the *Notes of Decisions* did not. Interestingly, the same search on Lexis delivers slightly different results, further impressing upon a researcher to get into the habit of using both platforms.

Figure 3-4. Searching Within the Citing References

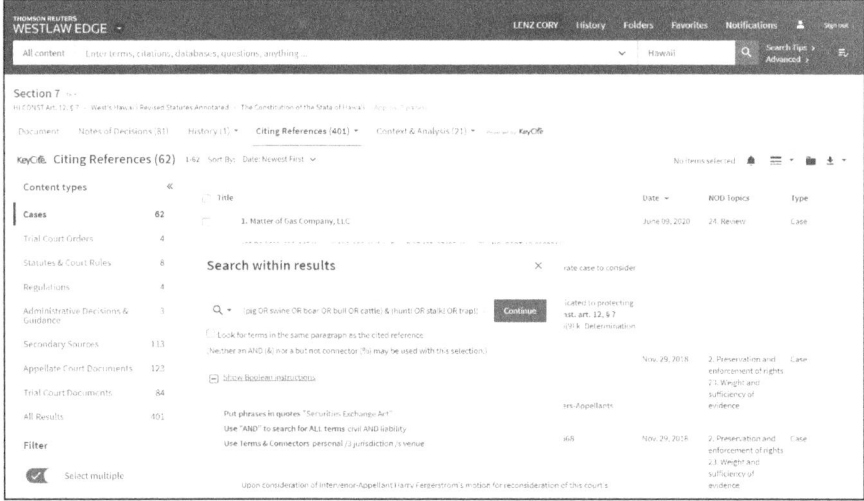

Source: Westlaw. Reprinted with permission of Thomson Reuters.

IV. Updating the Constitution of the State of Hawai'i

Revisions of, or amendments to, the Constitution must be proposed by constitutional convention at least once every ten years or may be proposed by the Hawai'i legislature.[49] If revised or amended by the legislature, a two-thirds vote of each chamber must send it to the electorate as a proposition, at which point the conditions of and requirements for ratification are the same as those for ratification at a general election.[50] Each proposition to revise or amend the Constitution is submitted to the voters in the form of a question embracing only one subject and spaces to mark YES or NO on the amendment.[51] The revision or amendments are effective only if approved at a general election by a majority of all the votes tallied upon the question.[52] Thus, similar to statutory research, you have to carefully track developments at the legislature to confirm that you are relying on the most current text of the Constitution.

To update the Hawai'i Constitution, published by the state of Hawai'i, LexisNexis, or Thomson Reuters, check the pocket part or supplement at the back of the appropriate volume of the annotated statutory code. The pocket part updates any changes to the language of the Constitution and includes new cases interpreting and applying the Constitution, as well as other research references providing additional context and background information that followed the publication of the main volume. But because the pocket parts are published annually, other tools are needed to capture the most current information that falls between publications. The text of new public laws and constitutional amendments can be tracked with the *Session Laws of Hawai'i*, which have a faster publishing schedule at the close of each session

---

49. Haw. Const. art. XVII, § 1, states:

> The legislature may submit to the electorate at any general or special election the question, "Shall there be a convention to propose a revision of or amendments to the Constitution?" If any nine-year period shall elapse during which the question shall not have been submitted, the lieutenant governor shall certify the question, to be voted on at the first general election following the expiration of such period.

50. *Id.* § 3.
51. *Id.* § 2.
52. *Id.*

of the legislature. Free online resources, like those at the Hawaiʻi State Legislature,[53] and subscription-based platforms probably offer a researcher the most current text of the Constitution.

Updating a relevant constitutional section on the research platforms is slightly easier with Lexis' Shepard's than Westlaw's KeyCite. Westlaw does not apply the KeyCite treatment flags to sections of the Constitution as it does to statutes and regulations. Within the citing references to the Constitution, Westlaw also does not indicate each citing case's treatment of and depth of discussion about the relevant section as it does when case law is KeyCited. Thus, a researcher would have to spend more time skimming citing decisions to gauge treatment and the court's analysis. Conversely, while Lexis also does not indicate the citing cases' depth of discussion about the relevant constitutional section, Shepard's on Lexis does provide each citing decision's treatment of the relevant constitutional section. For instance, in using Shepard's to update the law governing your clients' issue, you quickly determine there is no negative treatment of article XII, section 7 of the Hawaiʻi Constitution and only positive (e.g., followed by) or neutral (e.g., interpreted or construed by) treatment, which you can use as filters to narrow the results.

V. Interpreting the Constitution of the State of Hawaiʻi

Understanding how the state's highest court has interpreted the state constitution is important to advancing the practitioner's research and argument. States and the federal government cannot interfere with the other's exercise of its constitutional powers. A state's exercise of its constitutional powers includes granting its citizens access to the courts and to remedies where none exist federally and providing greater protections than those offered by the federal constitution. Your Native Hawaiian clients seeking to protect pig hunting as a traditional and customary right is one illustration of the Hawaiʻi Constitution bestowing access to the courts and to remedies for an issue the federal constitution does not recognize. After listening to your clients' story for the first time, you did not know a remedy existed for them: that knowledge only came with research. You gained an understanding of the applicable law because your search within multiple secondary sources and the

---

53. Available at https://www.capitol.hawaii.gov/.

annotated code, guided by a checklist and research plan, uncovered the often-cited and -discussed state constitutional law governing the issue and the relevant cases interpreting the law. Accurate and thoughtful legal research sets the stage for accurate and thoughtful legal writing. Armed with the courts' interpretations, you would then apply them to your clients' facts, illustrating the significant analogies and distinctions between the instant and precedent cases, in a clear and concise written argument that persuades and assures the court that the law favors your clients and consistently so.

Moreover, a state's exercise of its constitutional powers also includes interpreting the state constitution equivalent of the federal constitution more broadly to provide greater protections. Were a practitioner to argue only the minimum protections under the federal constitution, unaware of the greater state protections, he would fail in his duty to fully advocate for the client under the law and likely face some form of punishment from the court. A thoughtful, well-organized research strategy would have safeguarded the practitioner's professional and ethical responsibility because searching within relevant resources would have uncovered discussions and analyses of these greater state protections that give the client a potential remedy that does not exist at the federal level.

Aside from the protections for Native Hawaiian traditional and customary rights,[54] the Hawai'i Constitution provides other protections that do not exist in the United States Constitution or other state constitutions, and still others the Hawai'i courts have interpreted more broadly than their federal equivalents to lend greater protections. For instance, the Hawai'i Constitution gives greater protections to its citizens with an explicit right to privacy,[55] an Equal Rights Amendment,[56] and an explicit right to a clean and healthful environment.[57] Article XI, section 9 has been used by citizens of Hawai'i to bring private rights of action under statutes related to "environmental quality."[58] Additionally, the Hawai'i Supreme Court has extended the protection of the

---

54. Haw. Const. art. XII, § 7; *see also Pub. Access Shoreline Haw. v. Haw. Cnty. Plan. Comm'n (PASH)*, 79 Hawai'i 425, 451, 903 P.2d 1246, 1272 (1995).

55. Haw. Const. art. I, §§ 6, 7; *see also State v. Lester*, 64 Haw. 659, 667, 649 P.2d 346, 353 (1982).

56. Haw. Const. art. I, §§ 1, 5.

57. Haw. Const. art. XI, § 9.

58. *See County of Hawai'i v. Ala Loop Homeowners*, 123 Hawai'i 391, 408, 235 P.3d 1103, 1120 (2010); *In re Maui Elec. Co.*, 141 Hawai'i 249, 264, 408 P.3d 1, 16 (2017).

Equal Protection Clause to a single peremptory challenge based on race,[59] beyond the federal protections against multiple peremptory challenges based on race.[60]

The Hawaiʻi Constitution also gives all citizens greater protections under its search and seizure laws,[61] criminal defendants receive additional protections than those articulated by the U.S. Supreme Court,[62] and Native Hawaiians receive greater protections of their culture and ancestry.[63] For instance,

---

59. *State v. Batson*, 71 Haw. 300, 302–03, 788 P.2d 841, 842 (1990).

60. *Batson v. Kentucky*, 476 U.S. 79 (1986).

61. Haw. Const. art. I, § 7; *see also State v. Wong*, 137 Hawaiʻi 330, 350, 372 P.3d 1065, 1085 (2015) (finding warrantless searches and seizures are "unreasonable *per se* absent a few specifically established and well-delineated exceptions."); *State v. Torres*, 125 Hawaiʻi 382, 394, 262 P.3d 1006, 1018 (2011) (holding that the exclusionary rule analysis requires consideration of all three principles set forth in *Mapp v. Ohio*, 367 U. S. 643, 657–59 (1961), judicial integrity, protection of individual privacy, and deterrence of illegal police misconduct, and not merely the latter principle as under federal law); *State v. Rothman*, 70 Haw. 546, 556, 779 P.2d 1, 7 (1989) (where the Hawaiʻi Supreme Court departed from the U.S. Supreme Court's decision in *Smith v. Maryland*, 442 U.S. 735 (1979), and held that the installation of a pen register by the State to tap a phone was a search for purposes of requiring a warrant).

62. *See State v. Eli*, 126 Hawaiʻi 510, 523, 273 P.3d 1196, 1209 (2012) (interpreting article I, section 10 of the Hawaiʻi Constitution, to hold that the initial solicitation of a statement by the police for the defendant's "side of the story" must be preceded by the Miranda advisement and a waiver of rights); *State v. Luilama*, 9 Haw. App 447, 462–63, 845 P.2d 1194, 1204 (1992) (holding that the government cannot conduct a post-indictment interrogation until the accused has been advised by the court or by counsel of his parallel Sixth Amendment rights under article I, section 14 of the Hawaiʻi Constitution, and Fifth Amendment Miranda warnings do not suffice as an advisement of Sixth Amendment rights as they do under federal law); *State v. Matafeo*, 71 Haw. 183, 187, 787 P.2d 671, 673 (1990) (stating a defendant does not have to show that the police acted in bad faith in destroying evidence if the evidence was "so critical to the defense as to make a criminal trial fundamentally unfair without it."); *State v. Batangan*, 71 Haw. 552, 562, 799 P.2d 48, 54 (1990) (limiting expert testimony to explain behavior of child sex abuse victims, but *not* to establish credibility of the victim); *State v. Suka*, 70 Haw. 472, 476, 777 P.2d 240, 242 (1989) (finding that a defendant was denied his right to a fair trial because of the close physical presence of a neutral third party to the alleged victim); *State v. O'Brien*, 68 Haw. 39, 44, 704 P.2d 883, 887 (1985) (extending the constitutional right to a jury trial to those charged with driving under the influence even though the punishment does not include imprisonment exceeding six months); *see also* Jon M. Van Dyke, et al., *Protection of Individual Rights Under Hawaiʻi Constitution*, 14 U. Haw. L. Rev. 311, 340–41 (1992).

63. Haw. Const. art. XII, §§ 4–7.

the Constitution of the State of Hawai'i affirms that the State holds 1.2 million acres of land, conveyed by Congress back to the State from lands ceded to the United States in 1898, as a Public Land Trust with Native Hawaiians and the general public as the two distinct named beneficiaries.[64] The Constitution requires the State to allocate a pro rata share of the revenue from the Public Land Trust to the Office of Hawaiian Affairs for the betterment of Native Hawaiians.[65] Finally, the Public Trust Doctrine is a fundamental principle of the constitutional law of Hawai'i, used to protect and conserve the scenic beauty, natural resources, and ecological balance of the islands for present and future generations.[66]

---

64. *Id.* § 4; *see also* Jon M. Van Dyke, *The Political Status of the Native Hawaiian People*, 17 Yale L. & Pol'y Rev. 95, 105, 108–09 (1998).

65. Haw. Const. art. XII, §§ 5–6; *see also* Van Dyke, *supra* note 64, at 109.

66. Haw. Const. art. XI, §§ 1, 7.

The modern expression of the public trust doctrine was first advanced in the United States Supreme Court decision *Illinois Central Railroad v. Illinois*, 146 U.S. 387, 452 (1892), where the Court stated that title for the land at issue was "held in trust for the people of the State that they may enjoy the navigation of the waters, carry on commerce over them, and have liberty of fishing therein freed from the obstruction or interference of private parties." Several years later, the Hawai'i Supreme Court first endorsed the public trust doctrine in *King v. Oahu Railway & Land Co.*, 11 Haw. 717, 725 (1899), where the Court affirmed that "[t]he people of Hawai'i hold the absolute rights to all its navigable waters and the soils under them for their own common use... [and that] [t]he lands under the navigable waters... are held in trust for the public uses of navigation." Later court decisions confirmed and expanded Hawai'i's embrace of the public trust doctrine. *See, e.g., Kauai Springs, Inc. v. Plan. Comm'n of Kauai*, 130 Hawai'i 407, 426, 312 P.3d 283, 302 (Ct. App. 2013); *Kelly v. 1250 Oceanside Partners*, 111 Hawai'i 205, 226, 140 P.3d 985, 1006 (2006); *In re Water Use Permit Application (Waiāhole I)*, 94 Hawai'i 97, 135, 9 P.3d 409, 447 (2000).

Chapter 4

Researching *Kānaka Maoli*[1] (Native Hawaiian) Custom and Law

I. Introduction

Researching Native Hawaiian custom and law demands a thorough understanding of Hawai'i's unique history and many documents, including sections of the U.S. Constitution, sections of the Hawai'i Constitution amended in 1978, particular Hawai'i Administrative Rules, particular chapters in the Hawai'i Revised Statutes and associated legislative materials, and court decisions that interpret and enforce these laws.

II. Checklist for Researching Native Hawaiian Custom and Law

- ☐ Consult *Native Hawaiian Law, a Treatise* for your legal issue.
- ☐ Note the primary authority precedents.
- ☐ If necessary, locate original or historic documents.

---

1. *Kānaka Maoli* means "true people." It is how Native Hawaiians refer to themselves. Melody Kapilialoha MacKenzie, Native Hawaiian Law, A Treatise, xv (2015).

III. Native Hawaiian Law, a Treatise

For a thorough examination of each Native Hawaiian legal issue see *Native Hawaiian Law, a Treatise* edited by Melody Kapilialoha MacKenzie (2015). The book includes a table of contents in the front of the book as well as a general index at the back. Additional aids for research include an Index of Cases on page 1351 and an Index of Statutes, Regulations and Other Documents begins on page 1356, and the General Index begins on page 1365.

Always begin your research with a consultation of *Native Hawaiian Law, a Treatise* to become grounded in the legal issue and precedents. The customary and cultural differences between Native Hawaiians and those from a western society are significant and succinctly described in chapter 18 in *Native Hawaiian Law, a Treatise*, as "[w]estern culture ... stresses the independence of the individual rather than interdependence on extended family."[2]

For example, throughout the history of Hawai'i, real property litigation and western ideas of property where ownership gives exclusive rights often clash with *Kānaka Maoli* who trace their ancestry to the 'āina (land) and cultivated land communally. Begin by noting the precedents as you read chapter 14 "Traditional and Customary Access and Gathering Rights" in *Native Hawaiian Law, a Treatise* by David M. Forman and Susan K. Serrano.[3] In it they examine the legal precedents of gathering rights that began with the 1840 Constitution in the "Exposition of the Principles on Which the Present Dynasty is Founded."[4] Followed by the "Law Creating the Board of Commissioners to Quiet Land Titles" that was passed by the House of Nobles and House of Representatives October 4, 1845.[5] The *Māhele* or land division began January 27, 1848, with a division of land between King Kamehameha

---

2. N. Kanale Sadowski & K. Kaanoi Walk *Pili Ohana: Family Relationships*, Ch. 18 in Native Hawaiian Law, A Treatise 1138 (Melody Kapilialoha MacKenzie ed. 2015).

3. David M. Forman & Susan K. Serrano *Traditional and Customary Access and Gathering Rights*, Ch. 14 in Native Hawaiian Law, A Treatise (2015).

4. Lorrin A. Thurston, The Fundamental Law of Hawai'i, Lorrin A. Thurston, ed., 1902, 3, *available at* https://books.google.com/books/about/The_Fundamental_Law_of_Hawai'i.html?id=vW9LAQAAIAAJ.

5. Joint Resolution to promulgate Art. IV, [Of the Board of Commissioners to Quiet Land Titles] ch. VII [Of the Hawaiian Land Office], 81. Originally passed Oct. 4, 1845, p. 65 in Records of the Legislators 1841–1845 (typescript in English) available at http://www.llmc.com/OpenAccess/docDisplay5.aspx?textid=46870310.

III and the chiefs coming first, the *konohiki* (landlords) second, and native tenants third.

This was followed in 1850 by the Kuleana Act.[6] This important piece of legislation guaranteed native tenants' rights to gather necessary natural resources for subsistence living within their *ahupua'a*, a wedge of land that typically ran from the sea to the top of the mountain. As a result, Hawaiian gathering rights, a defense to trespass, have been protected since Aug. 6, 1850. The Constitutional Convention of 1978 incorporated Article XII, section 7 to further protect the traditional and customary rights of the native population. Then you would follow the case law for each identified provision.[7]

Your research when reading might look something like this to begin:

Table 4-1. Example of Research Log for Native Hawaiian Topic

From Ch. 14 Native Hawaiian Law, a Treatise

David M. Forman and Susan K. Serrano, Ch. 14 *Traditional and Customary Access and Gathering Rights* in NATIVE HAWAIIAN LAW, A TREATISE (2015).

Page	Authority	Where Found
784	1840 Constitution	Lorrin A. Thurston, ed. THE FUNDAMENTAL LAW OF HAWAI'I, Honolulu: Hawaiian Gazette, 3, 1902, *available at* https://books.google.com/books/about/The_Fundamental_Law_of_Hawai'i.html?id=vW9LAQAAIAAJ.

---

6. The Kuleana Act passed Aug. 6, 1850, was titled *An Act Confirming Certain Resolutions of the King and Privy Council, Passed on the 21st Day of December, A. D. 1849, Granting to the Common People Allodial Titles for Their Own Lands and House Lots, and Certain Other Privileges*, L. 1850, p. 202–04. It was amended July 11, 1851, p. 98, by removing some language that seemed to allow *konohikis* (landlords) to prohibit tenants full rights to the awarded land.

7. The Hawai'i Supreme Court gives a thorough legal history of gathering rights in *Pub. Access Shoreline Haw. v. Haw. Cnty. Planning Comm'n*, 79 Hawai'i 425, 903 P.2d 1246 (1995), cert. denied, 517 U.S. 1163 (1996).

785	1845 Board of Commissioners to Quiet Land Titles	Joint Resolution to promulgate Art. IV, [Of the Board of Commissioners to Quiet Land Titles] ch. VII [Of the Hawaiian Land Office], 81. Originally passed Oct. 4, 1845, p. 65 in RECORDS OF THE LEGISLATORS 1841–1845 (typescript in English) *available at* http://www.llmc.com/OpenAccess/docDisplay5.aspx?textid=46870310.
785	1848 Māhele begins	Jon J. Chinen, *The Great Māhele: Hawai'i's Land Division of 1848* (1958) *available at* http://www.llmc.com/OpenAccess/docdisplay5.aspx?textid=39974848 noting [p. 29] that all Māhele awards were subject to the rights of native tenants (*koe nae ke kuleana o na kānaka*).
786, 790	1849–50 The Kuleana Act	Reprinted in Chinen, *Māhele*, 29–31

Table: Roberta F. Woods.

To research the gathering rights guaranteed under the original Kuleana Act, you will need to examine historic materials. To aid you in that pursuit, the University of Hawai'i School of Law Library offers a research guide to resources available online from 1822–1898.[8] Consider this illustration of how to track enacted law from the Kingdom era to current times. The Kuleana Act was passed in 1850. Section 7 of the 1850 Kuleana Act became section 7-1 in the Hawai'i Revised Statutes. However, the history of the current statute does not show its origin in 1850 nor its amendment in 1851.[9] Instead, you would need a good secondary authority such as *Native Hawai'i Law, A Treatise*, to guide you and knowledge of the publication of Kingdom and Territorial laws in order to get a full picture of this important law. By reviewing these historic materials, you would learn how the law came into being.

---

8. Most of the resources are freely available online: https://law-Hawai'i.libguides.com/Hawai'ilawsonline.

9. The Kuleana Act passed Aug. 6, 1850, was titled *An Act Confirming Certain Resolutions of the King and Privy Council, Passed on the 21st Day of December, A. D. 1849, Granting to the Common People Allodial Titles for Their Own Lands and House Lots, and Certain Other Privileges*, L. 1850, p. 202–04. It was amended July 11, 1851, p. 98, by removing some language that seemed to allow *konohikis* (landlords) to prohibit tenants full rights to the awarded land.

At a Privy Council[10] meeting in the Palace on December 21, 1849, William L. Lee, then Chief Justice of the Superior Court of Law and Equity who had served on the Board of Commissioners to Quiet Land Titles since 1847 suggested the changes to the *kuleana* lands, i.e. land of the native *hoa'āina* (tenants). The changes became known commonly as The Kuleana Act.[11]

---

10. Dec. 21, 1849. Freely available online http://llmc.com/OpenAccess/docDisplay5.aspx?textid=14174785.

11. William Little Lee arrived in Hawai'i Oct. 12, 1846 and was appointed Chief Justice of the Superior Court Jan. 15, 1848. *Appointments Under the Act to Organize the Judiciary*, 43 The Polynesian 139, Jan. 15, 1848, available at https://chroniclingamerica.loc.gov. The Superior Court created in 1847 eventually became the Supreme Court by the 1852 Constitution. *See* https://digitalcollections.hawaii.gov/greenstone3/sites/localsite/collect/governm1/index/assoc/HASH4282/af22b0e7.dir/doc.pdf.

Chapter 5

Secondary Sources

I. Introduction

This chapter will introduce you to different types of secondary authorities and illustrate how you can find topic specific references on your own. These tools will summarize the trends in the law and identify leading primary authorities on the subject. Lawyers use secondary sources to learn about the law and find citations to primary authority. They are particularly helpful for new lawyers who are just becoming conversant in their specialty, or experienced practitioners who are jumping into a new area of law. These research tools can also breakdown complicated areas of law so that your research path becomes clearer and more efficient.

As you begin your research project, consulting a secondary source first will help you organize your analysis and contextualize your primary authority. Because the law is varied and complicated, best practices dictate that you consult a few secondary sources to gain the best understanding of your subject area. Although using several of these resources is a highly recommended way to begin your research, secondary sources should be consulted throughout your research process as new issues emerge.

II. What Are Secondary Sources?

Secondary sources, also called secondary authorities, help you learn about the primary law (i.e., not a case, statute, regulation, or other type of authority issued by the government). You should think of secondary sources as a team of experts that can help you learn an area or facet of the law in various degrees of complexity and authority. Each "team member" has her own expertise and opinion for you to consider when building your argument or drafting your legal documents. As you read more about your legal issue in a secondary source, you will often be alerted to underlying sub-issues that you may have been unaware of and learn the lexicon of the courts when writing or discussing these issues.

A secondary source is also a time saver. It collects the important cases and statutes on an issue and can refer you to other secondary sources in order to gain a complete understanding of your client's legal issues. It will help you decide if you have a statutory or common law question to answer, or both, and if you are working with federal or state law, or both. Secondary sources include dictionaries, encyclopedias, articles, treatises, and form books just to name a few and you can use them at any point in your research process.

III. Features of and Tips for Finding Secondary Sources Online

The secondary sources discussed in this chapter are commercial products and not accessible on the internet for free. The three primary legal databases—Blomberg Law, Lexis, and Westlaw—are the typical points of access for these materials. There is some overlap, especially between Lexis and Westlaw; however, the interface for these resources present different opportunities and challenges. As a general matter, Westlaw will often provide an alphabetical index to their resources. An index compiles all the related content for a particular subject in one place, making it a convenient reference tool. This feature is typically not available on either Bloomberg Law or Lexis in which cases you can only rely upon your keyword searches.

We recommend that you begin your research within a specific title or type of secondary source rather than generating a generic results list that may not present the information you need comprehensively. Lexis, and Westlaw allow you to browse secondary sources and search specific titles rather than searching their entire database. The path to follow is provided in the description of each of these resources listed later in this chapter.

This recommendation is made for a couple of practical reasons. First, if you are using keyword searching to find secondary sources, the existence of an index or table of contents to the publication may not be obvious. For a novice researcher, these tools will be indispensable. Second, the number of hits you retrieve from a generic keyword search might be over- or under-whelming. This may be related to your choice of keywords and unfamiliarity with the formal language used by scholars and judges. Using a navigation tool like a table of contents or an index will avoid those frustrating moments.

IV. Types of Secondary Sources

Secondary sources can be divided roughly into four categories:

- finding aids,
- practitioner aids,
- highly persuasive authorities, and
- current awareness resources

Some publications can fit into more than one category. Those just learning about these resources may not appreciate the differences between these categories at first, but with practice it will become apparent when it is appropriate to refer to one type or another. The common features among them include explanations of legal doctrine and citations to primary law and other secondary sources. In practice, you will cite only the types of publications that bear the standards of highly persuasive secondary sources. Highly persuasive secondary sources are distinguished due to the high quality of analysis and the authors' reputation in the legal community.

A few of the more popular, general secondary sources are described below. Most of these resources are not jurisdiction specific, so you will need to look for binding authority in the narrative or footnotes or use what you learn to find the controlling law in Hawai'i or the Ninth Circuit. There are very few Hawai'i specific secondary sources. Those that exist are listed under Practitioner Aids: and they are not available in digital format. Both the University of Hawai'i Law Library and the Hawai'i Supreme Court Library have multiple copies of these books that can be checked out for review.

A. Finding Aids

Finding aids include legal encyclopedias and a series called the American Law Reports. These are basic sources that will lift you up and get you on your way. They are an excellent way for new attorneys to learn the basics of the legal issue they are researching in order to get to the next level of analysis. Because they are helper tools, they are not regarded with the same level of gravitas by the courts as are more authoritative sources discussed below. As a result, you should not cite to finding aids in your briefs or memos. For example, an article in the American Law Reports may provide an analysis that fits your research question perfectly, but rather than cite the finding aid, you should consult the primary authority or a better secondary authority supporting the information provided in the American Law Report article. These resources are described in more detail below.

1. Legal Encyclopedias

Encyclopedias provide short entries that focus on particular phrases or issues. There are two national legal encyclopedias: *American Jurisprudence 2d* (also called Am Jur) and *Corpus Juris Secundum* (also called C.J.S.). In print, these encyclopedias arrange legal topics alphabetically and consist of more than 100 volumes. For example, the first topic in Volume 1 of Am Jur 2d is "Abandoned, Lost and Unclaimed Property" and the last topic in Volume 83 is "Zoning and Planning." You can scan the spine of the volumes in your library to identify the topic you are interested in or use the multi-volume index. Entries on specific legal topics are typically only a few paragraphs long, will cite to relevant primary authority, and cross reference other secondary sources to help you advance your research. Encyclopedias are a recommended starting point for researchers especially if you are unfamiliar with the area of law that you are researching.

In order to demonstrate how a secondary source like a legal encyclopedia will help you with your research plan, consider the following hypothetical. Your supervising attorney tells you that in October, a client's eight-year-old daughter broke her arm swinging on a neighbor's home- made swing in his backyard when the cord broke. She might then ask you to research the doctrine of attractive nuisance to determine if you should take the case and sue the neighbor. Starting your research with secondary sources will help you navigate this tort.

To demonstrate a possible layout for a research plan and log and to illustrate what your preliminary work might look like, review Table 5-1, Preliminary research plan for attractive nuisance:

Table 5-1. Preliminary Research Plan for Attractive Nuisance

Jurisdiction	Hawai'i
Applicable Law	Hawai'i State law
Preliminary Issue	Under Hawai'i state law, can a landowner be held liable under the doctrine of attractive nuisance when a swing he made and installed on his property resulted in a child breaking their arm when playing on it without permission?
Keywords	"attractive nuisance" child! swing
Description of relevant facts should include synonyms and draw attention to any relationship that exist between the parties/facts.	
When	October 2020
Who—Plaintiff	Child! (girl, 8 years), her parents, guest? Trespasser? Invitee?
Who—Defendant	Landowner, property owners, host?
What—caused the event	Child played on homemade swing, the swing rope broke, the child fell
What—was the harm	The child broke her arm
What—are the potential claims and defenses	Attractive nuisance Trespass

Table: Victoria Szymczak

To find relevant information, you can search for *attractive nuisance* or use an index to find all entries related to *attractive nuisance* in the specific database for this title. In this example from Lexis, you are looking at one section of a larger chapter in Am Jur 2d. If you only look at the one section, you will miss out on other useful information and citations. Review Figures 5-1, Am Jur 2d Section 295 and 5-2. Am Jur 2d Cross References to Other Resources.

Figure 5-1. Am Jur 2d Section 295

62 Am Jur 2d Premises Liability § 295

Copy Citation

American Jurisprudence 2d (AMJUR) > Premises Liability > V. Duties and Liabilities to Children > C. Attractive Nuisance Doctrine and Related Rules > 4. Restatement Rule

Author

Paul M. Coltoff, J.D.; Janice Holben, J.D.; Sonja Larsen, J.D.; Jack K. Levin, J.D.; Lucas Martin, J.D.; Karl Oakes, J.D.; and Eric C. Surette, J.D.

§ 295 Relation of Restatement rule governing attractive nuisance to attractive nuisance doctrine

There is considerable disagreement among the courts as to whether the Restatement [1] primarily reformulated the **attractive nuisance** doctrine or adopted a basically new approach. Some courts, focusing on the similarities between the two rules, rather than on their differences, apparently treat them as if they are the same. [2] It has also been said that the **attractive nuisance** doctrine is not contrary to the principles set forth in the Restatement. [3]

Source: Lexis+, reprinted with permission from LexisNexis.

Figure 5-2. Am Jur 2d Cross References to Other Resources

Reference
West's Key Number Digest, Negligence [westkey]1016, 1172 to 1177
A.L.R. Index, Attractive Nuisances
West's A.L.R. Digest, Negligence [westkey]1016, 1172 to 1177
West's Key Number Digest, Negligence [westkey]1173

Source: Lexis+, reprinted with permission from LexisNexis.

After thoroughly reading all sections in this Am Jur 2d, chapter, your research plan will continue to develop. For example, now you know that in law, this type of action is properly called premises liability, and you need to add that to your search words. You also learned that there is a *Restatement (Second) of the Law of Torts* section to review, and you need to find out if Hawai'i has adopted this Restatement of the Law. This chapter tells you that there are seven West key numbers related to this topic and that there are entries in the *American Law Reports* for you to read.[1] Although there are no Hawai'i cases cited in these sections, you can use the methods outlined in chapter 7 to find related case law for Hawai'i. Your evolved research plan should now look more like this and you should have additional questions about your client's situation to make a full analysis. Review Table 5-2. Developed research plan with secondary sources.

---

1. See Chapter 1 for a discussion about the West key number system.

Table 5-2. Developed Research Plan with Secondary Sources

Issue Statement	Under Hawai'i state law, can a landowner be held liable for premises liability when an eight year old girl falls from a broken swing on his property?
Additional Questions	Has Hawai'i adopted the Restatement (Second) of Torts, Ch. 13? Was the child a guest or trespasser? Is the defendant the property owner or a lessee? Did the defendant know about the swing? Did the defendant maintain the swing?
Working Keywords and Search Strings	"premises liability" /p child! /p "guest or invitee" "premises liability" /p child! /p trespass!
Digest Topics	Negligence, 272
Key Numbers	1172–1178, attractive nuisance • K1174, Persons to whom it applies • K1175, Things constituting A.N. generally • K1176, Particular cases

Secondary Sources—Finding Aids

Source	Keyword/Index Term	Lexis/Westlaw	Cite
Am Jur 2d	Premises Liability	Lexis	62 Am. Jur. 2d Premises Liability §230-247, child as guest §268-279, child as trespasser §280-287, related rules
ALR			Am Jur referred to attractive nuisance in ALR—TO DO

Secondary Sources—Persuasive Authorities

Source	Keyword/Index Term	Lexis/Westlaw	Cite
Restatement (Second) of Torts	Ch. 13—Liability for conditions and use of land		Return to this chapter when status of child as trespasser or guest is known.

Table: Victoria Szymczak

Continue to develop your research plan as you work through other secondary and primary sources.

American Jurisprudence 2d appears in online form on both Lexis and Westlaw; however, only Westlaw provides an index entry to the publication. Corpus Juris Secundum is available online on Westlaw only, along with an index to help find relevant entries. It is recommended that you search or browse individual secondary sources rather than run a generic search so that your results are more exact and manageable. Below are the paths to follow on Lexis and Westlaw in order access these national legal encyclopedias:

Lexis: Browse > By Category > Secondary Materials > Jurisprudence > Am Jur

Westlaw: Secondary Sources > Texts and Treatises > (Choose Am Jur or CJS).

2. *American Law Reports* (A.L.R.s)

American Law Reports is a multi-volume, multi-series collection of legal essays written by practitioners on narrow legal topics. Each essay is called an *article.* An article summarizes the case law relevant to a specific legal point across multiple jurisdictions. The authors point out distinctions among cases in the same jurisdiction and and compare them other jurisdictions to provide a balanced representation of judicial doctrine regarding that issue. This secondary source is published in print and is available on Lexis and Westlaw.

American Law Reports is divided into three sets that represent state law, federal law, and international law. The state law volumes are published into seven series and are designated A.L.R., A.L.R. 2d, A.L.R. 3d and so forth. The federal series is published into three series and are designated A.L.R. Fed., A.L.R. Fed 2d, and A.L.R. 3d. The international law series is only 7 volumes and is no longer being published. It is designated A.L.R. Intl. When a new series is designated, it starts with volume 1. Subsequent A.L.R. articles do not necessarily supersede earlier essays in an earlier series. The publisher updates the print series with supplements called pocket parts to keep the case law current. In an online environment, the case law is automatically updated, and the series are merged into one. So you need to pay attention to the citation information to know in which set you are researching. If an annotation is superseded, the print supplement and the online counterpart will indicate that you should no longer rely on the information in that annotation because it was superseded.

Figure 5-3. Example of an A.L.R. Article

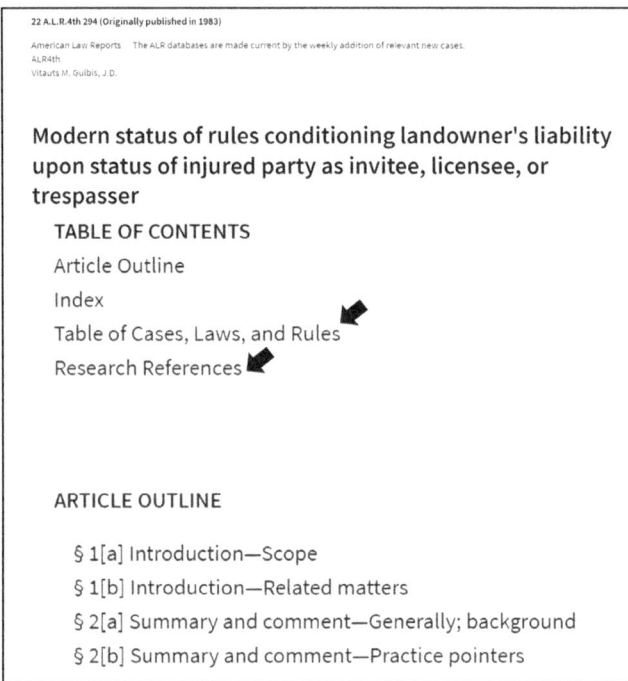

Source: Westlaw, reprinted with permission from Thomson Reuters.

To further your research on premises liability, you would use the state law volumes. If using an index, you can look up the phrase *premises liability* to find ALR Articles, or, if you prefer to do an online keyword search, you can be more exact and search for *premises liability" /25 child!* to find relevant entries. ALR Articles will review the status of the legal doctrine, point you to other secondary sources, and provide case law organized by jurisdiction. See Figure 5-3. Example of an A.L.R. Article.

It is recommended that you search or browse individual secondary sources rather than run a generic search so that your results are more exact and manageable. Below are the paths to follow on Lexis and Westlaw in order to access the *American Law Reports*:

    Lexis: Browse > Sources > By Category > Secondary Materials > Jurisprudence

    Westlaw: Secondary Sources > American Law Reports.

B. Highly Persuasive Secondary Authorities

1. Law Review and Law Journal Articles

Articles are written by subject experts who thoroughly examine new legal developments and issues, provide serious analysis of important decisions or statutes, and present policy issues related to these concerns. They are typically published by a law school and edited by a group of students under the supervision of a faculty member. Usually, the school will publish a general topic law review and other subject specific journals. For example, the William S. Richardson School of Law publishes the *University of Hawai'i Law Review* and the *Asia Pacific Law and Policy Journal*.

Attorney's use journal articles to identify policy issues related to the law, flaws in the current or historical versions of the law, and to collect citations to important cases and other secondary authority discussed by the author. Since scholars are often writing about legal developments, a journal or law review may be particularly helpful to learn about the legal discourse surrounding new laws or legal doctrine at the time they were enacted or adopted.

Authors of academic journal articles examine an issue and often advocate action or changes in the law. Most journals and law reviews also publish articles called "Comments" or "Notes" which are written by students. Although it is not uncommon for attorneys and judges to cite to law journal articles, they will do so depending on the author's reputation or while the law is still developing and there are no better authorities to consider. For example, a student's Comment is not a highly persuasive authority. But what if the student became a Supreme Court justice? You might look at that article a little more closely.

The most popular database to retrieve articles is on the HeinOnline database because, unlike Lexis and Westlaw, HeinOnline has a robust searchable collection of legal articles beginning in 1789 from the United States in a PDF format. Lexis and Westlaw provide access to law reviews and law journals in standard html form, and their coverage begins around 1980. If a researcher is reviewing materials on laws passed prior to 1980, it is important to review the literature at the time the law was passed. For example, to find the legal thoughts surrounding the Civil Rights Act of 1964 during that time period, you will need to extract the literature from HeinOnline, as it is unavailable on Lexis and Westlaw. Note that Bloomberg does not host any law journals or law reviews on their platform.

HeinOnline is available at most law schools. To access it from the William S. Richardson School of Law, go to the Law Library web page > research databases > HeinOnline. The search interface of HeinOnline is not as robust as what you can use on Lexis or Westlaw. You might prefer to perform a keyword search to identify journal articles, but then retrieve the articles from HeinOnline (see above) because it is easier to read and cite a PDF version.

The paths to follow on Lexis and Westlaw in order to access law journals are:

Lexis: Browse > Sources > By Category > Secondary Materials > Law Reviews and Journals

Westlaw: Secondary > Law Reviews and Journals > Full text articles from 1980 to present.

The following free, online resources will also provide access to journal articles, although the full-text versions of the articles are available only if available online for free; however, they will still prove useful to advance your research:

- American Bar Association Free Full-Text Online Journal/Law Review Search[2]
- Google Scholar[3]
- Social Science Research Network—Legal Scholarship[4]

2. Dictionaries

Frequently, the definition of a term is at the crux of a disagreement between parties. General dictionaries will provide researchers with the general meaning of a word, while more specialized legal dictionaries will define legal terms. There are also even more specialized legal dictionaries that provide definition for a specific area of law. For example, an environmental law dictionary will define terms related to environmental law. Obviously, the more

---

2. https://www.lawtechnologytoday.org/free-full-text-online-law-review-journal-search/.

3. http://scholar.google.com.

4. The SSRN network is an access point for scholarship across many disciplines including law. This network includes pre-publication journal articles and working papers. This is a good resource for cutting edge issues or when the standard publication routes prove fruitless. https://www.ssrn.com/index.cfm/en/lsn.

specialized dictionaries will include more terms of art than the general dictionaries.

Dictionary terms are often cited in legal arguments and are considered authoritative sources. Legal dictionaries may also cite case law for further explanation. You will undoubtedly find a collection of dictionaries in your law library's print or online collections. Additionally, because Hawai'i designates both English and Hawaiian as official languages, there is often need to consult a Hawaiian language dictionary to give meaning to terms. Refer to Table 5.3. Dictionaries.

Table 5.3. Dictionaries

General Dictionaries	The *Oxford English Dictionary* is the definitive resource on the history and meaning of words in the English language. In print, it exists is multiple volumes. Most libraries subscribe to the online version of this resource.
	Merriam Webster produces several highly acclaimed dictionaries and makes their online tool freely available.[5] Although this is a general dictionary, it will include definitions of common "legal terms."
Hawaiian Language Dictionary	Mary Kawena Pukui, *Hawaiian Dictionary: Hawaiian-English, English-Hawaiian* was last published as a revised, enlarged edition in 1986 by the University of Hawai'i Press. This dictionary is used by the Hawai'i courts when defining terms in Hawaiian.
Law Dictionaries	*Black's Law Dictionary* is currently in its 11th printed edition and is published by West publishing. The current edition often includes West key numbers to help researchers cross reference to other West products using the key number system. Black Law Dictionary is available in online format on Westlaw under the Secondary Sources tools bar.
	Ballentine's Law Dictionary, 3rd Edition is published by a Lexis sister company and is available on Lexis under Secondary Sources > Dictionaries. Definitions of legal terms are based on the construction of those terms by courts of last resort. Each cited case provides a pin cite to where the term is defined by the court.

---

5. https://www.merriam-webster.com.

The Wolters Kluwer *Bouvier Law Dictionary* was published in 2012 and is the latest version of the popular legal dictionary called *Bouvier's Law Dictionary* first published in 1853. The current edition includes the complete derivation of a legal term and quotations to illustrate how it is used in a legal context. This dictionary is made available on Lexis under the Secondary Sources > Dictionary content area.

Table: Victoria Szymczak

3. Treatises

A treatise is a scholarly commentary or book on the law in a particular subject group. It provides you with an in-depth analysis and explanation of the law with citations to relevant primary law that supports the author's narrative.

To find a print format treatise, use your keywords to search your library's discovery platform or catalog, or consult a library map that will identify the area of the library where you will find treatises on your topic. You can also consult a law librarian who will be able to point you in the right direction.

If you prefer, you can use one of these online treatise finders to identify a treatise by title, then consult your Law Library or one of your online tools for access. Bloomberg, Lexis and Westlaw also provide access to treatises by topic.

- William S. Richardson School of Law, Treatises in Electronic Format.[6]
- Harvard Law School Library Treatise Finder.[7]
- Lexis: You can find treatises in the Secondary Materials content area or select a Practice Area subject specialty and then select treatises. For example, if you are looking for a property treatise to research attractive nuisance, select Practice Area > Real Property Law > Treatises, Practice Guides & Jurisprudence. Select a treatise from the list and search for "attractive nuisance."
- Westlaw: You can find treatises on Westlaw by navigating to Secondary Sources > Texts and Treatises. Alternatively, you can select a Practice area and navigate to subject specific treatises. For example, select the

---

6. https://law-Hawaiʻi.libguides.com/treatises_online.
7. https://guides.library.harvard.edu/legaltreatises.

practice area of Real Property > secondary sources, then use your filters to select texts & treatises from the Publications filter on the left. At that point, you can scroll through the list or enter your search terms on the top of the page to customize your list.

Once you find a treatise, review the table of contents at the front of the book, or the index at the end of the book that will point you to the portion of the treatise in which you are interested. Online counterparts will usually have a table of contents that will give you a broad outline of the chapters but may not have an index for quickly locating specific commentary. For example, when looking for background on the tort of nuisance, browse the table of contents of a torts treatise for the chapter on negligence. If you want to specifically find commentary on the law of "premises liability," it will be more efficient to use the index and look for that phrase.

4. Restatements and Principles of the Law

These two types of publications are published by the American Law Institute (ALI). A Restatement of Law reports on the rules that make up an area of common law and is aimed at the judiciary. Principles of the Law identify the goals to achieve when drafting legislation or regulations on a specific matter and its intended audience is legislatures, administrative agencies, and the private bar. These publications are written and reviewed by subject area experts including legal scholars, judges, private practitioners, and policy experts. Due to the stature of the ALI and the reputation of the Restatement authors, they are considered highly authoritative especially if a jurisdiction has adopted the Restatement in its jurisprudence.

Restatements and Principles of the Law are organized into broad chapters for browsing and have an index to look up terms and case law doctrine. You can either conduct a keyword search or browse the table of contents to help orient you to the publication. Due to complicated and irregular updating, it is best to update both of these publications using Lexis or Westlaw.

a. Restatements

In a Restatement, the law is expressed in clear rules gleaned from thousands of judicial opinions. Restatements exist for many topics like Contracts, Torts, and Property. For example, Chapter 13 in the Restatement (Second) of Torts has a section dealing with premises liability that provides the rules for different situations and case law to support the rule.

The rules are often referred to as "black letter law."[8] Each rule is given a section number and is followed by "Comments" which explain the rule and the reasons for its adoption. Sometimes the Comments are followed by "Illustrations," which show how the rule would apply in specific fact situations. The narrative usually concludes with "Reporters Notes," which give the history of the provision and cite to the authority from which the rule is derived. Finally, the section is supported by the case law evidencing the rule under consideration. Opinions are organized by jurisdiction and are gathered from every jurisdiction in the country. After reading the pertinent rule and accompanying narrative, start exploring the case law relevant to your jurisdiction.

Restatements are one of the most highly regarded types of secondary authority and are frequently cited by judges in their opinions. To determine if Hawai'i has adopted a Restatement rule, you can view the rule on Lexis or Westlaw and then employ their citator tool (Shepard's or KeyCite respectively) to see if the Hawai'i Supreme Court has treated the rule positively in its opinions. Even if the Supreme Court has not specifically adopted a provision, it is still considered a very persuasive secondary authority. Review Figure 5-4. Example of a rule in the *Restatement (Second) of Torts* displayed on Westlaw.

Figure 5-4. Example of a Rule in the Restatement (Second) of Torts Displayed on Westlaw

§ 339 Artificial Conditions Highly Dangerous to Trespassing Children

Comment on Clause
Case Citations - by Jurisdiction

A possessor of land is subject to liability for bodily harm to young children trespassing thereon caused by a structure or other artificial condition which he maintains upon the land, if
 (a) the place where the condition is maintained is one upon which the possessor knows or should know that such children are likely to trespass, and
 (b) the condition is one of which the possessor knows or should know and which he realizes or should realize as involving an unreasonable risk of death or serious bodily harm to such children, and

Source: Westlaw, reprinted with permission from Thomson Reuters.

---

8. This phrase refers to the historic practice of setting law books and citing legal precedents in blackletter type, which is different than Roman or italics type.

b. Principles of the Law

Principles of the law are intensive studies of areas in need of statutory or regulatory reform. A Principle of the Law will begin with recommendations on how to draft legislation or regulations that clearly outline the best practices identified in the subject area. This will be followed by a thorough explanation that will typically include citations to primary and secondary authorities that you may use for further research. Unlike a Restatement of Law, you will not find an exhaustive list of case law organized by jurisdiction.

It is recommended that you search or browse individual Restatements and Principles of Law rather than run a generic search so that your results are more exact and manageable. Below is the path to follow on Lexis and Westlaw in order to get to this specific title:

Lexis: Browse > Sources > By Category> Secondary Materials > Restatements

Westlaw: Secondary Sources > Restatements and Principles of Law.

C. Practitioner Aids

These types of research aids are similar to finding aids; however, they are geared more toward the attorney who is preparing for trial or closing a transactional deal. These aids will often provide the outline of forms (e.g., depositions, bill of sale, etc.) and cite to appropriate primary authority to support the legal issue behind each element of the form. Due to their practice orientation, they are straight forward and easily understood; however, only those produced by the Hawaiʻi Bar Association are specific to Hawaiʻi. Others are general in nature and it is up to researchers to adapt it for their jurisdiction.

1. Hawaiʻi Specific Practitioner Aids published by the Hawaiʻi State Bar Association

The Hawaiʻi State Bar Association (HSBA) publishes numerous titles to support the local bar. None of these titles are available online. Print copies of these publications are found in the main collection of the William S. Richardson School of Law Library and also at the circulation desk in the Library. More information about these publications can be found at the HSBA website including how to order a copy.[9]

---

9. https://hsba.org > Events and Programs > Manuals

- *Family Law Hawai'i Divorce Manual* (9th ed.) 2 Volume Manual, Supplement (2016).
- *Hawai'i Divorce Manual* (9th Ed) Supplement (2017).
- *Estate Planning and Elder Law Estate Planning Forms Manual* 2012.
- *Hawai'i Appellate Practice Manual* 2012 with 2013 Supplement.
- *Federal Appellate Practice Manual* 2013.
- *Corporations & Business Limited Liability Company Manual*, September 2011.
- *Hawai'i Corporations Manual* (September 2011).
- *A Manual of Style for Contract Drafting* (ABA 4th ed. 2017).
- *Real Estate Hawai'i Real Estate Manual* 2011, Volume 3.
- *Hawai'i Real Estate Manual* 2013, Volume 4.
- *Probate Hawai'i Probate Forms Manual* (4th Edition).

2. Pattern Jury Instructions: Hawai'i and Ninth Circuit

Civil and criminal pattern jury instructions restate the law surrounding a legal issue by outlining the elements of a legal claim, identifying who bears the burden of proof in a case, provides defenses to assert, and cites to primary authority. For example, the State of Hawai'i model jury instructions for premises liability lay out the six elements that the plaintiff must prove in order to maintain an action for premises liability. Attorneys uses pattern jury instructions to mold their own prospective jury instructions for approval by a judge hearing their clients' case. Jury instructions are written for the lay jury member. They are meant to be clear and easy to understand so that the average person can understand the law. Jury instructions are helpful to get a basic understanding of the law, but you should limit them to a starting point in your research process as they often do not provide extensive authority to further your research.

Hawai'i State Civil and Criminal Jury Instructions are found on the Hawai'i State Judiciary website.[10] The Ninth Circuit's Manual of Model Civil

---

10. https://www.courts.state.hi.us/legal_references/circuit_court_standard_jury_instructions.

Jury Instructions and Manual of Model Criminal Jury Instructions is available on the Ninth Circuit's website.[11]

In addition to the court sponsored model jury instructions, commercial versions are produced that may have more primary law citations and explanation. There are also model jury instructions for specific types of actions (i.e., the American Bar Association produces the Model Jury Instructions for Business Torts). You can search a law library catalog or discovery platform using the phrase "jury instructions" to find different versions of published jury instructions, and you can follow these paths on Lexis and Westlaw to find jury instructions. Finally, in the general sources included here, entries will often include model jury instructions for the types of cases considered.

The following paths on Lexis and Westlaw will lead you to the jury instructions on each platform:

Lexis > Jury Instructions

Westlaw > Secondary Instructions > Jury Instructions.

3. General Practice Aids

These resources have a generic national focus. When using these resources, remember that the information must be verified in Hawai'i before relying on it.

a. *Am Jur Proof of Facts (POF)*

POF explains and illustrates how to prove particular facts that are essential to a cause of action or a defense. It provides detailed articles on the elements of proof for very specific evidentiary issues. Each article begins with a scope note and has a detailed table of contents and index to the article. For example, under attractive nuisance an article on Negligent Operation of a Private Swimming Pool reviews the elements of the action, proof necessary to collect damages, review of and how to collect testimony to establish proof. Sample documentation covers a wide range of civil litigation and select criminal defense actions. Each entry includes cross references to other secondary sources to help establish your case. To locate your topic, use the general index in either print or on Westlaw, or conduct a keyword search. The direct path to *Am Jur Proof of Facts* on Westlaw is provided here:

Westlaw > Secondary Sources > Texts and Treatises > A.

---

11. https://www.ca9.uscourts.gov/judicial_council/judicial_council.php.

b. Am Jur Trials

The articles in this publication are based on completed trials throughout the United States covering a wide variety of commonly litigated matters. The articles provide litigation tools and strategies to be successful at trial and to secure better settlements. For example, the article on attractive nuisance will cover an introduction to the topic including how to conduct a client interview, investigating and collecting evidence, when and where to bring an action, writing pleadings, pre-trial procedures, trial procedures, asserting defenses, examining witnesses, and managing the jury. The articles are not jurisdiction specific but cite to appellate level cases and authoritative secondary sources to further your research in Hawai'i. The direct path to *Am Jur Trials* on Westlaw is provided here:

Westlaw > Secondary Sources > Texts and Treatises > A.

c. Causes of Action

This publication provides articles and case studies focusing on different types of actions (i.e., personal injury, employment, business, etc.) and provides guidance on specific instances of a cause of action. To illustrate, under "attractive nuisance" you will find seventeen entries on different types of attractive nuisance rather than a general claim.[12] Each article or case study identifies the elements of each case and provides a summary of the substantive law with detailed research and procedural guidelines. The direct path to *Causes of Action* on Westlaw is provided here:

Westlaw > Secondary Sources > Texts and Treatises > C

d. Federal Practice and Procedure (Wright and Miller)

This treatise—commonly referred to as Wright and Miller, the original authors—is designed to provide extensive coverage of all aspects of federal civil, criminal, and appellate procedure. For researchers, it offers analysis of each procedural rule and joins keywords and legal concepts to its index and the cited decisions used in its commentary. The first part of the book centers around the Rules of Procedure and jurisdiction, the second part provides further commentary on application of the Rules, and the third part is a supplement to the commentary and provides citations to cases and secondary

---

12. For example, *Cause of Action for Death or Injury Caused by Residential Swimming Pools* compared to *Cause of Action for Loss or Injury to an Animal by an Animal*.

sources. In print, this set has many volumes. Use the comprehensive index in the last volume to find the material you need. As a Westlaw produce, the index is also available in its online counterpart. The direct path to *Federal Practice and Procedure* on Westlaw is provided here:

Westlaw > Secondary Sources > Texts & Treatises > F.

e. Moore's Federal Practice

This is a standard treatise on federal civil, criminal, appellate, and admiralty procedure for federal practitioners. It reprints the full text of the federal rules, extensive commentary and analysis of the rules, expert opinions on issues that are unclear or unsettled and cases interpreting the rules. The Lexis online counterpart to this treatise includes only the federal civil rules of procedure and commentary. Both the online and print version of this treatise have an extensive index. In print, the index is located at the end of the set; on Lexis the index is located at the beginning of the publication—before chapter 1. The direct path to *Moore's Federal Practice* on Lexis is provided here:

Lexis > Secondary Materials > Treatises, Practice Guides and Jurisprudence.

f. Weinstein's Federal Evidence (Weinstein's)

Weinstein's is a comprehensive treatise devoted specifically to federal evidentiary rules and their application. It is widely cited in federal court opinions. The treatise is arranged according to the federal rules of evidence, each rule is reviewed in terms of history and application. At the end of the multi-volume set and at the end of the online version, the publisher includes a Chart of State Adaptions. Using this chart, you can see which rules Hawai'i has adopted and how each rule differs from the corresponding federal version. The direct path to *Weinstein's Federal Evidence* on Lexis is provided here:

Lexis > Secondary Materials > Treatises, Practice Guides and Jurisprudence.

4. Current Awareness Resources

Bar association journals tend to be more practice oriented and will examine issues relevant to the practicing bar membership. The Hawai'i State Bar Association publishes the *Hawai'i Bar Journal* on a monthly basis. The journal contains articles written by practitioners and judges in the local legal community on legal issues of interest to the jurisdiction. The monthly publication is supplement by a special issue referred to as *Issue 13*. This supplement is irregularly published. The monthly publication is available in full text on Blomberg Law, Lexis, and Westlaw, though Issue 13 is indexed on Lexis only and not available in full text electronically on any of these platforms. The Law Library maintains a complete set of Issue 13 in print.

At the national level, The *ABA Journal* and the *National Law Journal* report on matters of interest to the practice of law generally. Both journals are available on Lexis and Westlaw, and both provide subscriptions directly through their websites. The *ABA Journal* is published by the American Bar Association on a bi-monthly basis.[13] The *National Law Journal* is published monthly by ALM.[14] Both offer updating services on evolving topics on their website between formal publication dates and are a good way to stay on top of national trends in the law.

V. Using Subject Oriented Approaches on Bloomberg Law, Lexis, and Westlaw

Another way to identify secondary sources on Bloomberg Law, Lexis, and Westlaw is to take advantage of their Practice Area arrangements of their content that are available from their main content screen. For example, by selecting Immigration Law from from Westlaw's Practice Area pages will organize all the primary law (cases, statutes, regulations) and secondary sources (treatises, practice aids, etc.) that relate to the topic of immigration in one place.[15] On Lexis and Westlaw, the editors will also list a few of their most popular treatises to help you decide which ones might be most appropriate to use; otherwise, each service will provide a long list of secondary sources in their massive databases that relate to the selected Practice Area.

---

13. American Bar Journal, https://www.abajournal.com.
14. National Law Journal, https://www.law.com/nationallawjournal.
15. Although this might be a convenient way to identify all your primary authority, it is not recommended that you simply rely on the editors at these publishing houses to identify all relevant primary authority for your legal issue. That task falls to you and is at best a starting point. We suggest that you follow the recommendations for primary research in those relevant chapters in this book.

VI. Locating Additional Secondary Sources

Use the following suggestions to find additional secondary sources by topic. More specific suggestions are listed under each category of secondary sources:

- Work with your Law Librarian to identify the best resources on your topic. Not all secondary authority is available online or on Bloomberg Law, Lexis, or Westlaw.
- A Law Librarian may refer you to a bibliography or research guide on point that will list the relevant secondary and primary sources.
- Ask to learn how to use a Law Library's discovery platform to find secondary sources by topic in your Law Library.
- Consult the Practice area content and follow the links to secondary sources in your online resources like Bloomberg Law, Lexis, and Westlaw.
- Keyword searches from the main screen will also pick up secondary sources. You can use your navigation filters to limit your search results to secondary sources and then to more specific types of secondary sources.
- Use B-Cite, KeyCite, and Shepard's citator services for your primary law and filter your results to secondary sources. This is probably the most convenient way to collect background material related to your legal issue or case. However, remember that the results will be tailored to each publishers' proprietary material and it is to your advantage to consult more than one resource.

VII. Updating Secondary Sources

Secondary sources in print are kept up-to-date in a few different ways. The most common is using a supplement to a hard volume. The supplement might appear as a little booklet slipped into the back of the hard volume and commonly referred to as a *pocket part* in reference to the little pocket at the back of the book into which it is slipped. Instead of using a pocket part, a print volume may be updated by a separately issued supplementary pamphlet that will sit next to its parent volume on the bookshelf. Both types of supplements are usually updated once each year so be sure to check the date on the front of the supplement to see when coverage ends.

A second type of updating service involves publications that are published in two- or three-ringed binders. As the law changes, the publisher issues new pages that are sent to replace the obsolete pages in the binder. These types of publications are called *looseleaf services*. They tend to be updated more frequently than those publications using supplements, but that is not always true. It is important to check the date when the binder was last updated. You can usually find this information in the beginning of the publication.

You may think that online equivalents to these secondary sources will be updated more frequently than they are in print format. This is a false presumption. Typically, the two formats will be updated at the same time. It is not uncommon that the digital counterpart will be updated after the print edition. Like the print edition, you should always check the currency of an online resource.

Chapter 6

The Judiciary and Case Reporters

I. The Hawai'i Courts

A. Introduction

The Hawai'i State Judiciary has a unified court system that is administered by the Chief Justice of the Hawai'i Supreme Court. The current Hawai'i State Court System includes the Hawai'i Supreme Court, Intermediate Appeals Court, and these trial level courts: Circuit, District, and Family Courts. Hawai'i is divided into four judicial districts called "circuits." The circuits are represented by four of the five counties in the state and encompass one or more islands:[1]

- First Circuit—Includes the island of O'ahu and other islands of the State not in any other circuit.
- Second Circuit—Consists of the islands of Maui, Moloka'i, Lana'i, Kaho'olawe and Molokini.

---

1. The islands which make up the state of Hawai'i are: Hawai'i, Maui, Oahu, Kahoolawe, Lanai, Molokai, Kauai and Niiha, and Kaala (near Niihau). The outer Hawaiian Islands (also known as the Northwest Hawaiian Islands are a series of 9 small islands and several shallow banks that sit northwest of Kauai, extending from Nihoa to Kure. Together outer islands and the main islands make a total of 18 commonly accepted islands. Depending on how you count them, there are also more than a hundred additional small rocks and islets among the Hawaiian Islands which when combined with the other 18, total approximately 137 land masses. The five counties in the State of Hawai'i are organized around the largest islands. Hawai'i County includes the island of Hawai'i; Honolulu County includes the islands of Oahu and the Northwest Hawaiian Islands; Kalawao includes the Kalaupapa Peninsula on the island of Molokai; Kauai County includes the islands of Kauai, Ni'ihau, Lehua, and Ka'ula; and Maui County which includes the islands of Maui, Kaho'olawe, Lāna'i, Molokai (except the Kalaupapa Peninsula), and Molokini.

- Third Circuit—Consists of the island of Hawai'i.
- Fifth Circuit—Consists of the islands of Kaua'i and Ni'ihau.

The Fourth Circuit, which represented a portion of the island of Hawai'i, was eliminated in 1943 when it merged into the Third Circuit.

There are three specialized courts which function within the District and Circuit courts: The Environmental Courts, Land Court, and Tax Appeal Court. Table 6-1 represents the hierarchical structure of the Hawaiian Judiciary system:

Table 6-1. Chart of Hawai'i Judiciary

```
                    Supreme Court
                         |
              Intermediate Appeals Court
               /         |          \
    District Court   Family Court   Circuit Court
    First Circuit—Land & Tax        All Circuits—Environmental
    Appeals Court                   Courts
    All Districts—Environmental
    Courts
```

Table: Victoria Szymczak

B. The Appellate Courts of the State of Hawai'i

The Supreme Court of the State of Hawai'i is the court of last resort in the State of Hawai'i. It is composed of five justices: a Chief Justice and four Associate Justices. The court sits in the state capitol of Honolulu. The Supreme Court hears appeals that are brought before the court upon applications for writs of certiorari to the Intermediate Court of Appeals (ICA) and applications for transfer from the ICA. The ICA is composed of six judges who sit on panels of three when hearing an appeal. This court also sits in the state capitol of Honolulu. The ICA hears appeals from all the trial level courts and some state agencies.

When a seat is vacant on either the Supreme Court or the ICA, the Governor selects a new appointee from a list of names provided by the Judicial Selection Committee. The initial appointment for a judge or justice is ten years. After ten years, the Judicial Selection Committee decides if an individual will continue or leave the bench.

C. The Trial Level Courts of the State of Hawai'i

The Circuit Courts have general jurisdiction in civil and criminal cases and can hear jury trials. They also have exclusive jurisdiction in probate, guardianship and criminal felony cases, as well as civil cases where the contested amount exceeds $40,000. Other cases heard by the Circuit Courts include mechanics' liens and misdemeanor violations transferred from the District Courts for jury trials. Circuit Courts share concurrent jurisdiction with District Courts in civil non-jury cases in which the amounts in controversy are between $10,000 and $40,000.

The District Courts are further divided into Regular Claims (for civil actions involving amounts under $40,000); Small Claims (for civil actions involving amounts under $5,000) and Landlord Tenant Claims. The District Court has jurisdiction over criminal offenses punishable by imprisonment not exceeding one year. It issues temporary restraining orders and injunctions against harassment involving parties who are not related to each other and who have never been in a dating relationship.

Family Courts rule in all legal matters involving children, such as delinquency, waiver, status offenses, abuse and neglect, termination of parental rights, adoption, guardianships, and detention. They also hear traditional domestic-relations cases, including divorce, nonsupport, parentage, uniform child custody jurisdiction cases, and miscellaneous custody matters. There is a Family Court in each Circuit.

D. The Specialized Courts of the State of Hawai'i

Hawai'i's Environmental Courts are divisions of the Circuit and District courts. There is an Environmental Court in each judicial district. The environmental courts have broad jurisdiction, covering water, forests, streams, beaches, air, and mountains, along with terrestrial and marine life, and hear both civil and criminal matters within their jurisdiction. Hawai'i is one of two states that have an Environmental Court.[2] These courts were established in 2014 and began operations on July 1, 2015. They were established to help

---

2. The State of Vermont Superior Court has an environmental division that hears appeals and enforcement actions. See https://www.vermontjudiciary.org/environmental for more information. Other states have divisions or appeals boards for specific types of environmental issues. For example, within the Colorado judiciary, there are seven Water Court divisions for each of the seven drainage patterns in the state. See https://www.courts.state.co.us/Courts/Water/Index.cfm for more information.

fulfill obligations creates by the 1978 Hawai'i State Constitution, Article IX, Sections 1, 9.[3] Appeals from these courts are made to the IAC and/or to the Hawai'i Supreme Court in accordance with the Hawai'i Rules of Appellate Procedure.

The Land Court has exclusive original jurisdiction over all applications for the registration of title to land, easements, or rights in land held and possessed in fee simple within the State.[4] It also has jurisdiction over other questions brought forth under the Land Court Registration law, Hawai'i Revised Statutes 501. The State of Hawai'i adopted the Torrens system of land registration in 1903 on which the current land court system is based.[5] However, it should be noted that registration of land in Land Court is optional in Hawai'i. Non-registered land is conveyed instead by recording deeds or other documents in the Bureau of Conveyances.[6] The Land Court is embedded in the District Court, First Circuit. The Administrative Judge of the Circuit Court

---

Another example is the Environmental and Land Use Hearings Board in Washington State, https://www.eluho.wa.gov/Board/SHB.

3. Article XI, Section 1 states: "For the benefit of present and future generations, the State and its political subdivisions shall conserve and protect Hawai'i's natural beauty and all natural resources, including land, water, air, minerals and energy sources, and shall promote the development and utilization of these resources in a manner consistent with their conservation and in furtherance of the self-sufficiency of the State. All public natural resources are held in trust by the State for the benefit of the people."

Article XI, Section 9 states: "Each person has the right to a clean and healthful environment, as defined by laws relating to environmental quality, including control of pollution and conservation, protection and enhancement of natural resources. Any person may enforce this right against any party, public or private, through appropriate legal proceedings […]."

4. During the Territorial period, the Land Court was called the Court of Land Registration.

5. Act 56 of the Session Laws of Hawai'i, 1903, Chapter 144, Revised Laws of Hawai'i, 1935. This system, also known as the Land Court system in Hawai'i, was established by Robert Torrens, an Australian government official. Under this system, the Hawai'i Department of Land and Natural Resources issues a certificate of title and the property is immune to adverse possession claims.

6. This method is commonly referred to in Hawai'i as the "Regular" or "Abstract" system, as opposed to the Land Court system. Under this system, recording does not prove ownership. Buyers instead protect themselves through title companies which guarantee their purchase.

of the First Circuit assigns all Land Court matters to the appropriate judge or judges of the First Circuit Court, subject to the approval of the Chief Justice.

The Tax Appeal Court hears appeals regarding real property taxation directly from assessments or from the Boards of Review. It is a court of record and decides all questions of fact and law, including constitutional questions involving real property taxation. Like the Land Court, the Tax Appeal Court is embedded in the District Court, First Circuit. The Administrative Judge of the Circuit Court of the First Circuit assigns all Tax Appeal matters to the appropriate judge or judges of the First Circuit Court, subject to the approval of the Chief Justice.

The web site for the judiciary includes in a wide variety of information.[7] You can find the decisions and orders of the courts from 1998 to the present, listen to oral arguments, download forms, access the court rules and find contact information for the various departments within the judicial system.

II. The Federal Courts

In the federal judicial system, the trial courts are called United States District Courts. These are courts of general jurisdiction and they hear both civil and criminal cases. Bankruptcy Courts operate within the Federal District Courts and have exclusive jurisdiction over bankruptcy cases. There are ninety-four district courts with at least one district court located in each state. In large states, like California, there is more than one district court spread out geographically to serve the state. In less populated states, such as Hawai'i, there is only one district court for the entire state. The Federal District Court for the District of Hawai'i sits in the state capitol of Honolulu, Oahu.

The ninety-four Judicial District Courts are organized into twelve regional circuits, each of which has a Court of Appeals. Appeals from the Federal District Court are made to the Court of Appeals in their circuit. In addition to the twelve regional circuits, there is a thirteenth circuit called the Federal Circuit. The Federal Circuit hears appeals from district courts in all circuits on matters related to patent law, the International Court of Trade, and the Court of Federal Claims.

---

7. https://www.courts.state.hi.us.

Hawai'i is in the Ninth Circuit. Cases from the United States District Court for the District of Hawai'i are appealed to the United States Court of Appeals for the Ninth Circuit. Besides Hawai'i, the Ninth Circuit hears appeals from the Federal District Courts in Alaska, Arizona, California, Guam, Idaho, Montana, Nevada, Northern Mariana Islands, Oregon, and Washington. When a case is heard by a Court of Appeals, three judges sit on the panel to hear and decide the case. In the Ninth Circuit, litigants may elect to appeal a three-judge opinion to an *en banc* court within the Ninth Circuit. An en banc panel is composed of eleven judges from the Ninth Circuit. This process is not as of right and parties may not be granted an en banc hearing. The litigants may also elect to bypass that process and seek review by the United States Supreme Court, the highest court in the federal system.

The United States Supreme Court sits in Washington D.C. and is composed of nine Justices appointed by the United States President upon approval by the United States Senate. The United States Supreme Court hears appeals on matters concerning federal statutes and United States Constitutional Law. Parties who wish to have their case heard by the Supreme Court must file a petition of certiorari which may or may not be granted by the court.

III. Case Reporters

A judicial opinion, or case, is a court's written explanation of its decision in a particular dispute. Opinions that are selected for publication provide guidance as to how courts will resolve similar disputes in the future. These opinions are published in rough chronological order in books called *case reporters*, or simply, *reporters*. Case reporters are republished in online databases with the same organization so that case citations are easily transferable between print and online resources. Since case law databases mimic their print counterparts, learning the organization of case reporting in your jurisdiction is necessary whether you complete your research online or in a print environment.

A. Reported v. Unreported Opinions

When an opinion appears in a case reporter, it is said to be a *reported* case as opposed to an unreported case. A reported case is selected by the court for publication due to its perceived precedential value. Unreported cases are infrequently published; however Bloomberg Law, Lexis and West include unreported cases in their online database and include them in your search results unless you specifically filter them out.[8] Although unreported cases do not present binding authority, they can be used in many jurisdictions, including Hawai'i, as persuasive authority.[9] If you will be relying on unreported decisions, you need to check the local court rules in your jurisdiction to determine if and how they may be utilized.

Reported cases can be found in print case reporters and online databases, while unreported cases can typically be found only in online resources with few exceptions.[10] When you cite to a court opinion, you need to include the volume number of the case reporter, followed by the name of the reporter properly abbreviated according to the Bluebook rules, and then the page number where the opinion can be located. There are different types of case reporters. Some report cases decided by a certain court, for example, the *United States Reports* publishes decisions from the United States Supreme Court. Other reporters, like the *Hawai'i Reports*, include decisions from the appellate courts in the state. Still others include cases from courts within a specific geographic region. For example, the *Pacific Reporter* includes opinions from the state appellate courts in the western region of the United States, including Hawai'i. Cases can be reported in more than one case reporter. A Hawai'i State Supreme Court decision can be found in both the *Hawai'i Reports* and in the *Pacific Reporter*. When a case appears in more than one reporter, the citations are called *parallel citations*. For example, *Honda v. Bd. of Trs. of the State Emps.' Ret. Sys.*, is reported in the Hawai'i Reports at 108 Haw. 212 and also in the Pacific Reporter at 118 P.3d 1155.

---

8. Under the Federal Rules of Appellate Procedure, Rule 32.1, as of December 1 2016, a federal court may not prohibit or restrict the citation of federal judicial opinions, orders, judgments, or other written dispositions that have been designated as "unpublished," "not for publication," "non-precedential," "not precedent," or the like; and were issued on or after January 1, 2007. If a party cites a federal judicial opinion, order, judgment, or other written disposition that is not available in a publicly accessible electronic database, the party must file and serve a copy of that opinion, order, judgment, or disposition with the brief or other paper in which it is cited. It is unclear from the FRAP what precedential value the Ninth Circuit assigns to "unreported" decisions.

9. Rule 35 of the Hawai'i Rules of Appellate Procedure permit unreported cases filed after July 1, 2008 to be used for persuasive authority only. This means that courts are not required to follow the decisions made in these unreported cases.

10. For example, unreported federal court opinions are produced by West in a publication called the Federal Appendix.

Each volume of a print case reporters typically includes the following research aids that are not repeated in their online counterparts: Table of Cases Reported, Table of Cases Cited, Table of Statutes Cited, and a subject index to the cases for each volume. The subject index to the cases in each volume is also known as a digest.

B. State Case Reporters

Like most states, the appellate courts of Hawai'i report their decisions in an official and unofficial case reporter. Up until the Territorial Period, trial level decisions were reported in the *Hawai'i Reports*. Since then, trial level decisions are not reported, although some case information is available for these courts through the eCourt Kokua and Ho'ohiki databases located on the judiciary web site.[11] The eCourt Kokua website began by publishing traffic offenses. It now includes Land Court and Tax Appeals cases (beginning from November 18, 2019), Circuit Court civil cases (beginning from October 28, 2019), District Court civil cases (beginning from October 7, 2019), Circuit Court criminal cases and Family Court adult criminal cases (beginning from January 23, 2017). The Ho'ohiki database provides access to Family Court civil cases only (beginning from 1983).

The different types of government in power since the Kingdom Era create a complicated case reporting structure. Since 1994, case reporting has become more standardized and is similar to most states that have relegated case reporting to a commercial entity. Nevertheless, it is important to understand the historical structure of case reporting because these cases remain valid and hold precedential value in today's courts.

1. Official Reporters

Hawai'i received statehood on August 21, 1959; however, cases decided during the time when Hawai'i was a United States Territory, a Republic, a Provisional Government, and a sovereign Kingdom still hold precedential value. The official reporter for the State Supreme Court is the *Hawai'i Reports*. The cases printed in volume 1, which covers the Kingdom years from 1847 to 1856, were published in a reporter titled the *Law Reports*, or *Ke Alakai o Ki*

---

11. Hawai'i State Judiciary > Legal References > Search Court Records, https://www.courts.state.hi.us/legal_references/records/jims_system_availability.

Kānaka Hawai'i.[12] Volume 1 was reprinted in the current series with different pagination from the original reporter that was prepared by the Kingdom. The original page numbers appear in the margins of the case reporter. This is important to note when researching the case law from 1847–1856 because materials from that time period will match the original pagination, not the current pagination. See Figure 6-1, an illustration from volume 1 of the *Hawai'i Reports*. *Judd v. Ladd* et al appears on page 17 of this volume but appeared on page 13 of the original reporter. If you view this case on a commercial provider, it will use the original pagination in the Hawai'i Reports.[13]

Figure 6-1. Example from Volume 1 Hawai'i Reports

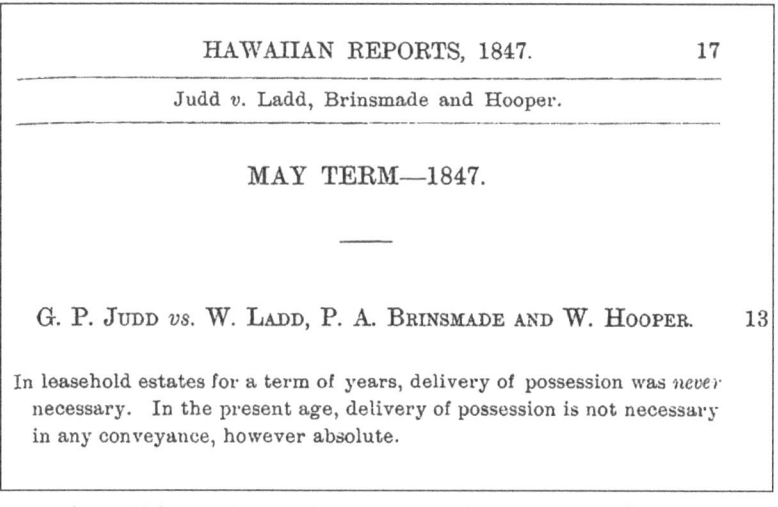

Source: Volume 1 Hawaiian Reports, Reprinted 1889, Kingdom of Hawai'i.

---

12. These cases were also published in *Reports of Some of the Judgments and Decisions of the Courts of Record of the Hawaiian Islands for the Years Ending with 1856*, compiled by George Robertson. The cases reported from 1847 to 1856, along with those decided prior to 1847, can also be found in the *Polynesian*, an Hawaiian newspaper. The *Polynesian* was published weekly in from June 6, 1840 to December 11, 1841 (first series), and again from May 18, 1844 to February 6, 1864 (second series). It was the "Official Journal of the Hawaiian Government" from 1844 to 1861. The *Polynesian* is digitized (1844–1864) at the Library of Congress' website Chronicling America. URL: http://chroniclingamerica.loc.gov/lccn/sn82015408/issues.

13. Hawaiian and Hawai'i Reports volumes 1–27 (1847–1924) are freely available online http://www.llmc.com/OpenAccess/Volumes.aspx?set=77101.

Up until volume 55 (including the reprinted volume 1), this case reporter series was called the *Hawaiian Reports*. In 1974, beginning with volume 56, the name was changed to *Hawai'i Reports*; however, for citation purposes, the abbreviation Haw. applies to both. State court decisions appear in this series beginning in 1959 with volume 44 when Hawai'i became the 50th state.[14] Table 6-2 below provides a timeline of case reporting for the different time periods.

Table 6-2. Timeline of Case Reporting for Different Eras of Governance

Status	Time Period	Volume #s of Hawai'i/an Reporter	Courts Covered by Reporter
Kingdom Era	1847–1856	1	Trial, IAC and Supreme Courts of Hawai'i
Kingdom Era	1857–1893	2–8	Trial, IAC and Supreme Courts of Hawai'i
Provisional Government	January 17, 1893–July 3, 1894	9	Trial, IAC and Supreme Courts of Hawai'i
Republic of Hawai'i	July 4, 1894–July 6, 1898	9–12	Trial, IAC and Supreme Courts of Hawai'i
Territory of Hawai'i[15]	July 7, 1898–August 20, 1959	13–43	Supreme Court of the Territory of Hawai'i
State of Hawai'i	August 21, 1959–present	44–	IAC and Supreme Courts of Hawai'i

Table: Victoria Szymczak

---

14. The judicial system throughout the history of the Hawaiian islands was comprised of three sets of courts: Supreme Court, Superior Courts, and the District (or trial) level courts. While the composition of the judiciary is not significantly different, the jurisdiction for each and composition of the bench varied though the years.

15. Because the Territory of Hawai'i was a United States federal jurisdiction, some cases will appear in federal reporters in addition to the state reporters. See this Chapter section on Federal Cases.

The government of Hawai'i published the *Hawai'i Reports* up to and including volume 75. In these first 75 volumes, the syllabus or synopsis and the headnotes were prepared by the courts. Beginning with volume 76, the printing of the Hawai'i Reports was outsourced to West Publishing. Volumes 1 through 75 in print will not contain the editorial enhancements—such as key numbers—that are common to West case reporters; however, West editorial treatment has replaced the courts' written enhancements in their online counterpart on Westlaw. Lexis does not provide editorial treatment to decisions published in volumes 1 through 75 on their system; however, unlike Westlaw, Lexis does reproduce the courts' original syllabus and headnotes.

The Intermediate Appeals Court. Decisions from the IAC were first published by the government in a series called the *Hawai'i Appellate Reports*. This is a 10-volume set reporting cases from May 6, 1980 to September 1994 with the standard features associated with most case reporters. The IAC decisions appear in the *Hawai'i Reports* beginning in September 1979 with volume 79. This reporter is included on both Lexis and Westlaw.

2. Unofficial Regional Reporters

Like most states, Hawai'i's appellate decisions are published in West's Regional Reporter system. Regional reporters are roughly divided among the states in each region of the country and report the appellate decisions from those states. West has published several series of each reporter indicated by the abbreviations 2d for second series and 3d for third series.[16] The first series does not bear any special numerical designation. This table indicates which state cases are reported in each regional reporter.

---

16. West will start a new series of regional case reporters when the series reaches a designated number of volumes. For example, the Pacific Reporter 2d reached 999 volumes before West began the Pacific Reporter 3d. Each series begins with volume 1.

Table 6-3. West's Regional Reporters

Regional Reporter	States Included
Atlantic Reporter (A., A.2d, A.3d)	Connecticut, Delaware, District of Columbia, Maine, Maryland, New Hampshire, New Jersey, Pennsylvania, Rhode Island, Vermont
North Eastern Reporter (N.E., N.E.2d, N.E.3d)	Illinois, Indiana, Massachusetts, New York, Ohio
North Western Reporter (N.W., N.W.2d)	Iowa, Michigan, Minnesota, Nebraska, North Dakota, South Dakota, Wisconsin
Pacific Reporter (P., P.2d, P.3d)	Alaska, Arizona, California, Colorado, Hawai'i, Idaho, Kansas, Montana, Nevada, New Mexico, Oklahoma, Oregon, Utah, Washington, Wyoming
South Eastern Reporter (S.E., S.E.2d, S.E.3d)	Georgia, North Carolina, South Carolina, Virginia, West Virginia
South Western Reporter (S.W., S.W.2d, S.W.3d)	Arkansas, Florida, Louisiana, Mississippi

Table: Victoria Szymczak

The unofficial regional reporter for the State of Hawai'i Supreme Court and IAC decisions is *West's Pacific Reporter*. Coverage for Hawai'i state cases begins in 1959 with *State v. Peters* which is reported in volume 352, page 329 of the *Pacific Reporter*, 2d Series. Similarly, the IAC decisions published in the *Hawai'i Appellate Reports* are also found in the *Pacific Reporter*, 2d series beginning with volume 612. The cases from the pre-statehood period are not reprinted in the *Pacific Reporter* and will not have a parallel citation to a regional reporter.

3. *Hawai'i Legal Reporter*

The *Hawai'i Legal Reporter* was active between November 1, 1976 and February 19, 1988. It published significant state civil and criminal opinions from the Circuit Court and District Court and Administrative decisions from the following agencies:

- Contractor's Licensing Board,
- Real Estate Commission,
- Public Utilities Commission,

- Hawai'i Public Employment Relations Board,
- Labor and Industrial Relations Appeals Board,
- Board of Nursing,
- Business Registration Division, and
- Opinions of the Attorney General.

According to its preface, this reporter emphasized matters unique to Hawai'i statutory, administrative, case law, and/or involve cultural questions not common to other states. Although this reporter has ceased operation, researchers will still come across citations to it in judicial opinions. These decisions are not found in other reporters and are not available online.

The *Hawai'i Legal Reporter* begins with volume 76 because it began reporting cases in 1976. Most years had more than a single volume. These volumes were called issues and were numbered consecutively within each year. For example, 77-1 corresponds to the first issue in volume 77, published in 1977. This set has a detailed subject index.

C. Federal Case Reporters

Federal trial level decisions from the Federal District Courts have been published in the *West's Federal Supplement* case reporter since 1933. Prior to 1933, they were published in the *West's Federal Reporter*. The Federal Reporter publishes the opinions from the federal Courts of Appeals that are selected by the Court for publication. Like the state regional reporters, West has produced multiple series of these reporters. The *Federal Supplement* is currently in its 3d series and the *Federal Reporter* is in its 3d series. These are the official reporters for the District Courts and Courts of Appeal at the federal level.

When the Territory of Hawai'i was formed in 1900, jurisdiction was placed in the Ninth Circuit. The decisions from August 19, 1900 to December 30, 1916 from this court are published in *Reports of Causes Determined in the United States District Court for the District of Hawai'i*.[17] Informally, this reporter is referred to "Estee's Reports," named after Judge Morris March Estee who was an early case reporter in the Hawaiian Territory. It is a four-volume set and includes the standard research aids for most case reporters. Volume 4 also includes the Rules of Court in effect for the time period covered by this reporter series. It is available electronically through HeinOnline

---

17. Act of Congress of April 30th, 1900, 31 U.S. St. 141.

as part of the "State Reports: A Historical Archive Library." These decisions do not appear on either Lexis or Westlaw. The first District Court case from the District of Hawai'i that is published in the *Federal Supplement* does not appear until 1940 in volume 66 of that series. There are no reported opinions issued by the Federal District Court for the Territory between the years of 1917 and 1940.[18]

The official reporter for the United States Supreme Court is the *United States Reports* and is published by the federal government. A popular unofficial reporter for U.S. Supreme Court decisions is West's *Supreme Court Reporter* and Lexis's *United States Supreme Court Reports, Lawyer's Edition*. Since these reporters are produced more quickly than their government counterpart, you will often see citations to these reporters in place of the official reporter for the United States Supreme Court.

D. Updates to Case Reporters

Judicial decisions first appear as slip opinions. They are typically found on a court's website and may later be issued in an advance sheet before being collected and organized into a hard copy reporter that bears the volume number and reporter series. Advance sheets are a collection of recent opinions published in paper that updates the case reporter. This is a relatively quick, inexpensive way to publish a decision in print. It also allows the court and publisher an opportunity to correct any mistakes in a decision before it is published in its permanent case reporter home.

Online databases that republish court decisions are generally updated between 24 and 48 hours after a slip decision appears. You can easily identify slip opinions and those decisions still in advance sheets in online format because they will lack the volume and page numbers for the reporter in which they will eventually appear.

---

18. Cases for this court and related documents are available at the San Francisco office of the National Archives and Records Administration, Leo J. Ryan Building, 1000 Commodore Drive, San Bruno, CA 94066-2350. Records originating at the US District Court for the District of Hawai'i are in Records Group 21.

Chapter 7

Using and Finding Cases

I. Introduction

In this chapter we are going to identify the different parts of a judicial opinion and suggest methods of case law research using those parts that will make you a more efficient researcher. Understanding how an opinion is structured will enhance your ability to skim cases quickly because you will know the important parts of the opinion to focus on that would interest you in your research project. For example, discerning between a majority or dissenting opinion may influence your decision to cite to that case. Likewise, comprehending the validity of a case for a specific point of law will enable you to cite to that authority with confidence or leave it alone because it lacks traction in the jurisdiction in which you are practicing law.

II. The Structure of a Judicial Opinion

Cases published in a reporter reprint the exact language of the opinion. The publishers of case reporters will add research aids or enhancements—such as headnotes—to the opinion that will assist you in your research. A publisher may be a government entity or a commercial operation. Notwithstanding who the publisher is, the enhancements are not part of the court's opinion and should not be cited. The following discussion explains the information and enhancements included in the *Hawai'i Reports* and *Pacific Reporter*, both published by West. Other publishers include similar research aids in their presentation of a case, though the wording and order of presentation will be different. For example, in an online format, Lexis provides a different arrangement and wording of their headnotes than the West version on Westlaw. Similarly, the structure of the research aids and the language used on Bloomberg Law are different than Lexis and Westlaw.

A. Parts of a Judicial Opinion

Many reporters are published by West and follow a standard pattern. Consult the image in Figure 7-1 of a case reported in West's *Pacific Reporter* as you read about the different elements that make up a reported case.

Citation. The case reporter volume and page number appear at the top of the page. In this example, it is 118 P.3d 115 (Hawai'i 2005). The parallel citation to the official reporter appears above the title of the case: 108 Hawai'i 212.

A note about online versions: Bloomberg, Lexis and Westlaw display the corresponding volume and page numbers for multiple reporters using asterisks to mark pages in the text of the display. At the state level, for example, the

Figure 7-1. Example of a Case from the Hawai'i Reports

```
                          Parallel Citations

            HONDA v. ERS                    Haw. 1155
          Cite as 118 P.3d 1155 (Hawai'i 2005)
being conclusive proof of his gross income,    108 Hawai'i 212
the court may, in its discretion, deny the    Katsumi HONDA, Deceased, by Helen        Caption or Title
motion and requested relief prayed for by        S. Honda, Petitioner, Appellant-
[Father].                                              Appellee
Clearly, it was not "shown to the satisfac-              v.
tion" of the family court "that there were
good reasons for [Father's] failure to present  BOARD OF TRUSTEES OF THE EM-
... in the proceeding before the agency" the   PLOYEES' RETIREMENT SYSTEM
additional evidence Father sought to intro-    OF THE STATE of Hawai'i, Appellee-
duce.                                           Appellant.
                                                                                        Docket Number
          CONCLUSION                             No. 23625.
The following parts of the family court's     Supreme Court of Hawai'i.                 Court
September 18, 2002 Order Affirming in Part,
Reversing in Part, and Remanding Adminis-         June 17, 2005.
trative Findings and Order Filed on June 14,                                            Date of Opinion
2001 are vacated:                             Reconsideration Denied Sept. 15, 2005.
   The [CSEA's] determination of child       Background: Wife of deceased civil ser-
support was based on the finding that Fa-    vice employee petitioned for review of de-
ther's total income available to pay child   cision of state Employees' Retirement Sys-
support includes $20,000 per year (that      tem Board (ERS Board) that wife was not
Father admitted he is capable of earning)    entitled to alter employee's retirement
and his retirement annuity. The Court        election, which left no survivor benefits.    Syllabus
disagrees that the resulting increase was    The First Circuit Court, Allene Suemori,
error, in light of evidence on the record.   J., entered final judgment for wife. ERS      (or
    ....                                     Board appealed.                               Synopsis)
```

7 · USING AND FINDING CASES 101

> Syllabus (or Synopsis) cont.
>
> Second, [Alice] testified that the $51,517 retirement annuity can be withdrawn, and has in fact been withdrawn from, to pay for expenses.... This is evidence that the retirement annuity is available for child support. The 1998 Amended Child Support Guidelines ... states that "[i]f the parent owns assets, he/she may be required to convert all or some portion of said assets for cash for payment of support." ... Hence, the administrative finding that the $51,517 retirement annuity is income available for child support, less 10% penalty for withdrawal, is supported by the record and is not clearly erroneous.
>
> Except as stated above, the September 18, 2002 Order Affirming in Part, Reversing in Part, and Remanding Administrative Findings and Order Filed on June 14, 2001 is affirmed.
>
> We remand this matter to the Family Court of the First Circuit for further proceedings consistent with this opinion.
>
>
>
> **Holdings:** The Supreme Court, Acoba, J., held that:
>
> (1) evidence did not support ERS Board's finding that employee had no trouble understanding retirement options;
>
> (2) employee's choice might have been voidable under doctrine of unilateral mistake;
>
> (3) ERS Board had fiduciary duty to provide retirees sufficient information to make informed decision in electing retirement options; and
>
> (4) wife's claim sounded as negligent representation.
>
> Vacated and remanded with directions.
>
> Levinson, J., filed dissenting opinion, in which Moon, C.J., joined.
>
> **1. Administrative Law and Procedure**
> ⚖═683
>
> The standard of review for secondary appeals of administrative decisions is one in which the Supreme Court must determine
>
> > First headnote indicating the digest topic Administrative Law and Procedure and the key number 683 (standards of review).

Source: Hawai'i Reports, West, reprinted with permission from Thomson Reuters.

official *Hawai'i Reporter* page number is marked using a single asterisk. Double asterisks are used to indicate the corresponding pagination for the regional Pacific Reporter if it exists. On Lexis and Westlaw, the pagination is displayed automatically. On Bloomberg Law, you must use the Pagination feature on the page to select which case reporter pages you want to see displayed, if any.

Caption or Title. The caption or title of a case gives the names of the parties and, at the trial level, the parties are identified as *Plaintiff* (the party bringing the suit) and *Defendant* (the party defending the charge brought by the Plaintiff). In appellate level cases, the caption indicates if they are the *Appellee* (the party who is answering the appeal and hoping to confirm the lower court decision) or *Appellant* (the party who is appealing the lower court decision). Not infrequently, the word *Petitioner* will take the place of *Appellant* and the word *Respondent* will take the place of the word *Appellee*. The parties may be further identified at the appellate level as *Plaintiff-Appellant* or *Defendant-Appellee* or vice versa. The order of the parties in the caption does not change in Hawai'i cases or Federal cases.

Docket Number. The docket number is bolded under the caption. This number is assigned by the court clerk to the case and provides the court with a way to keep track of the documents and briefs filed in the case. Decisions which have not been published but are available as slip opinions, or are otherwise unreported, are usually cited by their docket number. If several cases have been consolidated into one case, there may be multiple docket numbers listed.

Name of Court. The name of the court writing the opinion is provided under the docket number.

Date. The date listed is the date that the decision was rendered and should be included in your citation.

The Syllabus or Synopsis. Although this is not part of the court's opinion and should never be cited, a syllabus or synopsis provides a succinct summary of the case that includes procedural background information, key legal points and facts, and the holdings by the court. Prior to Volume 76 of the print version of the *Hawai'i Reports*, the syllabus was written by the judge or his/her clerk. In the online equivalent on Westlaw, and all other West case reporters, the syllabus is written by West editors. Similarly, the syllabus on Lexis and Bloomberg Law are written by their editors.

Headnotes. Headnotes provide a brief statement of the propositions of law decided in a case. They are designed to serve as an outline to the legal issues presented in each case and are organized according to where in the opinion that point of law is discussed. A Headnote will begin by identifying the area of law being addressed in bold followed by the language used by the court in its opinion when discussing that point. Researchers can then use the sequential number of that headnote to locate the specific part of the opinion where that language appears in order to read the full analysis. Like the Syllabus or Synopsis, the Headnotes may be written by the court if the case reporter is published by the government, or by the editors if the case reporter is prepared by a commercial publisher. Therefore, the headnotes will differ from one publication source to the next. For example, headnotes produced by West are different than those case reporters produced by Lexis. While Headnotes are powerful research aids, they should never be cited in a memorandum or brief because they do not represent the opinion of the court.[1]

A note about online versions: Both Lexis and Westlaw reproduce headnotes in their online databases that appear in line with the case. Bloomberg Law does not reproduce headnotes in its opinions. Instead, it uses "Points of Law" which are accessed via a navigation pane separate from the opinion. Nevertheless, they serve the same function as the headnotes in print case reporters and online equivalents on Lexis and Westlaw.

Name of Attorneys. The names of the lawyers who represented the parties usually appear after the Headnotes.

Opinion. The names of the judges who heard the case and the name of the judge who wrote the opinion appear at the beginning of the opinion. If the name of the judge who wrote the opinion is not provided, the opinion is called a *per curiam opinion*. At the trial level, there is typically only one judge who hears and writes the opinion. At the appellate level, there are panels of judges that hear a case. At the IAC, the judges sit in panels of three while the Hawai'i Supreme Court sits in a panel of five justices. The Ninth Circuit Court of Appeals also sits in panels of three.[2] The U.S. Supreme Court convenes a full panel of nine justices when it hears a case.

---

1. Volumes 1 through 75 of the Hawai'i Reports were published by the government of Hawai'i. The headnotes in these 75 print volumes were written by the court. The West online counterpart to the Hawai'i Reports volumes 1 to 75 does not reproduce the court's added enhancements. West replaced them with their own so that the full set of the Hawai'i Reports on Westlaw show editorial enhancements made only by West editors. On LexisAdvance, volumes 1 to 75 of the Hawai'i Reports display the headnotes written by the court.

2. Following the issuance of a three judge panel order or opinion, parties may seek rehearing before an *en banc court*. An en banc court is, generally, a session in which a case is heard before all the judges of a court. The Ninth Circuit variation of an en banc court limits the number of judges for this type of proceeding to 11. Parties may also elect to bypass an en banc hearing and submit a writ of certiorari to the United States Supreme Court. Another type of review in the Ninth Circuit is a *sua sponte en banc call*. This type of review is initiated by a circuit judge. The judge can also request that a vote be held on whether a decision should be reheard by an en banc panel, even

When multiple judges hear a case, they may discuss and compromise among themselves to reach unanimity in the opinion. If the judges cannot reach unanimity in the outcome or reasoning, there may be more than one opinion. The opinion supported by a majority of the judges is called the *majority opinion*. The majority opinion appears first in order and is the only part of the opinion that creates binding precedent. If there is no majority on both the outcome and the reasoning, the case will be decided by whichever opinion has the most support. In this case, the decision is called a *plurality decision*.

There are two other types of opinions which do not present binding precedent but can be considered persuasive authority and can provide further insight into the court's reasoning. The first is called a *concurring opinion*. A concurring opinion is written to agree with the outcome of the majority opinion but not the reasoning. There can be more than one concurring opinion. The second type is the *dissenting opinion*. These are opinions written by judges who disagree with the majority opinion's outcome and reasoning.

Procedural History. Following the names of the judges, the procedural history of the case will be recited. It will identify the court where the case originated along with the dates and citations to statutes if applicable. The procedural history will also indicate what issues the petitioner is appealing.

Opinion, Dicta, and Holding. The opinion of the judge(s) is the legal reasoning he or she used to reach the decision or holding. The decision or holding is succinct and identified at the end of the opinion by the words "we hold that..." or similar language. Under the doctrine of *stare decisis*, only the holding in a case will govern other cases in the same jurisdiction in which the facts and issues are substantially the same. The legal reasoning of the judge or any other extraneous comments made in the opinion is called *dicta*. When writing a legal brief or memorandum and citing to the judge's reasons for reaching his or her holding, it is inappropriate to use language such as "the court held that...." Although dicta is not binding, the language used by the court to explain its decision helps establish the narrowness or extent of its holding. Although it cannot be relied upon for precedent, dictum should not be ignored in your research.

---

if the parties have not requested it. Federal Rule of Procedure 35, Ninth Circuit Rules 27 and 35, and the Ninth Circuit General Orders.

III. Weight of Case Law Authority

One of the foundational doctrines that underlie our legal system is precedent. Precedent, or stare decisis, is a legal case that is used by courts to guide their decisions when deciding later cases with similar issues or facts.

A. Similarity of Cases

When researching case law, the object is to find cases with similar facts and legal issues in the same jurisdiction where your client's issue arose. It is rare to find a single case with all of the exact facts and legal issues as the matter that you are researching. Your role is to determine whether the facts are similar enough to apply the law in the same way. If a court reached a decision favorable to your position, you will want to stress the similarities between the two matters. If, on the other hand, a court reached a decision unfavorable to your position, you will want to differentiate your situation from the facts in that case. Similarly, it would be unusual to use one case to address all the issues in your matter. Legal claims typically involve several factors or elements. Factors are important aspects of a case; elements are required subparts of a claim. Each element will require its own research trial. Often you will need to use several cases to support your legal reasoning.

B. Binding and Persuasive Authority

The jurisdiction of the court is another point to consider when identifying cases dealing with similar facts and legal issues. Courts must follow the holdings of higher courts in the same jurisdiction. We call this binding or mandatory authority. Decisions made by courts from another jurisdiction, or from courts lower in the hierarchy within your jurisdiction represent persuasive authority only. This concept embodies the doctrine of stare decisis. In Hawai'i, the trial level courts are bound by the holdings of the IAC and the Hawai'i Supreme Court on matters of state law. The IAC is bound only by the Hawai'i Supreme Court. The Hawai'i Supreme Court is the highest court in Hawai'i and is not bound by the decisions of lower courts.

At the federal level, the Federal District Court of Hawai'i is bound on matters of federal law by the Ninth Circuit Court of Appeals and the United States Supreme Court. The Ninth Circuit Court of Appeals is bound on matters of federal law by the United State Supreme Court. As the highest court at the federal level, the United States Supreme Court is not bound by the decisions of Circuit Courts of Appeal or trial level courts. When researching case law, it is recommended to limit your research to the jurisdiction that binds the courts unless that jurisdiction has no case law on that legal issue, or you want to present a new trend to the judiciary in that jurisdiction.

C. State Law in Federal Court

It is not uncommon that a case may include matters concerning both state and federal law. This could occur when state and federal claims are so closely related that they form part of the same controversy under Article III of the U.S. Constitution. In this situation, 28 U.S.C. § 1367 authorizes the federal court to exercise supplemental jurisdiction over the related state law claims. Another common situation arises if the parties to the case are from different states and the amount in controversy exceeds $75,000.[3] In this situation, the federal courts will have original jurisdiction over that matter even if the litigation concerns state law claims. This is called diversity jurisdiction. When exercising diversity jurisdiction, the federal courts are required to follow and apply state law as interpreted by the State of Hawai'i Supreme Court.[4]

When federal courts apply state law, their holdings are not binding on the state courts. Only state courts can create a binding precedent in their jurisdiction on matters of state law.

IV. Case Finding

There are many ways to start your case law research, and the way you start it depends on what information you are beginning your research. For example, you may be directed to case law from a secondary authority that you are reading, from an annotated statutory code, or even from another case. In that instance, you would simply find the case using its citation.

In this section, we will look at ways to find cases when you don't already have a citation, by using digests to identify case law, the role of headnotes in furthering your research, managing keyword searching online, and, finally, how to use citators to update and verify your cases, as well as expand your research.

---

3. 28 U.S.C. § 1332.
4. 28 U.S.C. § 1367(b).

A. West Digests Topic and Key Numbers

Digests are research tools that organize cases according to subject. Under each subject, cases are listed along with a brief paragraph, or annotation, about the case. Because case reporters are organized chronologically, it would be nearly impossible to locate relevant case law in print without the use of a digest. The most widely used digest is published by West. West published a digest for the *Hawaiʻi Reports*, the *Pacific Reporter*, and a Federal Digest that indexes both the *Federal Supplement* and *Federal Reporter*. There is also a digest for the Supreme Court Reporter. In each digest, West organizes cases into 400+ legal topics (*Digest Topics*) which are further divided into discrete legal issues (*Key Numbers*).[5] The annotated cases under each topic will change between jurisdictions, but the legal topics and issues will always be the same regardless of the jurisdiction that you are consulting.

There are several ways to find the Digest Topics and Key Numbers relevant to your research. You can be directed to the topic in a secondary source, or from another case. Each headnote in a West published case is assigned at least one Digest Topic and Key Number. To complete a full review of relevant digest topics and key numbers for your research project, there are two methods that can be accomplished in print and online. They are:

- Topical Analysis or Browsing, and
- Descriptive Word Index.

Each of these methods is reviewed in print and on Westlaw.

1. Print Research Using the West Digest Topic and Key Number System

Method 1. Topical Analysis or Browsing. One way to find the best topic that describes your research is to just browse the full list of Digest Topics and select those that seem most promising. The Digest Topics are listed at the front of each digest volume and assigned a digest number. In Figure 7-2, for example, Abandoned and Lost Property is assigned the number 1, while Arrest is assigned number 35. Figure 7-2 illustrates an example of Digest Topics in Print.

Then, select the corresponding volume of that digest and turn to the beginning of that topic in the book. Each topic begins with a detailed outline that

---

5. See Chapter 1 for a description of the West Digest Topic and Key Number System.

Figure 7-2. Example of Digest Topics in Print

DIGEST TOPICS AND ABBREVIATIONS

See, also, Outline of the Law by Seven Main Divisions of Law preceding this section.

The topic numbers shown below may be used in WESTLAW searches for cases within the topic and within specified key numbers.

1	Abandoned and Lost Property............ Aband L P	36	Arson....................... Arson
2	Abatement and Revival............... Abate & R	37	Assault and Battery.......... Assault
		38	Assignments................ Assign
4	Abortion and Birth Control............ Abort	40	Assistance, Writ of.......... Assist
		41	Associations................ Assoc
		42	Assumpsit, Action of....... Assumpsit

Source: Hawai'i Digest, West, reprinted with permission from Thomson Reuters.

identifies discrete legal issues or elements frequently associated with the digest topic. Each of these sub-topics is also assigned a number called a Key Number. In Figure 7-3, Mistake is assigned Key Number 93. Do not confuse Digest Topic numbers with Key Numbers. Notice that a sub-topic can be further divided to even more precise legal issues. Mistake, for example, is further divided into 5 smaller topics. See Figure 7-3 for an example of Key Numbers in Print Digest.

Figure 7-3. Example of Key Numbers in Print Digest

2C Hawaii D—7   **CONTRACTS**

I. REQUISITES AND VALIDITY.—Continued.
  (E) VALIDITY OF ASSENT.
    ⚛92. Physical or mental condition of party.
    93. Mistake.
      (1). In general.
      (2). Signing in ignorance of contents in general.
      (3). Signing by illiterate persons.
      (4). Mistake of law.
      (5). Mutual mistake.
    94. Fraud and misrepresentation.
      (1). In general.
      (2). Materiality of representation.
      (3). Intent to deceive.

Source: Hawai'i Digest, West, reprinted with permission from Thomson Reuters.

To find the cases associated with Mistake, locate the Contracts volume in the digest set and follow the outline until you reach 93—Mistake. The cases discussing *mistake* are listed along with brief annotations for you to consider. Federal cases are listed first in order of procedural hierarchy, followed by state cases which are also listed in procedural hierarchy (Supreme Court first, followed by the intermediate appellate level, and then trial level courts). Figure 7-4 illustrates an example of a Case Annotation in a Print Digest.

Figure 7-4. Example of a Case Annotation in a Print Digest

> MIRROR image rule,
>   Acceptance of offer, **Contracts ⚎ 24**
>
> MISREPRESENTATION. See subheading
>   FRAUD and misrepresentation,
>   generally, under this heading.
>
> MISTAKE,
>   Generally, **Contracts ⚎ 93**
>   Burden of proof, **Contracts ⚎ 99(1)**
>   Certificate of architect, engineer, or others as to performance of contract,
>   **Contracts ⚎ 291**
>   Duty to read contract, **Contracts ⚎ 93(2)**
>   Effect of invalidity, **Contracts ⚎ 98**
>   Estoppel, **Contracts ⚎ 97**
>   Evidence,
>   Admissibility, **Contracts ⚎ 99(2)**
>   Sufficiency, **Contracts ⚎ 99(3)**

Source: Hawai'i Digest, West, reprinted with permission from Thomson Reuters.

You can then use the citations provided to retrieve the full case from the corresponding print case reporter, any online service, or the internet.

Method 2. Descriptive Word Index. As an alternative to browsing the digest topics and outlines for the appropriate Key Numbers, you can start with the digest's *Descriptive Word Index*. Every digest has a Descriptive Word Index. The Index is typically several volumes long and located at the end of the corresponding digest set. A Descriptive Word Index is a detailed subject index that points you to the appropriate Digest Topic and Key Number for your research. Figure 7-5 shows an example of an Entry in the Descriptive Word Index for Mistake.

Figure 7-5. Entry in the Descriptive Word Index for Mistake

> **Hawai'i Terr. 1914.** Equity will set aside an unconscionable bargain consummated with a person of weak or impaired mind through advantage taken of such person.
> Sumner v. Jones, 22 Haw. 23.
>
> ⬤⇒93. **Mistake.**
>
> ⬤⇒93(1). **In general.**
>
> **D.Hawai'i 2001.** Contract is voidable under Hawaii law where one party is mistaken as to basic assumption supporting the contract at time of its making, if mistake is material and has adverse effect to agreed exchange of performances, so long as (1) mistaken party has not borne risk of

Source: Descriptive Word Index, Hawai'i Digest, West, reprinted with permission from Thomson Reuters.

Like most indexes, it is important to use the most specific terms possible to describe your situation. If we were looking for cases discussing who has the burden of proof in a contracts case when there was a mistake made by one of the parties, you have the choice to look under Burden of Proof, Contracts, or Mistake. Burden of Proof is too general to be helpful here as it can relate to so many types of cases; however, if you look under Contracts—Mistake, or simply look under Mistake, you will see an entry for Burden of Proof with the digest topic Contracts and the Key Number 99(1). You would then select the Contracts volume of the digest and turn to the pages with the annotations relevant to Key Number 99(1), Burden of Proof in Contracts.

When accessing cases on Westlaw using Method 1 or 2 as described below, the cases will not be displayed with filters to help you refine your results further. A good strategy is to find your Digest Topics and Key Numbers using Method 1 or 2, but then run your Digest Topic and Key Number search from the main search screen to take full advantage of the West filters.

Figure 7-6. Example of Key Number Search Results with Filters

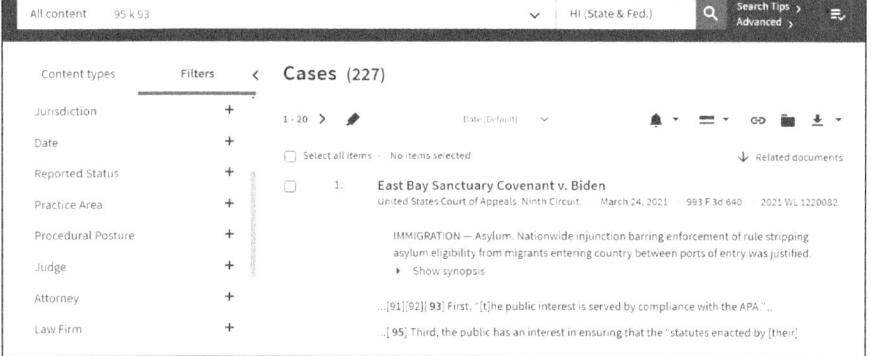

Source: Westlaw, reprinted with permission from Thomson Reuters.

B. Online Methods for Finding Relevant Case

1. Finding Case Law on Westlaw

Method 1. Digest Topics and Key Numbers. If you are conducting your research online, you can access the Digest Topics and Key Numbers on Westlaw by selecting "Key Numbers" on the Westlaw home screen and then selecting the appropriate topic, like Contracts. The sub-topics, or key numbers, are accessed by clicking on the digest topic link. At this point, you can simply click the topic/key number in which you are interested. The Westlaw algorithm will retrieve cases that discuss the topic in whatever jurisdiction to which your account is set. You can change the jurisdiction in the top right corner of your screen.

If you already know your Digest Topic and Key Number, you can use their numerical equivalents to type a search from the home screen with similar results. In this case, you would type in the search box: 95k93. The number 95 stands for the topic Contracts, the k before the number 93 indicates that 93 is the key number, and 93 stands for the sub-topic mistake. In the example below, you see that this search yielded 47 cases. When searching this way, Westlaw will provide filters on the left side of the screen to refine your results further. This is particularly helpful when you retrieve many cases. For example, you can limit your results to only reported cases or cases decided in a certain date range. The algorithm will also retrieve other West products tagged with the same digest topic and key number. See Figure 7-7 for an example of Key Numbers on Westlaw.

Figure 7-7. Example of Key Numbers on Westlaw

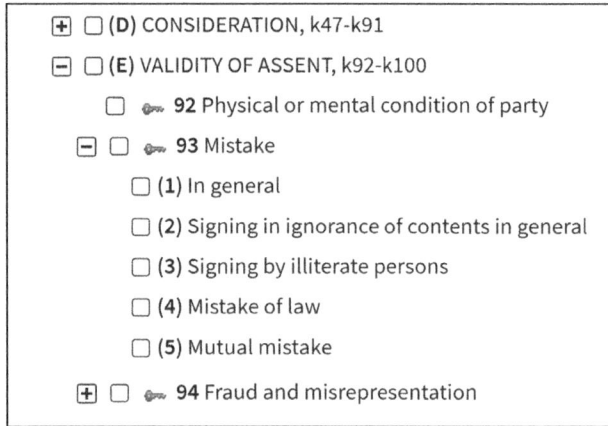

Source: Westlaw, reprinted with permission from Thomson Reuters.

Method 2. Descriptive Word Index. You can also search for Key Numbers on Westlaw using your keywords. This serves as a parallel to using the Descriptive Word Index to take you directly to the Key Number(s). See Figure 7-8 Searching for Key Numbers on Westlaw.

As in Method 1, if you click on the topic/key number in which you are interested to retrieve the cases organized under that legal issue. See Figure 7-9 that illustrates Search results from key number search on Westlaw.

C. Keyword Searching in Case Law Databases

Using digests and headnotes to further your research presents a structured methodology that takes advantage of an extensive classification system. Sometimes, your research project will not neatly fit into that classification, or you simply have a preference for a more liberated approach to case law research that entails performing keyword searches. Others might not have access to West print products or Westlaw and are forced to use a more generic

7 · USING AND FINDING CASES   113

Figure 7-8. Searching for Key Numbers on Westlaw

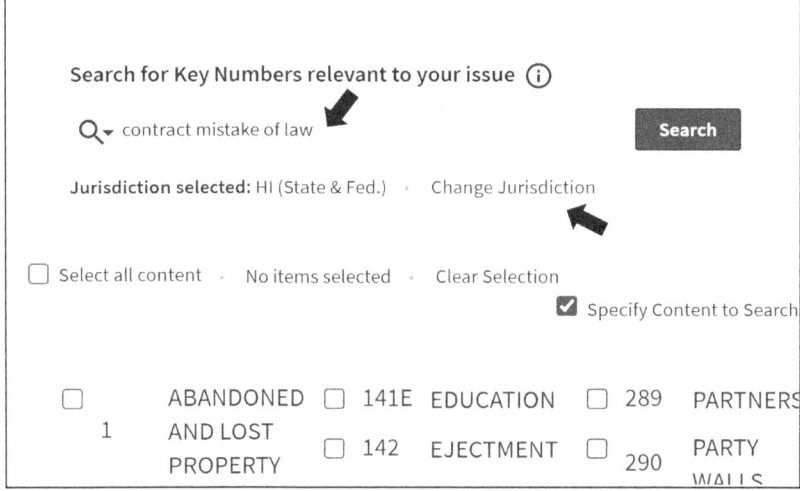

Source: Westlaw, reprinted with permission from Thomson Reuters.

Figure 7-9. Search Results from Key Number Search on Westlaw

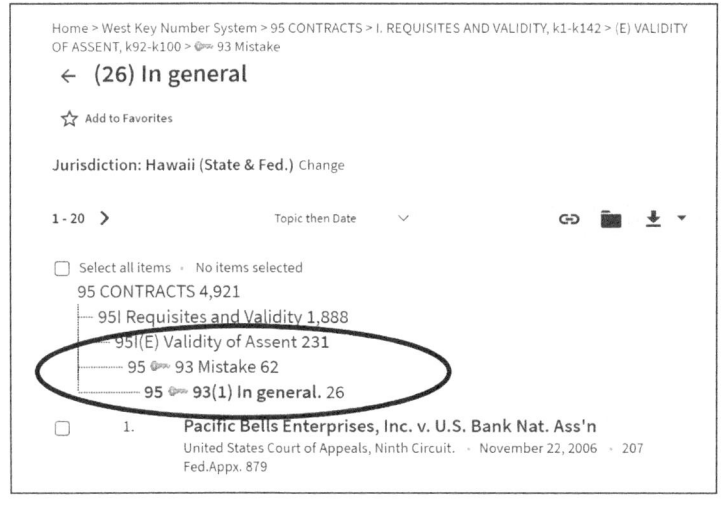

Source: Westlaw, reproduced with permission from Thomson Reuters.

keyword approach to finding their case law. Researchers complain frequently that they retrieve too many or too few results when doing keyword searches. There are some tips and tricks to making this approach more manageable for researchers.

1. Develop a list of keywords and define your issue, then call the 1-800 helpline at which database vendor you are using. Researchers like to use keyword searching because it is familiar to them; however, it requires you to use the correct terminology to find your cases. This may be tricky for new lawyers or those who are entering a new specialty of law and are just learning their legal vocabulary. Researchers should have a legal thesaurus or dictionary handy to help them develop their vocabulary. Using the thesaurus tools on Microsoft Word or the one provided on Westlaw are good ways to expand your keywords. Before accessing a database and searching with those keywords, you should consider discussing it with a research attorney. Research attorneys are employed by Bloomberg (888.560.2529), Lexis (800-455-53947), and Westlaw (1-800-733-2889) to consult with customers about their research projects. The legal database platforms are very expensive to use in the commercial settings and the research attorneys will help you craft your search query and make sure you are looking in the right place. They are accessible via live chat from the database platform or from the toll-free numbers listed here.

2. Begin your research by trying to find cases that discuss the law and then you can search within your results to try to find cases with similar facts. New law researchers tend to look for the facts first, and then try to fit it into the legal framework that they are trying to develop. For example, first you can find cases that discuss a mistake of law in the context of contract law. Then, within those cases, you might look for cases dealing with zoning errors for construction projects. You can narrow your initial results using keywords that describe your factual situation (i.e., *zon! /10 construction*). Law first, facts second.

3. Use the *advanced* search interfaces on Lexis and Westlaw, especially if you are not familiar with Boolean search language. If you do not use the advanced search features, or you are using Bloomberg Law which does not have advanced search features, make sure you use Boolean connectors that keep your terms together. You should also get in the habit of using synonyms

to capture different ways judges discuss the issue. If you are retrieving too few results, augment your search string with synonyms for your terms. For example, agreement or contract /s "mistake of law" looks for the words *agreement* OR *contract* in the same sentence (/s) as mistake of law. Using agreement or contract expands your possibilities; however, agreement AND contract limits your possibilities because the connector AND requires a document to have both words within the same sentence as mistake of law. Notice that the phrase "mistake of law" is in quotation marks. This helps the algorithm search for the correct phrase. Appendix 2 lists the standard Boolean connectors for Bloomberg, Lexis, and Westlaw. While each platform recognizes natural language searching (where Boolean operators are not being used), researchers can become more precise with their results by mastering more sophisticated search techniques.

4. Limit your results to reported cases in the jurisdiction(s) that you are researching. If you start by researching all federal and all state cases, you are likely to be overwhelmed with the number of cases you retrieve. Since you need to rely on mandatory or binding authority, limit yourself to the appropriate jurisdiction. Use your filters to limit results to *reported* cases from the *appellate level* courts in your jurisdiction. Unreported cases are persuasive authority at best. Trial level cases do not present any binding authority. The gold standard would be appellate level cases that have been selected for publication in a case reporter.

5. Identify cases that are cited frequently if you need to select from a large result list. Lexis provides a filter in your case results that identifies the most cited authorities (not just cases) from your results list. On Westlaw, this tool takes the form of a sorting mechanism that reorders your case results from your preferred default, set in your profile, to the most popular cases rising to the top. The reasoning behind this is that the court is showing a preference for how an opinion discusses the issue and one with which they are familiar; however, this method of selection should not be substituted for cases that are legally and factually directly on point for your legal issue. See Figure 7-10 Lexis Filters for Case Law and Figure 7-11 Westlaw Filters for Case Law.

116   7 · USING AND FINDING CASES

Figure 7-10. Lexis Filters for Case Law

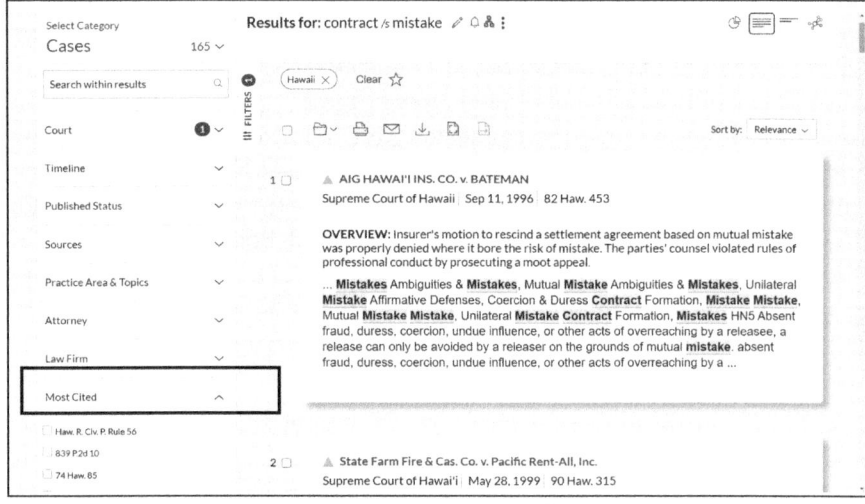

Source: Lexis, reprinted with permission from LexisNexis.

Figure 7-11. Westlaw Filters for Case Law

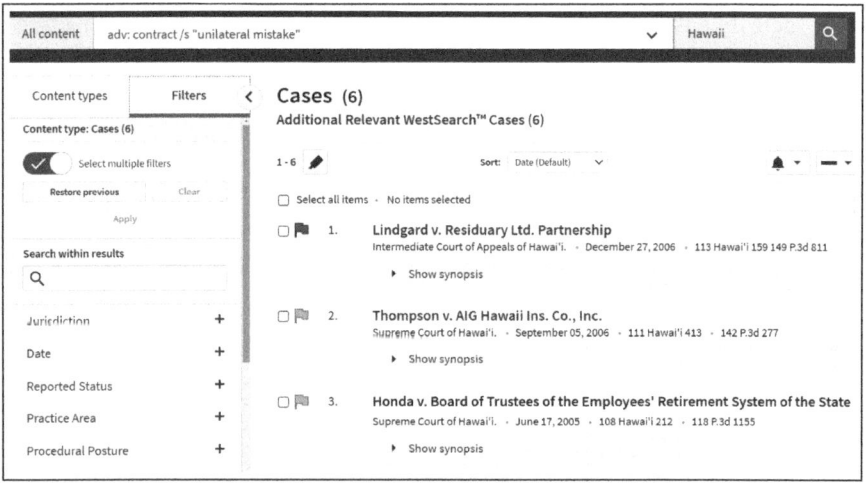

Source: Westlaw, reprinted with permission from Thomson Reuters.

D. Chasing Headnotes

One of the most important parts of an opinion when reading cases is the headnotes. As discussed above, the headnote summarizes a point of law discussed in the opinion. In case reporters published by West, each headnote is assigned a digest topic and key number. In the Figure 7-12, you can see that headnote number 5 is assigned the Digest Topic Contracts (95) and Key Number 93 (Mistake). If you click on the link to the Digest Topic and Key Number, it will run a search similar to that described in Method 1 above. A case typically has more than one issue under consideration by the court and each headnote will be assigned its own digest topic and key number. When a legal issue is sufficiently complex, West may assign it more than one Digest Topic and Key Number to one headnote. In the above example from *Honda v. Bd. of Trs. of the State Emps.' Ret. Sys.*, 108 Haw. 212, 118 P.3d 1155 (2005), headnote 4 is assigned two Digest Topics with their respective Key Numbers.

When you are reading a case that has relevance for your research, you can use the headnotes to find additional cases discussing that headnote. Under each headnote summary, there is a link that invites you to read cases that also discuss that particular point of law discussed in the case you are currently reading. See Figure 7-12 Example of Headnotes on Westlaw with Key Numbers.

In Figure 7-12, headnote number 4 has links to four other cases that discuss the same point of law, while headnote number 5 links to one case that discusses that point of law.

Using headnotes for your research on Lexis and Bloomberg Law is not much different than using them on Westlaw, except that there are no print counterparts to their headnote systems. The headnotes are written by the editors of these publishing houses, and they will organize them and summarize them differently from each other. Figure 7-13 displays headnotes 4 and 5 from the *Honda v. Bd. of Trs. of the State Emps.' Ret. Sys.* as they appear on Lexis. Compare headnotes 4 and 5 from the Westlaw version illustrated in Figure 7-12 to this version of the case displayed on Lexis. Notice the difference in the language and organization. On Lexis, the system offers to retrieve cases related to particular headnotes. Headnote 4 in this example does not have any cases that pertain to the legal issue embodies by that headnote, while headnote 5 is tagged by only one case See Figure 7-13 for an example of Headnotes on Lexis.

118   7 · USING AND FINDING CASES

Figure 7-12. Example of Headnotes on Westlaw with Key Numbers

4	Public Employment		
	States		
	Civil service employee's choosing, shortly before he died of cancer, retirement option designated "normal," which left no survivor benefits, might have been voidable under doctrine of **unilateral mistake**; at time of **contract** for retirement benefits was made employee believed his wife would receive benefits as he named her as "beneficiary" and did not change option when diagnosed with cancer, risk of mistake was not allocated to employee under agreement between him and state Employees' Retirement System (ERS), and allocating risk of mistake to ERS was reasonable as its explanation of "normal" and other options, which included use of confusing statutory language, might have caused mistake. HRS §§ 88–282, 88–283 (2000).		
		316P	Public Employment
		316PVII	Employment Practices
		316PVII(H)	Pensions and Benefits
		316PK383	Eligibility and Right to Benefits
		316PK390	Death and survivors' benefits
		🗝 360	States
		360II	Government and Officers
		360k56	Compensation of Officers, Agents and Employees
		360k64.1	Retirement and Incidental Benefits
		360k64.1(3)	Right to benefits, and amount
	4 Cases that cite this headnote		
5	Contracts		
	Under doctrine of **unilateral mistake**, where mistake of one party at time **contract** was made as to basic assumption on which he or she made **contract** has material effect on agreed exchange of performances that is adverse to him or her, **contract** is voidable by him or her if he or she does not bear risk of the mistake, and (1) effect of mistake is such that enforcement of **contract** would be unconscionable, or (2) other party had reason to know of mistake or his or her fault caused mistake. Restatement (Second) of **Contracts** §§ 153, 154.		
		🗝 95	Contracts
		95I	Requisites and Validity
		95I(E)	Validity of Assent
		95k93	Mistake
		95k93(1)	In general
	1 Case that cites this headnote		

Source: Westlaw, reprinted with permission from Thomson Reuters.

Figure 7-13. Example of Headnotes on Lexis

> **HN4** ⤓ **Standards of Review, Clearly Erroneous Standard of Review**
>
> Findings of fact by an agency must be disregarded if clearly erroneous because of a lack of substantial evidence, or if the supreme court is left with a definite and firm conviction in reviewing the entire evidence that a mistake has been committed, despite evidence to support the finding. 🔍 More like this Headnote
>
> *Shepardize®* - Narrow by this Headnote
>
> Contracts Law > Defenses ▾ > Ambiguities & Mistakes ▾ > General Overview ▾
> View more legal topics
>
> **HN5** ⤓ **Defenses, Ambiguities & Mistakes**
>
> Where a mistake of one party at the time a contract is made as to a basic assumption on which he or she made the contract has a material effect on the agreed exchange of performances that is adverse to him or her, the contract is voidable by him or her if he or she does not bear the risk of the mistake, and (1) the effect of the mistake is such that enforcement of the contract would be unconscionable, or (2) the other party had reason to know of the mistake or his or her fault caused the mistake. 🔍 More like this Headnote
>
> *Shepardize®* - Narrow by this Headnote(1)

Source: Lexis, reprinted with permission from LexisNexis.

On Lexis, the digest treatment is located above the headnote. So, for example, if you look at headnote 5, you can discern that this point of law is classified by Lexis as Unconscionability and falls under Defenses for Contracts Law. To view more cases, you can use the digest trial and click on the appropriate link, or chase the headnote by clicking on "more like this headnote."

On Bloomberg Law, the headnotes are called Points of Law. When you first view a case on Bloomberg Law, the headnotes are not displayed. You must select Points of Law from the navigation menu to see them. Unlike Lexis and Westlaw, the headnotes are unnumbered, do not have a digest trial associated with them, and are not embedded in the opinion. To see more cases that discuss that point of law, you would click on Explore. See Figure 7-14 for an example of Points of Law on Bloomberg Law.

Figure 7-14. Example of Points of Law on Bloomberg Law

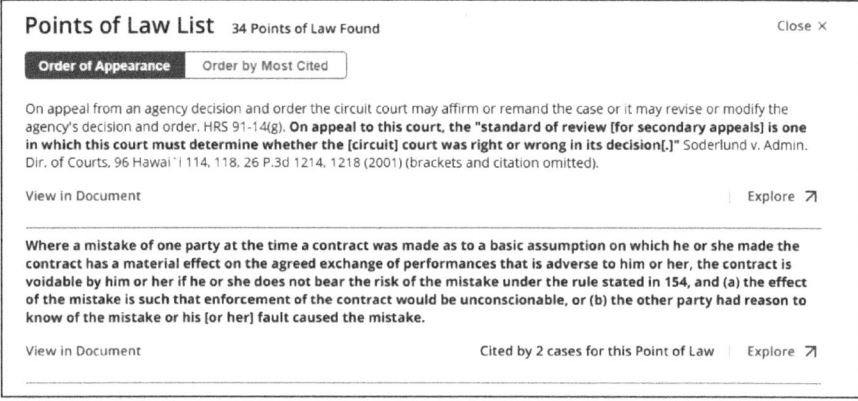

Source: Bloomberg Law, reprinted with permission from Bloomberg L.P.

V. Using Citators to Update, Verify, and Find More Authorities

Before relying on any case, you must determine if that case has reached its final disposition, and how other courts, legislatures, or agencies have treated it. A citator serves two functions: 1) it informs you if your case, or other primary authority, is still "good law," and 2) identifies what other primary or secondary sources have cited to your case. While citators can provide a preliminary analysis to help with your research, it is your job to read the citator report and pay special attention to those cases that negatively affect the case you are researching. Then you must read those citing cases to see what issues or points of law from your case are being affected. You cannot and should not rely on a citator to do the work of a lawyer. Doing so may result in malpractice because these systems are not foolproof. They will, however, make your research more efficient and are standards tools of the trade for lawyers.

A. Is It Still "Good Law"?

An authoritative decision can retain its binding effect for many years. However, a decision may lose its authority over time as legal norms evolve with society, and it may be overruled by a later decision or higher authority or rendered obsolete due to a change in the statutory or regulatory laws. A later decision may limit the holding of an opinion, distinguish it or criticize it to diminish its reach over other cases. The tool lawyers use to keep track of cases is called a "citator."

When you are trying to verify the binding authority of a case, you are checking two things. First, you want to be sure the *direct history* of the case has not changed. For example, has the case been appealed or was the decision reversed on appeal? Second, you want to evaluate how other courts have treated the case you are checking. Has it been cited widely? Have the courts followed the reasoning and rule set by your case? Are courts in your jurisdiction criticizing it or holding its application to a narrow set of circumstances? Before you rely on any case, you will want to check its validity.

When a court relies on the decision from another opinion, they might address only one point of law or the whole case. You will want to identify cases that discuss the point of law you are interested in, whether it be positive or negative treatment. You may find that it was criticized or overruled on one point of law, but not on others. In that case, the opinion remains "good law" for the points of law not criticized or overruled, but not for the point of law that was criticized or overruled. At this point, it will be good to recall how headnotes are organized in a case and remember that each publisher will produce its own headnotes that represent a point of law in the opinion.

B. Citators for Cases

There are three citators in regular use. The first, and oldest, is Shepard's which is owned by Lexis. It is not uncommon to refer to the updating process as "Shepardizing" a case. Shepard's Citations exists online though it began as a print resource and is still published in print. Westlaw also has a citator. It is called KeyCite. The third citator we will discuss is B-Cite on Bloomberg Law. A citator report will normally include the name of the court citing your case, the year that it was decided, how that court treated your case, and, in the case of Westlaw, the number(s) of the headnote(s) of your case that is referred to in the citing case.

Each citator uses a combination of symbols, colors, and language to alert you to how the citing case is treating your case. The following words are commonly used to describe negative treatment of a case by other courts:

- Distinguished,
- Criticized,

- Questioned,
- Abrogated, and
- Overruled.

Words that indicate positive treatment include:

- Cited,
- Discussed, and
- Affirmed

Bloomberg Law, Lexis and Westlaw use colorful symbols to further enhance the citator report. Generally, red symbols indicate serious negative history, yellow symbols indicate some negative treatment by the courts, while green symbols indicate positive treatment by courts. These companies continue to add editorial icons to produce more nuanced alerts. Appendix 3 charts the icon legends used by the companies in their online databases.

Beyond identifying how citing cases treated your case, a citator can help narrow your citator results making your research efforts more effective. Common filters include limiting results by jurisdiction, date, headnote topics, strength of discussion, and sorting reported cases from unreported cases.

Earlier in this chapter, we illustrated the difference in headnotes in *Honda v. Bd. of Trs. of the State Emps.' Ret. Sys.*, 108 Haw. 212, 118 P.3d 1155 (2005), on Westlaw, Lexis, and Bloomberg. Below are illustrations of how the citators on each of these services treat this case. Remember, the headnotes, or points of law, for each service are different.

1. Shepard's Citator Service

When viewing a case on Lexis, the Shepard's service provides a snapshot of both the direct history of the case as well as how other courts have treated that case. See Figure 7-15 for an example of a Case on Lexis with Shepard's Signals. The Subsequent and Prior History appear below the title of the case. On the right side, the Shepard's symbols and their meaning are provided, along with the number of cases providing that treatment that have cited your case. Below the symbol legend and directly above the link to fully "shepardize" this case, the citator indicates that there are 12 other citing sources. The "other" category typically includes secondary source material that can put

Figure 7-15. Case on Lexis with Shepard's Signals

Honda v. Bd. of Trs. of the Emples. Ret. Sys., 108 Haw. 212		Info	Notes
		Shepard's®	
Copy Citation	Request Law School Case Briefs	Caution	Why?
Supreme Court of Hawai'i		No negative subsequent appellate history.	
June 17, 2005, Decided			
NO. 23625		Citing Decisions	21
Reporter		Caution	1
108 Haw. 212 *	118 P.3d 1155 **	2005 Haw. LEXIS 313 ***		Positive	4
		Neutral	4
KATSUMI HONDA, Deceased, by HELEN S. HONDA, Petitioner, Appellant-Appellee vs. BOARD OF TRUSTEES OF THE EMPLOYEES' RETIREMENT SYSTEM OF THE STATE OF HAWAI'I, Appellee-Appellant		Cited	15
		Shepardize® document	

Source: Lexis, reprinted with permission from LexisNexis.

the case in context and help you understand the application and use of the legal rules at issue.

Clicking on "Shepardize this document" provides a full Shepard's Report. The Shepard's Report includes cases and secondary authority which cite back to your case. These cases may help further your research but, if there are too many to sift through, you can use multiple filters to select the most appropriate grouping in your results list. You can filter the results by treatment, jurisdiction, publication status (reported or unreported), depth of discussion, headnote of interest, and date. You can also execute a keyword search within the results. Cases citing your case will be assigned a Shepard's symbol as a preliminary way to gauge the strength of the citing case. In Figure 7-16, *State v. Miller*, a Hawaiian Supreme Court opinion, distinguished the *Honda* case. The yellow triangle to the right of the citation warns us to be cautious when relying on this case because it has received negative treatment. The next step in your research would be to read the *Miller* opinion to determine which legal issues from your case were of issue to the *Miller* court. See Figure 7-16 for an example of a Shepard's Report.

Figure 7-16. Shepard's Report

Shepard's® Honda v. Bd. of Trs. of the Emples. Ret. Sys., 1

Appellate History	**Citing Decisions (21)**
Citing Decisions	No negative subsequent appellate history
Other Citing Sources	
Table of Authorities	

Sort by: Date (Newest to Oldest) ⌄

View history report

FILTERS

Analysis ⌃
- Caution — 1
- Distinguished by — 1
- Positive — 4
- Followed by — 4
- Neutral — 4
- Cited in Dissenting Opinion at — 4

"Cited by" — 15

Court ⌃

Select multiple

Federal Courts — 3
- 9th Circuit — 3

Select multiple

State Courts — 18
- Hawaii — 15
- Louisiana — 2

1. ☐ **Baldauf v. Vt. State Treasurer, 2021 VT 29, 2021 Vt. LEXIS 37, 2021 WL 1707164**
   ▮▮▯▯▯ Vt. April 30, 2021 | **HN10**
   ▮ **Followed by**
   We find the analysis in Honda and Ricks persuasive in concluding that wife has failed to state a claim for breach of fiduciary duty here. Wife has failed to allege facts demonstrating that VSERS did not provide clear and comprehensive information to husband regarding his retirement allowance. Upon husband's hiring, VSERS provided him a form to designate a beneficiary and warned him that if he neglected to fill out the form, "your growing account could provide a very substantial survivorship protection.
   ▮ **Cited in Dissenting Opinion at**
   One of the cases relied upon by the majority in articulating VSERS' duty supports my position. There the Hawaii Supreme Court concluded that the state Employees' Retirement System failed to provide sufficient information to allow employees to make an informed choice regarding their retirement options. Honda v. Bd. of Trs. of the Emps: Ret. Sys. of the State, 108 Haw. 212, 118 P.3d 1155, 1164-65 (Haw. 2005). **(HN10)**
   ⌄ Show More
   🅐

2. ☐ **Wolcott v. Admin. Dir. of the Courts, 148 Haw. 407, 477 P.3d 847, 2020 Haw. LEXIS 385, 2020 WL 7487845**

Source: Lexis, reprinted with permission from LexisNexis.

A good strategy is to use Shepard's filters to limit your results by headnote. For example, if you were only interested in headnote 5 from your case, you can select HN5 in the Shepard's filter to limit your results to that legal issue. Your filtered results will include only cases that discuss the same issue addressed by HN5 in your case (HN5 in the Honda decision focuses on Unconscionability as a Defense). Other filters that are particularly helpful to whittle down large results sets are the publication status—to weed out unreported cases—and the strength of discussion bars. Cases with 3 or 4 bars have a more substantive analysis of your case than those cases assigned 1 or 2 bars.

You can also use the Analysis view of your Shepard's Report to gain a color-coded, visual sense of which courts have cited your case and how they treated it. See Figure 7-17 for an example of the Shepard's Citing Decisions Analysis.

Figure 7-17. Shepard's Grid View for Headnotes

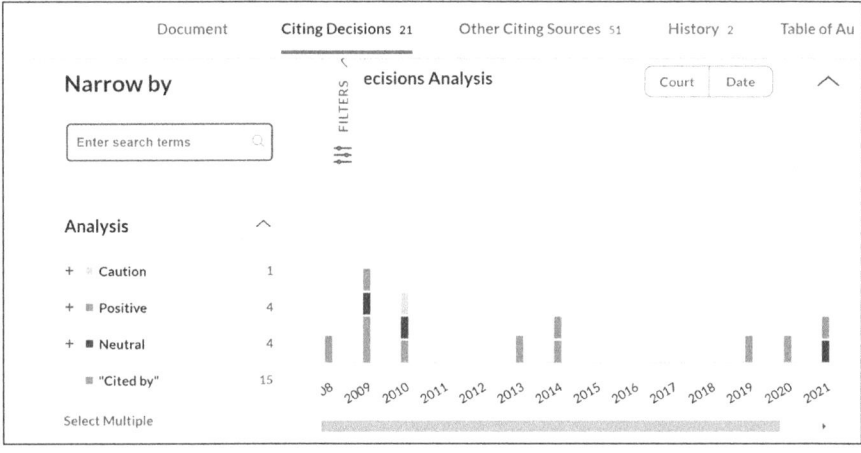

Source: Lexis, reprinted with permission from LexisNexis.

This view is particularly useful when you have many citing cases and you are trying to judge how the case has been considered by the courts.

To review the direct history of the case you are researching, you can click on the History link to make sure a higher court did not overrule your case. For our example case, you can see that there was a failed attempt to rehear the case after the final opinion, but otherwise, the case has reached its final phase of appeal. See Figure 7-18 for an example of the Direct History of a Case in Shepard's.

Figure 7-18. Example of Direct History of a Case in Shepard's

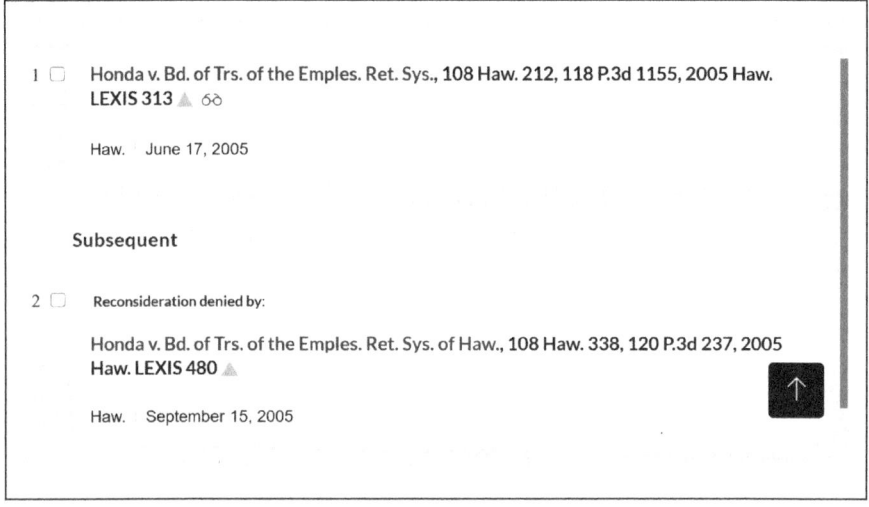

Source: Lexis, reprinted with permission from LexisNexis.

2. KeyCite

On Westlaw, the updating and verification of a case is accomplished using the KeyCite functions running in a ribbon across the top of the Westlaw screen. Figure 7-19 shows the order of the ribbon.

Figure 7-19. KeyCite Ribbon

Source: Westlaw, reprinted with permission from Thomson Reuters.

Westlaw isolates negative history of your case under the tab of the same name if you want a quick look at negative treatment without accessing the entire KeyCite report. To view the appellate or direct history of a case, you would select the History tab in the KeyCite ribbon. In this case, we are alerted that the history has 6 entries. When you open the History tab, you can see where, in the appellate history of this litigation that this particular instance of *Honda* takes place in graphical form. In this case, we can see the appeal from trial level court to the IAC. The IAC vacated and remanded the case, but before it went back to trial, an appeal was made to and denied by the Supreme Court to reconsider the IAC decision to remand the case. See Figure 7-20 for an example of a Graphical View of Direct History in KeyCite.

Figure 7-20. Graphical View of Direct History in KeyCite

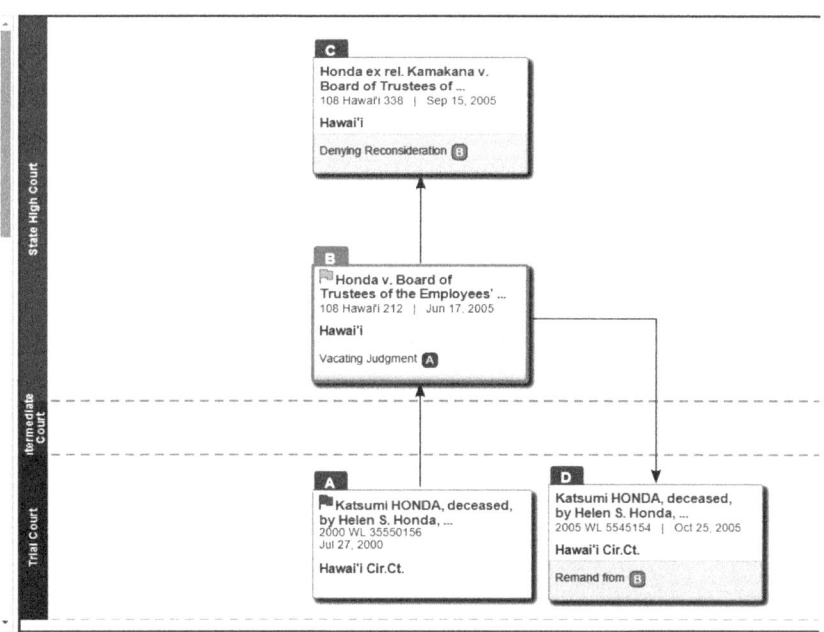

Source: Westlaw, reprinted with permission from Thomson Reuters.

The full KeyCite report is accessed via Citing References tab which is categorized by types of primary and secondary sources citing back to your case.[6] The full case report shows that there are sixteen cases citing the *Honda* opinion. For each case that cites *Honda*, KeyCite tells you the type of treatment that court accorded *Honda*, a quick indication that the case citing *Honda* is good law, when that case was decided, the type of document it is (remember, KeyCite provides access to many types of documents), the depth of treatment on a scale of 1 to 4 bars (4 being the highest), the headnote(s) under discussion and from which case reporter the headnote is identified. Westlaw takes the liberty of identifying what it considers the most negative treatment by labelling a case with a red "negative" label in the treatment column; however, the final analysis should be made by the researcher, not the Westlaw algorithm because many factors go into deciding how negative a case citing to your case actually is relevant to your research project.

3. B-Cite

The citator on Bloomberg Law is called B-Cite. From any case, the B-Cite function can be accessed on the right side of the screen. A click on B-Cite Analysis will release a summary of the results. To access the citing authorities, you must click on the type of authority you want to review. For example, clicking on Positive (18) will retrieve the 18 cases providing positive analysis of this case on Bloomberg Law. Clicking on Citing Documents, will display all authorities—including the positive cases—that discuss the case, or the rule(s) discussed in the case. Once you display the documents, there are only two filters to use: Content type or date. See Figure 7-21 for an example of B-Cite on Bloomberg Law.

---

6. In this example, there are 114 citing references but only 16 cases. Westlaw includes court filings in its KeyCite coverage which may be useful for research purposes but, like secondary materials, do not have a role in verifying the legal ruling of the case you are researching.

Figure 7-21. Example of B-Cite on Bloomberg Law

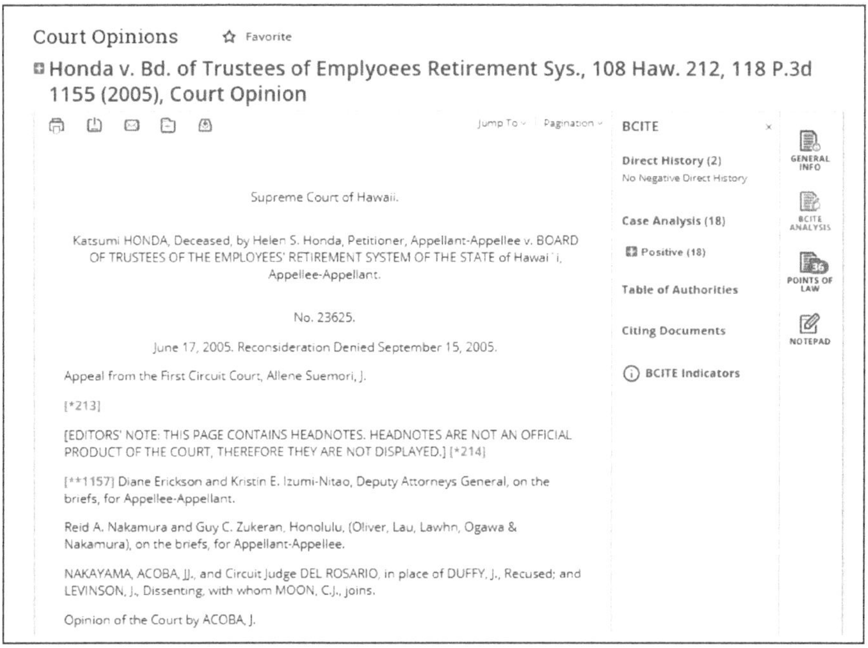

Court Opinions ☆ Favorite

Honda v. Bd. of Trustees of Emplyoees Retirement Sys., 108 Haw. 212, 118 P.3d 1155 (2005), Court Opinion

Jump To ∨ | Pagination ∨

BCITE ✕

Direct History (2)
No Negative Direct History

Case Analysis (18)
➕ Positive (18)

Table of Authorities

Citing Documents

ⓘ BCITE Indicators

GENERAL INFO

BCITE ANALYSIS

POINTS OF LAW

NOTEPAD

Supreme Court of Hawaii.

Katsumi HONDA, Deceased, by Helen S. Honda, Petitioner, Appellant-Appellee v. BOARD OF TRUSTEES OF THE EMPLOYEES' RETIREMENT SYSTEM OF THE STATE of Hawai`i, Appellee-Appellant.

No. 23625.

June 17, 2005. Reconsideration Denied September 15, 2005.

Appeal from the First Circuit Court, Allene Suemori, J.

[*213]

[EDITORS' NOTE: THIS PAGE CONTAINS HEADNOTES. HEADNOTES ARE NOT AN OFFICIAL PRODUCT OF THE COURT, THEREFORE THEY ARE NOT DISPLAYED.] [*214]

[**1157] Diane Erickson and Kristin E. Izumi-Nitao, Deputy Attorneys General, on the briefs, for Appellee-Appellant.

Reid A. Nakamura and Guy C. Zukeran, Honolulu, (Oliver, Lau, Lawhn, Ogawa & Nakamura), on the briefs, for Appellant-Appellee.

NAKAYAMA, ACOBA, JJ., and Circuit Judge DEL ROSARIO, in place of DUFFY, J., Recused; and LEVINSON, J., Dissenting, with whom MOON, C.J., joins.

Opinion of the Court by ACOBA, J.

Source: Bloomberg Law, reprinted with permission from Bloomberg L.P.

Chapter 8

Statutes

I. Introduction

This chapter will introduce you to statutes created by the Hawai'i Legislature and the federal government. Methodologies for searching current statutes is offered. You must evaluate your own knowledge of a legal issue and determine what you need to know before you start your research. Then develop a research plan and start a research log. You can follow the checklist for statutes and legislation to ensure thorough research:

- Determine the statutory scheme. Does it fall under the area of law for your facts?
- Look for definitions, exemptions, limitations.
- Check citing references.
- New or pending legislation? Check the Legislature website.
- For state jurisdictions, is it a Uniform or Model Act? Check uniformlaws.org to find other states that adopted the same law for case citations.
- Is it still "good law"? Validate with a citator.

II. Hawai'i State Statutes

The *Hawai'i Revised Statutes* are the general and permanent laws created by the Hawai'i State Legislature and put into a topical arrangement, *i.e*.

codified.[1] They are designed for a purpose and apply to the public prospectively. They are subject to change by amendment or repeal by the legislature or can be overturned by an appellate court. The Senate and House of Representatives comprises the Hawai'i State Legislature.

After the bill passes both houses of the Hawai'i Legislature, it is enrolled, certified, approved by the governor or passed over the governor's veto, and it becomes law. In the publication process, it goes from a "slip law," a law that just passed, to being collected at the end of the legislative session into the Session Laws of Hawai'i. In Hawai'i, a slip law and a session law are both called Acts and are abbreviated c. or ch. in the statute's history.[2]

After the session's laws are published, the Revisor of Statutes codifies them in broad general subject areas in the Hawai'i Revised Statutes. The Hawai'i Revised Statutes are organized into the following five divisions:

1. Government,
2. Business,
3. Property, Family,
4. Courts and Judicial Proceedings, and
5. Crime and Criminal Proceedings.

Each Division is further subdivided by Titles, and Titles are further subdivided by Chapters. See Figure 8-1 that shows an example of the subdivisions. Chapters are subdivided into sections. Sections are the basic units cited in Hawai'i statutes.

In Hawai'i, there are three sets of statutory codes in print and online:

Official: *Hawai'i Revised Statutes*, produced by the Authority. This set of statutes includes case annotations even though the title does not indicate it. However, case annotations are difficult to discern since they reference only the reporter citation rather than also listing the case name. Online the official *Hawai'i Revised Statutes* can be found at the Hawai'i Legislature site (http://www.capitol.hawaii.gov) and Bloomberg Law. Bloomberg Law shows the

---

[1]. Only laws of a general and permanent nature are codified. L. 1966, c. 29; L. 1968, c. 16; Haw. Rev. Stat. § 23G-14. See also the *Hawai'i Legislative Drafting Manual* available at https://lrb.Hawai'i.gov.

[2]. In print, both West and LexisNexis publish Hawai'i acts during the legislative session in pamphlet form to supplement their statutory codes.

Figure 8-1. Hawai'i Revised Statutes (Official)

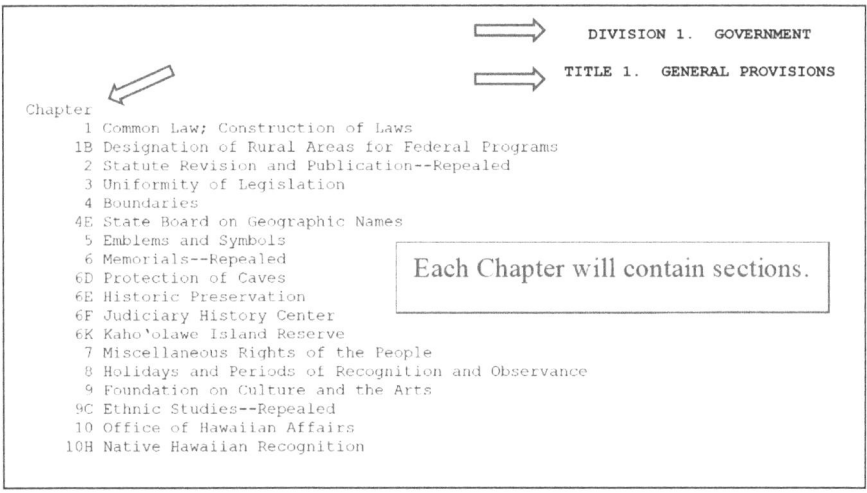

Source: Hawai'i State Legislature website, https://www.capitol.hawaii.gov..

official annotations after the text of the statute, but it links only to cases found by its algorithm in its Smart Code link. Bloomberg Law does not include the index to the statutes in its online offering.

Unofficial: *Michie's Hawai'i Revised Statutes Annotated* published by LexisNexis. Online you can find it at Lexis but without an index.

Unofficial: *West's Hawai'i Revised Statutes Annotated* published by West; online its available at Westlaw with an index.

An annotated code offers value added features including case annotations where this section of the code was implicated. Case annotations written by qualified personnel working for legal publishers summarize the case to give you context for evaluating its importance for your research. Secondary authorities, especially those published by the same publishing house, are typically included to help the researcher broaden their understanding of the law. Such editorial enhancements shorten the time needed to thoroughly research and understand the law. See Figures 8-2, 8-3, and 8-4.

Figure 8-2. Bloomberg Law Editorial Enhancements

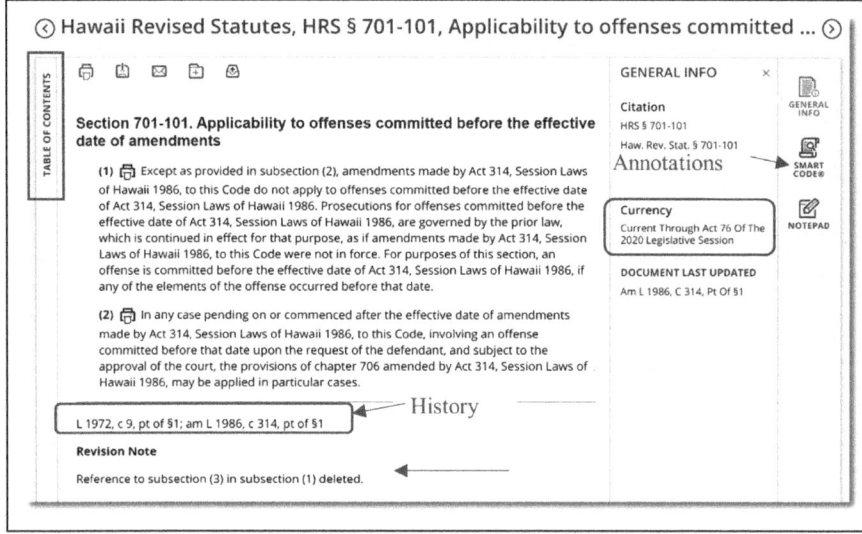

Source: Bloomberg Law, reprinted with permission from Bloomberg L.P.

Figure 8-3. Lexis Editorial Enhancements

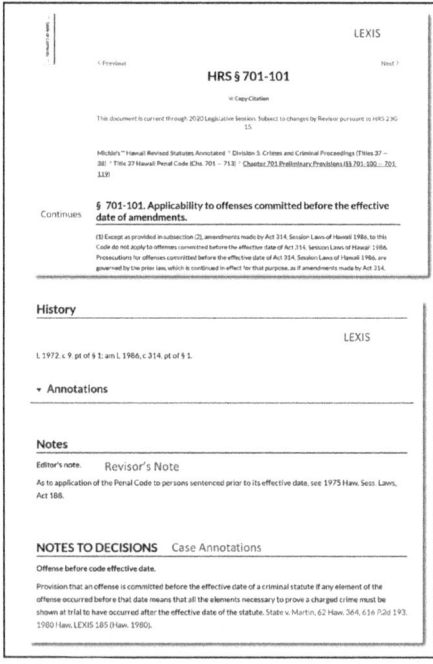

Source: Lexis, reprinted with permission from LexisNexis.

Figure 8-4. Westlaw Editorial Enhancements

§ 515-1. Construction
HI ST § 515-1 · West's Hawai'i Revised Statutes Annotated · Division 3. Property; Family (Approx. 2 pages)

Document | Notes of Decisions (3) | History (1) ▼ | Citing References (18) ▼ | Context & Analysis (1) ▼   Powered by **KeyCite**

Table of Contents   < § >

Annotations

Context:
West's Hawai'i Revised Statutes Annotated
 Division 3. Property; Family
  Title 28. Property
   Chapter 515. Discrimination in Real Property Transactions (Refs & Annos)

Citing References (18) ▼   Context & Ana
 Cases (5)
 Regulations (5)
 Secondary Sources (5)
 Appellate Court Documents (3)

Westlaw

HRS § 515-1
§ 515-1. Construction
Currentness

This chapter shall be construed according to the fair import of its terms and shall be liberally construed.

Credits
Laws 1967, ch. 193, § 1; H.R.S. § 515-1. ◄— History

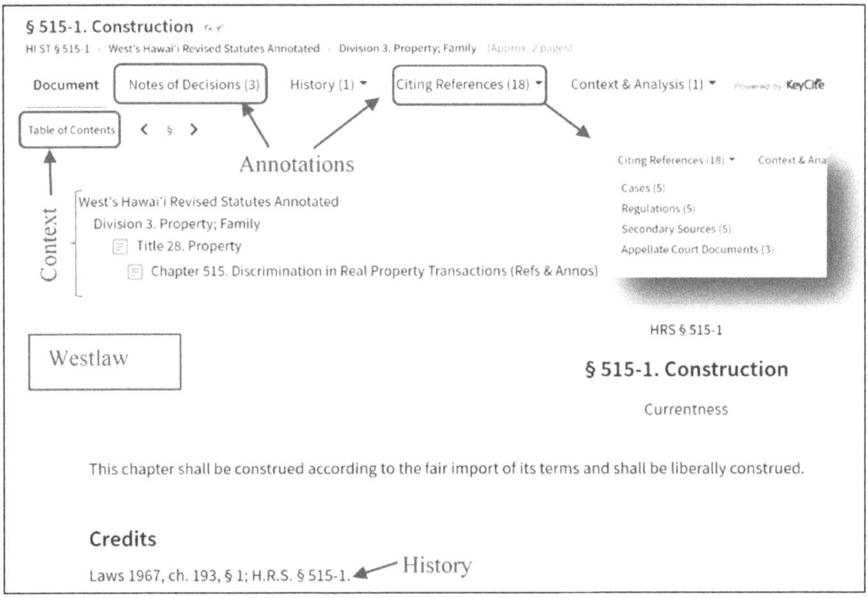

Source: Westlaw, reprinted with permission from Thomson Reuters.

Table 8-1 summarizes the four versions of the code and their features.

Table 8-1. Features of the Hawai'i Revised Statutes Online

Code	Online	Index?	Case Annotations?	Secondary Authorities?
Hawai'i Revised Statutes (official)	capitol.hawaii.gov (free)	yes—only at capitol site, publishing lags	yes—not with editorial enhancements	yes—limited
Hawai'i Revised Statutes (official)	Bloomberg Law (subscription)	no	yes—Smart Code	yes
Michie's Hawai'i Revised Statutes Annotated	Lexis (subscription)	only in print	yes—Research References & Practice Aids	yes
West's Hawai'i Revised Statutes Annotated	Westlaw (subscription)	yes (online and in print)	yes—Notes of Decisions; Citing References	yes

Table: Roberta F. Woods

A. Hawai'i Revised Statutes Online

The statutory organization as shown in online platforms reveals which statutory compilation forms the basis for the statutes being displayed.

Examine Figures 8-5, 8-6, and 8-7, the top line tells you the title of the resource. For Bloomberg Law, it is the *Hawai'i Revised Statutes* meaning Bloomberg uses the official statutory compilation published by legislative authority.[3] Lexis uses an unofficial code, *Michie's Hawai'i Revised Statutes Annotated*, a LexisNexis publication. Westlaw uses an unofficial code, *West's Hawai'i Revised Statutes Annotated*, a West publication. Lexis indicates the statutory scheme horizontally separated by a horizontal chevron while the others use a vertical indented format.

Figure 8-5. Bloomberg Law Example of Statutory Scheme

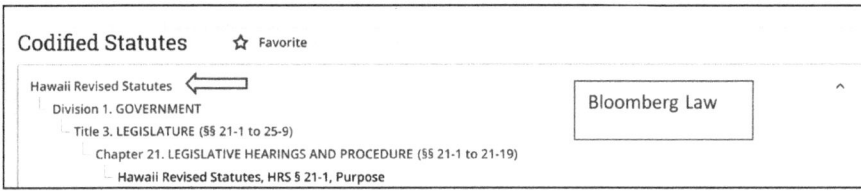

Source: Bloomberg Law, reprinted with permission from Bloomberg L.P.

---

3. In the section on Hawai'i in *The Bluebook: A Uniform System of Citation*, the first listed statutory compilation is the official and does not carry the word "annotated" in its title even if it is annotated.

8 · HAWAI'I STATE STATUTES

Figure 8-6. Lexis Example of Statutory Scheme

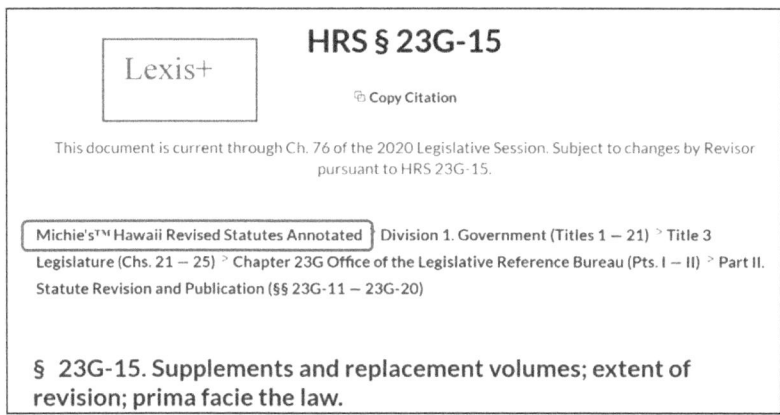

Source: Lexis, reprinted with permission from LexisNexis.

Figure 8-7. Westlaw Example of Statutory Scheme

Source: Westlaw, reprinted with permission from Thomson Reuters.

III. Understanding the Statute — Anatomy of a Statute and the Statutory Scheme

A section in the *Hawaiʻi Revised Statutes* typically operates within a statutory scheme, which contains groups of statutes that relate to one subject. For example, Chapter 6D, Protection of Caves has thirteen sections. See Figure 8-8.

Figure 8-8. Ch. 6D Statutory Scheme.

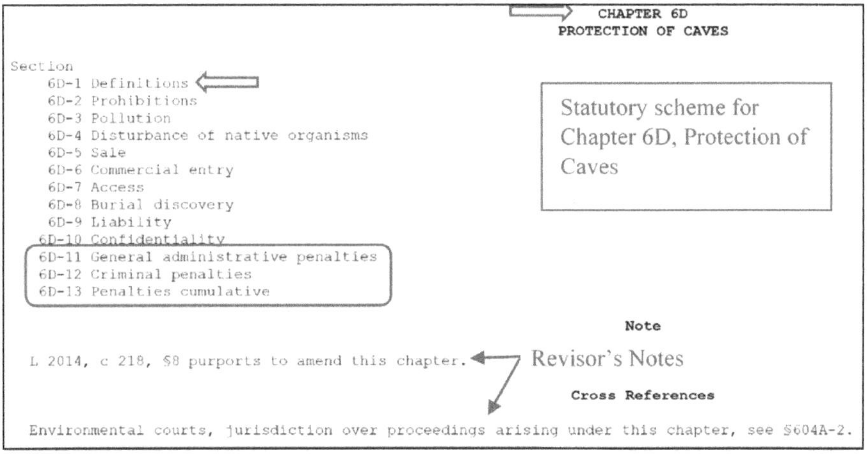

```
                                              ⟶ CHAPTER 6D
                                                PROTECTION OF CAVES
Section
   6D-1  Definitions ⟵
   6D-2  Prohibitions
   6D-3  Pollution                        Statutory scheme for
   6D-4  Disturbance of native organisms  Chapter 6D, Protection of
   6D-5  Sale                             Caves
   6D-6  Commercial entry
   6D-7  Access
   6D-8  Burial discovery
   6D-9  Liability
   6D-10 Confidentiality
   6D-11 General administrative penalties
   6D-12 Criminal penalties
   6D-13 Penalties cumulative

                                                       Note
  L 2014, c 218, §8 purports to amend this chapter. ⟵ Revisor's Notes
                                                       Cross References
  Environmental courts, jurisdiction over proceedings arising under this chapter, see §604A-2.
```

Source: Lexis, reprinted with permission from LexisNexis.

Vital to the task of research is reading and understanding the statutory text. Pay close attention to the definitions section of a statutory scheme. Very often definitions come toward the beginning of a chapter as they do in chapter 6D, but they can come anywhere and are not consistently called definitions. If definitions are found in the statutory scheme, they apply. If a word is not defined in your statutory scheme, then it goes by the plain-meaning rule.[4] Look further for any sections that include limitations or penalties. The

---

4. The doctrine that if a legal text is unambiguous it should be applied by its terms without recourse to policy arguments, legislative history, or any other matter extraneous to the text unless doing so would lead to an absurdity.

statutory scheme gives the researcher context for applying facts to law. Typically, you can find the statutory scheme by looking at the table of contents for the section.

Every word is important in the text of a statute. So much so that the Hawai'i Legislature codified important statutory construction rules found in Chapter 1 of the *Hawai'i Revised Statutes*. Here are some of the important rules:

§ 1-14 Words have usual meaning,

§ 1-15 Construction of ambiguous content,

§ 1-16 Laws in *pari materia* (on the same subject matter),

§ 1-17 Number and gender,

§ 1-18 "Or", "And",

§ 1-19 Person, others, any, etc., and

§ 1-20 Month; Year.

Consult the *Hawai'i Legislative Drafting Manual* on the Legislative Reference Bureau website for more guidance.[5]

There are four things to take note of when you first encounter a statutory section.

1. Context—where does this statute fit into the overall code? Remember to look in the Table of Contents for the statutory scheme.
2. History—when did this statute originate; when was it last amended?
3. Currentness—when was this statutory database or book last updated? If it doesn't include the most current session laws, then you will have to check pocket parts or slip laws since its last updating. You need this information for your citation.
4. Text—this was covered above in understanding the statute.

See, for example, Figure 8-9. Lexis Statutory Example.

---

5. *See Hawai'i Legislative Drafting Manual available at* https://lrb.hawaii.gov/drafting-manuals-guides.

Figure 8-9. Lexis Statutory Example

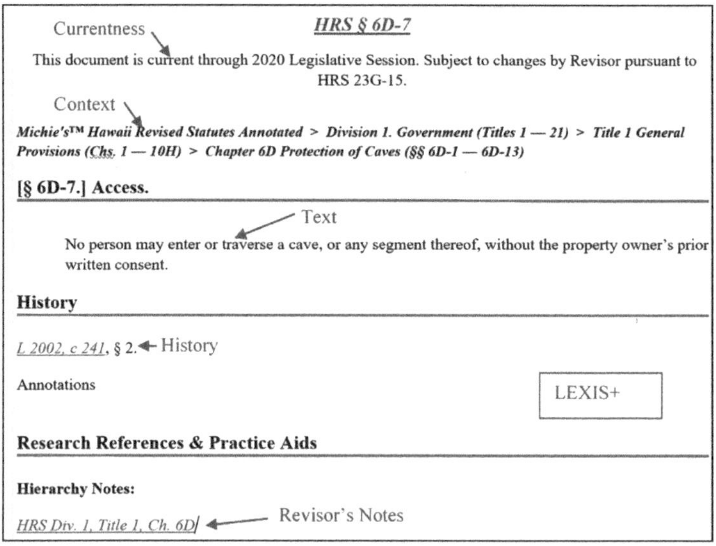

```
Currentness          HRS § 6D-7
This document is current through 2020 Legislative Session. Subject to changes by Revisor pursuant to
                              HRS 23G-15.
Context
Michie's™ Hawaii Revised Statutes Annotated > Division 1. Government (Titles 1 — 21) > Title 1 General
Provisions (Chs. 1 — 10H) > Chapter 6D Protection of Caves (§§ 6D-1 — 6D-13)

[§ 6D-7.] Access.
                                  ← Text
   No person may enter or traverse a cave, or any segment thereof, without the property owner's prior
   written consent.

History

L 2002, c 241, § 2. ← History

Annotations                                                   LEXIS+

Research References & Practice Aids

Hierarchy Notes:
HRS Div. 1, Title 1, Ch. 6D/  ← Revisor's Notes
```

Source: Lexis, reprinted with permission from LexisNexis.

A. Search Strategies for Hawai'i Statutes

1. Citation Method

If you know the statute's citation enter it or find it in the Table of Contents and go directly to it. This is quick and precisely targeted.

2. Index Method

If you can find one, using an index gives the researcher a head start in locating statutes. And you only need one search term or phrase to get into it. An index is a guide to the language of the text in brief but precise and accurate language.

Most indexes use a controlled vocabulary to group subjects together, consider other words used to find a topic, keywords, and synonyms. Typically, someone knowledgeable in the subject matter assigns the code provision to the appropriate place in the index and often leads the researcher to the appropriate term by using "see" or "see also" references. Importantly, it is much more efficient to use an index than to do a keyword search because of this intermediary help in the form of an index. However, online only two resources include an index to the *Hawaiʻi Revised Statutes*: Westlaw and the official legislative site. The two indexes are vastly different because their audiences are different.[6] Compare Figures 8-10 and 8-11 for the word "discrimination."

The current index to the official *Hawaiʻi Revised Statutes* was published in 1996 and has been supplemented since then making it necessary to search more than one index volume without knowing how up to date the information is. However, this index is for use by the general public not just those in the legal profession and is freely available online at the Legislature's site. Online, the Westlaw index is kept up to date and linked wherever the blue font indicates a link typically found in the right-hand panel. To determine the currency of the index, click on a blue circle with a small lowercase white "i" in the center at the top of the index page.

In print, all three statutory codes for Hawaiʻi have indexes.[7] Publication of the index volume in the official *Hawaiʻi Revised Statutes* lags the publication of other volumes. Table 8-2 shows the sets of official statutory codes and their indexes, which do not seem to be published regularly or with a set of statutes. Typically, the official index must be supplemented for years before a new one is published. The last full set of *Hawaiʻi Revised Statutes* was the 1993 Replacement. Since then, continuous statutory revision and replacement of individual volumes is the norm.

---

6. *See generally American Society for Indexing Best Practices available at* https://www.asindexing.org/best-indexing-practices/.

7. Westlaw's index follows *West's Analysis of American Law* (https://store.legal.thomsonreuters.com/law-products) a robust outline of the law that makes up the Digest and Key Numbers used by West throughout their products. The system was developed by lawyers for lawyers.

Table 8-2. Index Volumes to the Hawai'i Revised Statutes

Publication Year of Statutes	Matching Index Volumes
1968 Hawai'i Revised Statutes	8 includes index
1976 Replacement Hawai'i Revised Statutes	8 + 3a, 5a, & 7a vol. 8 is 1969 Index
1985 Replacement Hawai'i Revised Statutes	12 plus index vol. 1982 Replacement
1993 Replacement Hawai'i Revised Statutes	14 plus index vol. 1987 Replacement
Various depending on individual volume yyyy Replacement Hawai'i Revised Statutes[8]	Index vol. 1996 Replacement

Table: Roberta F. Woods

Figure 8-10. Official Index

```
DISCRIMINATION
  Actions
    appeals, 368-16
    civil rights commission powers generally,
      368-3
    class actions, 368-11
    damages, 489-7.5
    disabled persons, 347-13.5
    employment practices, 378-5
    limitation of actions, 368-11
    notice of right to sue, 368-12, 515-9
    public accommodations, 347-13.5, 489-7,
      489-7.5
    real estate transactions, 515-9
    restraining orders, 368-14
  Aiding and abetting, 378-2, 489-5
  Apprenticeship
    refusal to enter into apprenticeship
      agreements, 378-2
  Armed forces
    segregation in military prohibited, St Art I-9
  Boarding houses
    see BOARDING HOUSES, Unfair practices
  Child support
    discrimination based on assignment of
      income, 378-2
  Civil rights commission
    appeals, 368-16
    complaints, see Complaints, below
    compliance review, 368-15
    confidential information, 368-4
    established, 368-2
    intervening in civil action, 368-12
    jurisdiction, 368-11, 378-4, 489-6
```

Source: Hawai'i Revised Statutes, State of Hawai'i.

---

8. After 1993, Haw. Rev. Stat. §§ 23G-20, 23G-16 allow continuous statutory revision and publication of replacement volumes.

Figure 8-11. Westlaw Index

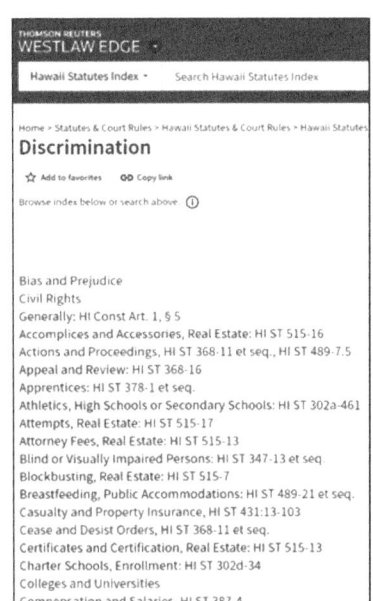

Source: Westlaw, reprinted with permission from Thomson Reuters.

Two other methods that use an index are the Definitions Method and the Popular Names Method that follow. These are both variations of the general Index Method.

3. Definition Method

When you have a key factual term to quickly find out if the legislature has defined it, use the index. In the official *Hawai'i Revised Statutes* look in the index main entry, "Definitions" for words defined in the statutes. In *Michie's Hawai'i Revised Statutes*, look in the index main entry, "Defined Terms" for words defined in the statutes. This is only available for Michie's if you have a print index. In *West's Hawai'i Revised Statutes*, look in the index main entry, "Words and Phrases" for words and phrases defined in the statutes.

4. Popular Name Method

Sometimes a law is known by its popular name rather than its official name. For example, in 2014 the Hawai'i Legislature passed "A Bill For An Act Relating To Child Abuse" to combat internet crimes against children. This law is known as "Alicia's Law" named for Alicia Kozakiewicz. The official *Hawai'i Revised Statutes* does not have a popular name entry in the index nor in a separate table. In *Michie's Hawai'i Revised Statutes*, look in the index main entry, "Popular Names and Short Titles," for the popular name of a statute. This is only available for Michie's if you have a print index. In *West's Hawai'i Revised Statutes*, look in the index main entry, "Popular Name Laws" for the popular name of a statute. Westlaw has a link to the Hawai'i Statutes Popular Name Table on the right-hand side panel in the Hawai'i Revised Statutes.

5. *Topical or Analytic Method*

Use the Division level table of contents when you know the broad area of law covered in your fact pattern. Perhaps you are sure it is a law but cannot determine whether it has been repealed or uses a term of art not familiar to you. As listed earlier, the *Hawai'i Revised Statutes* are divided into five broad groups called divisions. Starting at the Division level, drill down to the appropriate chapter and sections. For example, if you are researching a criminal matter, start at Division 5, Crimes and Criminal Proceedings. It has two titles, Title 37, Hawai'i Penal Code, and Title 38, Procedural and Supplementary Provisions. Scan the chapter titles for an appropriate topic. Once found, look at the sections and examine the statutory scheme. Find definitions, exceptions, exemptions, or limitations. Continually query yourself: Is the chapter relevant to your legal issue?

6. *Keyword Method*

This is the least effective way to search statutes because it usually returns too many irrelevant results. However, it works well if you have unique terms. Include Boolean search logic to narrow your results. Use of connectors like /p or /2, and the root expander (!) may aid in your search.

B. Finding Relevant Cases and Secondary Authorities Discussing a Statute

Statutes are subject to interpretation. Attorneys will look at legislative history to determine intent, secondary sources to gather expert analysis, and judicial opinions to determine application. As mentioned previously, one of the benefits of working with an annotated statutory code are the case annotations that the editors select to serve as examples of how courts are interpreting statutory language. Following the text of the statute, you will often—but not always—find references to secondary sources and another section listing cases with brief descriptions of the opinion. In the official version, the secondary sources are titled "Law Journals and Reviews" and the cases are designated "Case Notes." In *Michie's Hawai'i Revised Statutes Annotated*, commentary is listed under Research References and Practice Aids. Case annotations are organized under "Notes to Decisions." In *West's Hawai'i Revised Statutes Annotated*, secondary authority is found under Journals and Commentary, and Research References. Cases are listed under the section called "Notes of Decision." Frequently, in the commercial versions, there are many cases included in these sections, and the editors will insert subtopics within the annotations. This scheme is carried over to the online versions of the annotated codes and is similar to the United States Code.

Once you find a case, or cases, that are on point, you can then use that citation to read the full case and further your case law research as recommended in Chapter 5. Figures 8-12, 8-13, and 8-14 compare the annotations provided in the three online versions of the *Hawai'i Revised Statutes* and illustrate the statutes using the employment discrimination example first introduced in Chapter 1. If you are looking at the definitions section of the *Hawai'i Revised Statutes* on discrimination, you would look at the case annotations under the heading most relevant. In this example, we are exploring an allegation of race discrimination and you would select the subtopic that references cases discussing race discrimination. Since the official version does not provide a topical arrangement of case annotations, this comparison demonstrates the conveniences in commercial counterparts.

Figure 8-12. *Hawai'i Revised Statutes* **(Official) Example of a Case Annotation**

Case Notes

Not violated where employer discharged employees not merely because of their drug-related arrests but because of perceived harm to employer's reputation and business contracts. 803 F.2d 471 (1986).

Monocular pilot applicant's disability discrimination claim and retaliation claim not preempted by Airline Deregulation Act of 1978; pilot applicant's success or failure on the discrimination claim had no bearing on pilot applicant's retaliation claim. 128 F.3d 1301 (1997).

Source: Hawai'i Revised Statutes, State of Hawai'i.

Figure 8-13. Hawai'i Revised Statutes (Westlaw) Example of a Case Annotation

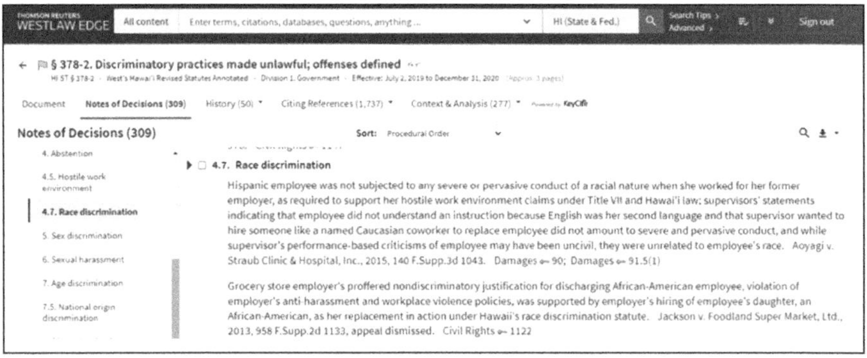

Source: Westlaw, reprinted with permission from Thomson Reuters.

Figure 8-14. Hawai'i Revised Statutes (Lexis) Example of a Case Annotation

Race discrimination.
Employee's discrimination claim under HRS § 378-2 was dismissed on summary judgment because the employee failed to show that the employer's reasons for terminating the employee's job was pretext for discrimination where the employee did not show that the negative performance reviews were inaccurate and biased against the employee because of race. Welch v. Haw. Med. Serv. Ass'n, 2002 U.S. Dist. LEXIS 25038 (D. Haw. July 12, 2002).

Source: Lexis, Reprinted with permission from LexisNexis

C. Temporary Laws

Sometimes you cannot find the statute by the methods mentioned above. It could mean that the statute was never codified and added to the *Hawai'i Revised Statutes*. Recall that a law once passed by both chambers of the legislature and signed into law by the executive is a statute even if it exists only in the form of a session law. Statutes containing clauses limiting the duration of their validity, sometimes called "sunset" or "duration clauses" are not codified but they are still law. They are considered temporary laws or temporary legislation. These laws govern for a limited time while permanent laws or legislation govern perpetually and are made part of the *Hawai'i Revised Statutes*. A typical example of this is the annual appropriations law.

If a statute isn't codified, *i.e.* made part of the *Hawai'i Revised Statutes*, then it is a temporary law. In Hawai'i, it is common for the legislature to enact temporary provisions that are effective for a few years. In some cases, these temporary provisions are extended for a further period. These provisions are not codified in the *Hawai'i Revised Statutes*. An Act that provides for its own repeal after, for example, five years is not permanent, and therefore, usually not codified. Researching temporary laws is conducted in the Session Laws and the legislative journals. See Chapter 9, Legislative History.

Statutes and statutory sections not included in the *Hawai'i Revised Statutes* can be tracked in the Tables of Disposition. See Figure 8-15. The current year's Table of Disposition is available on the Legislature's website.[9] In the official print set of *Hawai'i Revised Statutes*, a pamphlet usually shelved at the end of the set, includes many years of the Tables of Disposition. Check this Table to determine if all sections of the act signed into law appear in the *Hawai'i Revised Statutes*. Sections with an "O" indicate that it did not make it into the code. See Figure 8-16. Where there is a number, that is the section of the *Hawai'i Revised Statutes* where that provision is codified.

Figure 8-15. Tables of Disposition

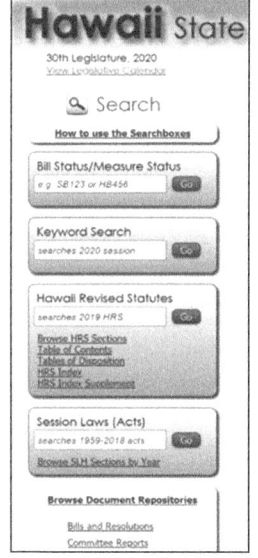

Source: Hawai'i State Legislature website, https://www.capitol.hawaii.gov.

---

9. Figure 8-16. https://www.capitol.hawaii.gov/docs/TablesofDisposition.pdf.

Figure 8-16. Table of Disposition Showing Omitted Section

TABLE OF DISPOSITION

Table 2. SESSION LAWS TO HAWAII REVISED STATUTES
(R = Repealed; O = Omitted)

Act	Section	HRS	Act	Section	HRS
SESSION LAWS OF 2019			26	1	201B-7
			27	1, 2	514B-3, 149
1		O ⇐	28	1 to 8	O
2	1	237-4.5		9	163D-19
	2	237-1	29	1 to 6	O
	3	238-1		7, 8	444-26, 29
3	1	236E-8		9	454F-41
4	1	O		10, 11	467-11, 16
	2	132-16		12	514B-72
5		O	30		O
6		O	31	1, 2	286-47, 271
7	1	514B-154	32	1	O
8	1	11-339		2	c 457J
9		O		3	26H-4
10	1	15-13.5	33		O
	2	15D-10.5	34		O
	3	15-14	35		O
	4	15-13 (R)	36	1	O
11	1	574-1		2	8-30
12	1	O	37		O

Source: Hawai'i Revised Statutes, State of Hawai'i.

D. Federal Statutes

Researching federal statutes is similar to researching state statutes with some vocabulary changes. Once a legislative bill has been signed into law by the President or the veto has been overridden, the nascent law is a "slip law" called a "Public Law" until its publication in the Statutes at Large, the federal government's session laws. Public Laws can be found online at congress.gov or in a law library in print. While it is a slip law, it is printed separately and when encountered the term "slip law" makes sense because many are merely slips of paper. They are easier to find online or in the bound editions of the *Statutes at Large*.

When it becomes a Public Law, it is numbered. The numerical representation of the Congress is the number before the dash and the law number of that Congress is after the dash. The Statutes at Large, the session laws for the federal legislature, is abbreviated Stat. in the history of the statute with the volume number coming before the abbreviation and the page number where the law begins following.[10] Thereafter it is distributed throughout the laws of the nation in the United States Code. Public Laws can be located online at www.congress.gov and the link for Public Laws can be found under the search bar from the landing page.

The *United States Code* (U.S.C.) is the official code of the general and permanent laws of the United States. Publication began in 1926, and it has been published in print every six years since 1934.[11] It does not include annotations to cases or secondary authorities, treaties, agency regulations, State or District of Columbia laws, or most acts that are temporary or special, such as those that appropriate money for specific years or that apply to only a limited number of people or a specific place.[12]

There are two unofficial codes that include annotations and you should use these. They are West Publishing's *United States Code Annotated* (U.S.C.A.) available on Westlaw and *the United States Code Service* (U.S.C.S.) published by LexisNexis available on Lexis.

Federal statutes are codified by first assigning them to one of 54 titles according to subject matter.[13] Each title of the Code is subdivided into a combination of smaller units such as subtitles, chapters, subchapters, parts, subparts, and sections, not necessarily in that order. The basic unit of every code title is the section, which is the same as Hawai'i.[14] In addition to the sections themselves, the United States Code includes statutory provisions set out as statutory notes, the Constitution, several sets of federal court rules, and certain presidential documents, such as executive orders, determinations, notices, and proclamations, that implement or relate to statutory provisions

---

10. Legislative materials can be found on https://www.congress.gov/.
11. The last six-year anniversary was 2018. You can view this publication at https://www.govinfo.gov/app/collection/uscode/2018/.
12. For more detailed explanation, *see* http://uscode.house.gov/detailed_guide.xhtml. It is also available online at https://www.govinfo.gov/app/collection/uscode and https://uscode.house.gov/.
13. Title 53 does not yet have any statutes. *See* https://uscode.house.gov/.
14. Citations are typically to sections of the Code and begin with Title number, abbreviation to code used (U.S.C., U.S.C.A. or U.S.C.S.) § section number (date).

in the Code. See Figure 8-17 to familiarize yourself with the parts of a federal statute.

Generally, begin your search for federal statutes in the unofficial annotated codes (U.S.C.A. or U.S.C.S.) because of the comprehensiveness of legal research related to the statutory section such annotations include. All of the search strategies mentioned in the section on Hawai'i Statutes are valid in researching federal statutes. They are:

1. Citation Method: If you know the statute's citation, enter it, and go directly to it. Typically, you get a citation by reading secondary authorities or judicial opinions.

2. Index Method: If you know the subject of a statute, use an index to locate statutory sections.

3. Definition Method: Legal publishers include an entry in the index for "definitions" or "defined terms" or "words and phrases" depending on the resource.

4. Popular Name Method: Many federal statutes have popular names that they are known by, for instance, "The Affordable Care Act" or "The Americans with Disabilities Act." Use the Popular Names Tables for the United States Code, U.S.C.A. or U.S.C.S.

5. Topic or Analytic Method: If you know the title that the law falls under, the outline at the beginning of the title can be used to drill down to a section. It also provides the necessary context to the law.

6. Keyword Method: Using a keyword to find a federal statute works well when the word is unique, but it is the least effective or efficient method of finding a federal statute. Using a keyword or a Boolean expression often returns too many results that have to be evaluated.

Start a new research log when you change jurisdictions and begin research in federal statutes. Because federal statutes can be especially large and cumbersome finding a treatise on the topic is critical to narrowing down the number of primary authorities one would need to examine and to gain an understanding of the laws that cover a legal issue.

Figure 8-17. Identifying Parts of a Federal Statute

Page 481   TITLE 46—SHIPPING ← Title   § 30305

§ 30106. Time limit on bringing maritime action for personal injury or death

Except as otherwise provided by law, a civil action for damages for personal injury or death arising out of a maritime tort must be brought within 3 years after the cause of action arose.

(Pub. L. 109–304, § 6(c), Oct. 6, 2006, 120 Stat. 1511.)

HISTORICAL AND REVISION NOTES

Revised Section	Source (U.S. Code)	Source (Statutes at Large)
30106	46 App.:763a.	Pub. L. 96–382, § 1, Oct. 6, 1980, 94 Stat. 1525.

The words "civil action" are substituted for "suit" for consistency with rule 2 of the Federal Rules of Civil Procedure (28 App. U.S.C.). The words "or both" are omitted as unnecessary. The words "must be brought" are substituted for "shall not be maintained unless commenced" for clarity and consistency. The word "arose" is substituted for "accrued" for consistency in the revised title.

Chapter → **CHAPTER 303—DEATH ON THE HIGH SEAS**

Chapter Outline
Sec.
30301. Short title.
30302. Cause of action.
30303. Amount and apportionment of recovery.
30304. Contributory negligence.
30305. Death of plaintiff in pending action.
30306. Foreign cause of action.
30307. Commercial aviation accidents.
30308. Nonapplication.

§ 30301. Short title ← Section title

Text → This chapter may be cited as the "Death on the High Seas Act".

History → (Pub. L. 109–304, § 6(c), Oct. 6, 2006, 120 Stat. 1511.)

HISTORICAL AND REVISION NOTES

Revised Section	Source (U.S. Code)	Source (Statutes at Large)
30301	46 App.:761 note.	

Revisor's Notes

SHORT TITLE

Act Mar. 30, 1920, ch. 111, 41 Stat. 537, which enacted chapter 21 (§ 761 et seq.) of the former Appendix to this title, was popularly known as the "Death on the High Seas Act", prior to being repealed and restated in this chapter by Pub. L. 109–304, §§ 6(c), 19, Oct. 6, 2006, 120 Stat. 1509, 1710.

§ 30302. Cause of action

When the death of an individual is caused by wrongful act, neglect, or default occurring on the high seas beyond 3 nautical miles from the shore of the United States, the personal representative of the decedent may bring a civil action in admiralty against the person or vessel responsible. The action shall be for the exclusive benefit of the decedent's spouse, parent, child, or dependent relative.

(Pub. L. 109–304, § 6(c), Oct. 6, 2006, 120 Stat. 1511.)

HISTORICAL AND REVISION NOTES

Revised Section	Source (U.S. Code)	Source (Statutes at Large)
30302	46 App.:761(a).	Mar. 30, 1920, ch. 111, § 1(a), 41 Stat. 537; Pub. L. 105–181, title IV, § 404(a)(1), Apr. 5, 2000, 114 Stat. 131.

The words "Subject to subsection (b) of this section" are omitted as unnecessary. The words "3 nautical miles" are substituted for "a marine league" for clarity. The words "United States" are substituted for "any State, or the District of Columbia, or the Territories or dependencies of the United States" because of the definition of "United States" in chapter 1 of the revised title. The words "bring a civil action" are substituted for "maintain a suit" for consistency with rule 2 of the Federal Rules of Civil Procedure (28 App. U.S.C.). The words "for damages" are omitted as unnecessary. The words "in the district courts of the United States" are omitted as unnecessary because of 28 U.S.C. 1333. The words "person or vessel" are substituted for "vessel, person, or corporation" because of 1 U.S.C. 1. The word "responsible" is substituted for "which would have been liable if death had not ensued" to eliminate unnecessary words.

§ 30303. Amount and apportionment of recovery

The recovery in an action under this chapter shall be a fair compensation for the pecuniary loss sustained by the individuals for whose benefit the action is brought. The court shall apportion the recovery among those individuals in proportion to the loss each has sustained.

(Pub. L. 109–304, § 6(c), Oct. 6, 2006, 120 Stat. 1511.)

HISTORICAL AND REVISION NOTES

Revised Section	Source (U.S. Code)	Source (Statutes at Large)
30303	46 App.:762(a).	Mar. 30, 1920, ch. 111, § 2(a), 41 Stat. 537; Pub. L. 105–181, title IV, § 404(b)(1), Apr. 5, 2000, 114 Stat. 131.

The words "and just" are omitted as redundant to "fair". The words "each has sustained" are substituted for "they may severally have suffered by reason of the death of the person by whose representative the suit is brought" to eliminate unnecessary words.

§ 30304. Contributory negligence

In an action under this chapter, contributory negligence of the decedent is not a bar to recovery. The court shall consider the degree of negligence of the decedent and reduce the recovery accordingly.

(Pub. L. 109–304, § 6(c), Oct. 6, 2006, 120 Stat. 1511.)

HISTORICAL AND REVISION NOTES

Revised Section	Source (U.S. Code)	Source (Statutes at Large)
30304	46 App.:766.	Mar. 30, 1920, ch. 111, § 6, 41 Stat. 537.

§ 30305. Death of plaintiff in pending action

If a civil action in admiralty is pending in a court of the United States to recover for personal injury caused by wrongful act, neglect, or default described in section 30302 of this title, and the individual dies during the action as a result of the wrongful act, neglect, or default, the personal representative of the decedent may be substituted as the plaintiff and the action may proceed under this chapter for the recovery authorized by this chapter.

(Pub. L. 109–304, § 6(c), Oct. 6, 2006, 120 Stat. 1511.)

HISTORICAL AND REVISION NOTES

Revised Section	Source (U.S. Code)	Source (Statutes at Large)
30305	46 App.:765.	Mar. 30, 1920, ch. 111, § 5, 41 Stat. 537.

Source: United States Code, Government Printing Office.

E. Using Citators in Your Statutory Research
1. Validating Statutes

The last step in legal research is making sure the law you are relying on is still good law. It is critical that you validate your research to ensure that the primary source authority you are relying upon has not been amended or repealed or declared unconstitutional by an appellate court. To confirm that your statute remains valid, you must use a citator.

The citator in Westlaw is KeyCite, and the citator in Lexis is Shepard's. Each of these services are quite good, but both are fallible and frequently disagree. Each is only as good as its algorithm and its editors. For most statutes, it is fine to rely on one service. However, if it is a statute that is frequently amended and/or relates to a topic where there is pending legislation, you may consider running it through both citators to double check that the statute remains good law.

When the citator reveals negative authority for your statute, you must read the materials to determine the extent on which you can rely on the statute. When courts declare statutes invalid or unconstitutional, frequently only a portion of the statute is impacted, and it could depend on a specific factual situation. The remaining portions continue to be valid and controlling. Or a statute may be held unconstitutional only when applied to a limited set of circumstances. There may be pending legislation that could impact your statute, but it may be that the legislation is unlikely to get passed. Reviewing the negative authorities will help you determine the extent to which the statute is controlling law.

Shepard's reports on Lexis display one of seven *Shepard's* Signal indicators to alert the researcher to a potential change in the status of a statutory section. To access the statute's Shepard's Report, simply click on the link on the right-hand side. See Figures 8-18 and 8-19. In Figure 8-19, some yellow triangles are circled to call your attention to the flags. Those flags belong to the document linked there not to the statute.

For statutes, the *Shepard's* signal described as a red exclamation mark in white circle is generated by a court's treatment of the statute. If the court has cited the statute but did not provide analysis of the statute, no signal is generated. The statute's history is never considered when determining Shepard's signal for a statute. *Shepard's* signals for statutes are only generated based on

8 · STATUTES   153

Figure 8-18. Shepard's Flag

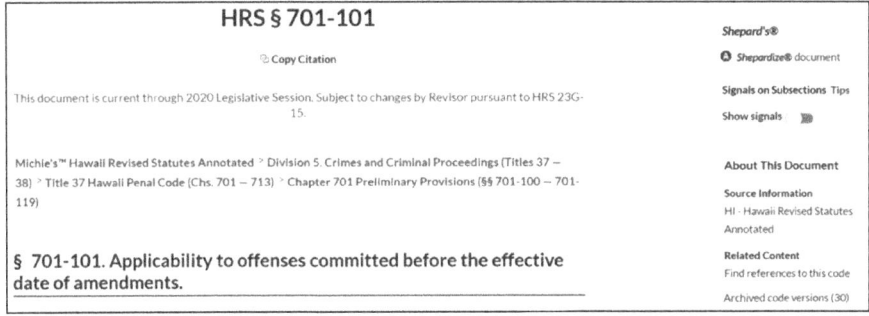

Source: Lexis, reprinted with permission from LexisNexis.

Figure 8-19. Shepard's Report

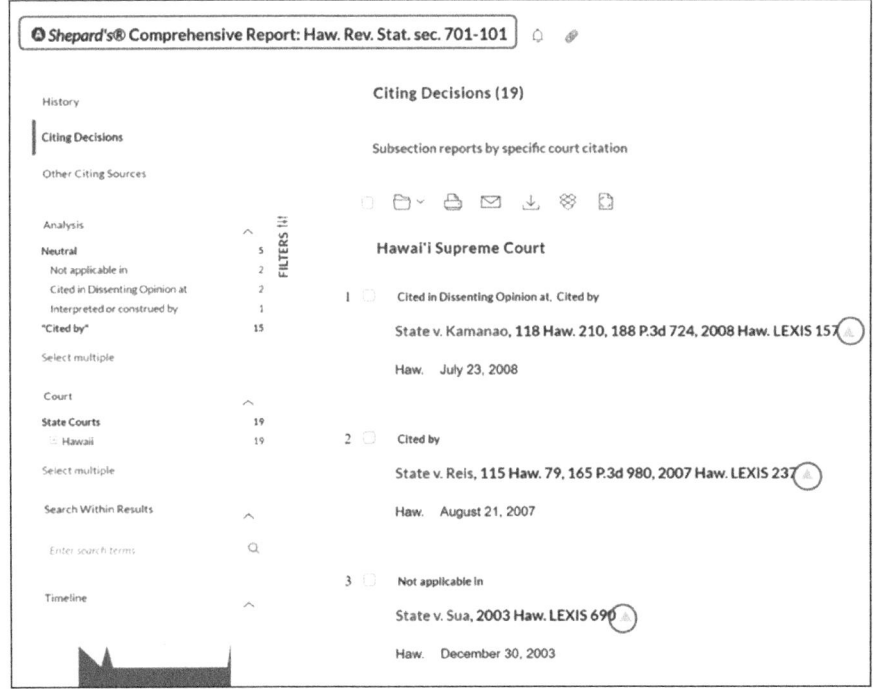

Source: Lexis, reprinted with permission from LexisNexis.

Figure 8-20. KeyCite Flag

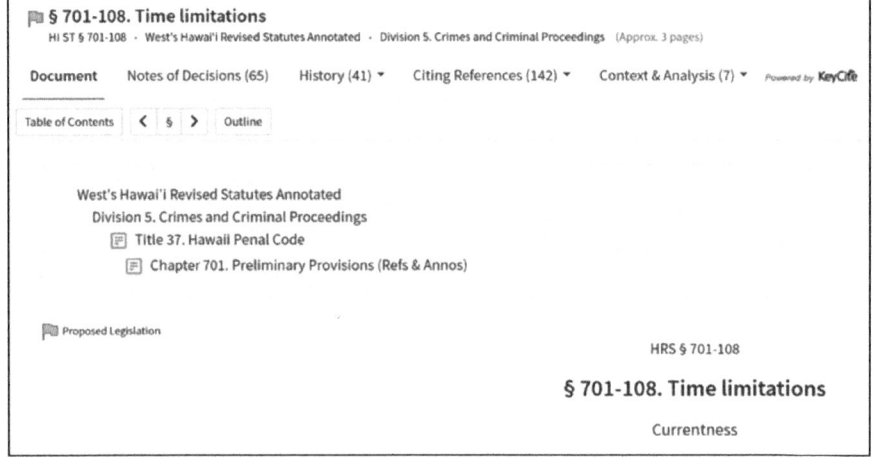

Source: Westlaw, reprinted with permission from Thomson Reuters.

Figure 8-21. KeyCite Report

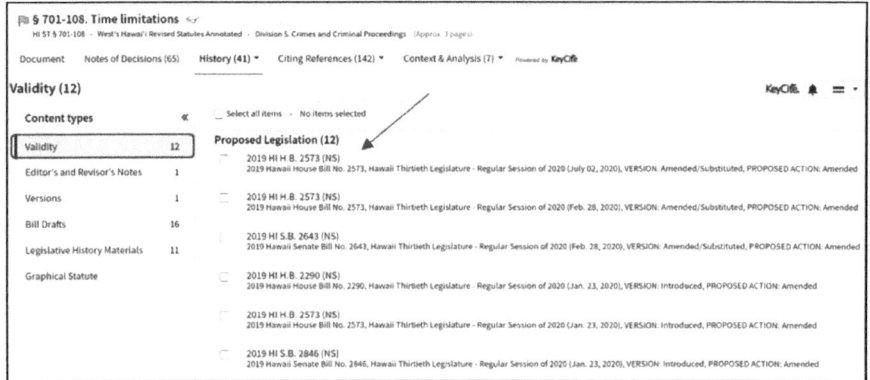

Source: Westlaw, reprinted with permission from Thomson Reuters.

Figure 8-22. Shepard's Comprehensive Report for Statutes

Source: Lexis+, reprinted with permission from LexisNexis.

the court's treatment of the statute. *Shepard's* never looks at the legislative treatment of a statute.

Westlaw's citator is KeyCite. Once you have found a statute upon which to base your legal argument, KeyCite Flags alert you to negative references or events that may impact the validity of that document. Simply click on the flag to access the report. See Figures 8-20 and 8-21.

A red flag alerts the researcher that a statute has been amended, repealed, superseded, held unconstitutional, or preempted in whole or in part. Take note and read the referenced document.

A yellow flag typically indicates proposed legislation but could also indicate that an appellate court has questioned the validity of the statute, or a prior version of the statute has received negative treatment from a court.

Yellow flags are often seen on statutes when the Hawaiʻi Legislature is in session. In the 2020 Regular Session, 2,336 bills were introduced yet only 82 passed.[15] With that many bills, a.k.a. "proposed legislation," many yellow

---

15. https://lrb.hawaii.gov/wp-content/uploads/2020LegislativeStatistics.pdf.

Figure 8-23. KeyCite Filters for Statutes

Source: Westlaw, reprinted with permission from Thomson Reuters.

flags are generated by citator services, but check the status of proposed legislation to determine its potential impact on the statute under consideration.

Two other flags seen less frequently on statutes are a blue-striped flag and an orange circle with a triangle. A blue-striped flag indicates a document is on appeal to the U.S. Courts of Appeals or the U.S. Supreme Court (federal courts only). The orange circle with a triangle indicates an overruling risk based on an otherwise invalid prior decision.

2. Using a Citator to Update Your Research

The annotated codes do not include all case or secondary source references. For a more thorough review, attorneys use a citator.[16] The advantage of using an online citator like Shepard's or KeyCite, is that you can customize your citator results. In the employment discrimination example, you might

---

16. See Chapter 1 for an introduction to citators.

limit your citing cases to specific courts, or specific date ranges if the statute has been amended. Using citators for your statutory research is an excellent way to find case law and commentary interpreting the statute. Citators should be used during your research process but should also be the last thing you do before finalizing your assignment to be sure that additional cases have not been reported since you last updated the law.

For example, the Shepard's Citator found 265 federal cases and 65 state cases discussing this statute under the heading citing decisions. This result can be refined by court, date of decision, and keyword searching. For example, if you select only cases from the state's highest court, the Hawai'i Supreme Court, and further limit your results with the phrase "race /s discrim!," your Shepard's report will display twenty one cases that are likely more on point than all sixty five cases and are binding on the Hawai'i judiciary because they are from the Supreme Court. Notice that the cases cited by Shepard's are marked by Shepard symbols to indicate how the case is being treated by the courts.

To find commentary in the Shepard's Report, you need to select Other Citing Sources at the top of the display. In this example, there are a total of 213 documents. These can also be limited using the filters to the left of the display. You can limit by publication type, date, and keyword searching within Shepard's initial results for this statutory section.

To continue this example on Westlaw, KeyCite retrieved 347 cases that are citing Haw. Rev. Stat. § 378-2. These are too many to be absorbed by a researcher, and not all of these will relate to Jacob's situation as described in Chapter 1. Using the KeyCite filters, we can trim the 347 cases by using multiple filters. Good choices include selecting only reported cases from the Hawai'i Supreme Court, the highest court of the state. KeyCite also allows keyword searching within the results. By adding the phrase "race /s dicrim!" the number of cases would be reduced to eighteen. Notice that only some of the cases listed will include a KeyCite symbol. Westlaw does not provide initial KeyCite symbols for cases not already included in their Notes of Decisions.

The filters for secondary sources on KeyCite are not as sophisticated as they are for primary law; however, you can select the type of secondary source to review, and you can also perform keyword searches within these titles.

Chapter 9

Hawai'i Legislative History

I. Introduction

This chapter is unlike the others in that it both explains the process for researching legislative history and provides a visual process. In order to capture the process of legislative history, all figures in this chapter are found at the end of the chapter for easy reference. The figures are intended to guide you visually through the online process at the Hawai'i Legislature website. By following the examples shown in the figures or the written process or both researching legislative history need not be as complicated as it may seem initially. The number and unique characteristics of the Hawai'i material make it seem difficult, but it is not. Think of it as ordering your meal from an *ala carte* menu where you get a little bit from many dishes to make an entire meal. Actually, there are only a few steps to this research process. See Table 9-1.

Table 9-1. Post 1984 Hawai'i Legislative History Checklist

Post 1984 Hawai'i Legislative History Checklist	
Action	Resource
Step 1. Get the statute's history following the text	Hawai'i Revised Statutes
Step 2. Find the bill number and committee report numbers in the "Table of Committee Reports on Measures Enacted and Vetoed"	Session Laws of Hawai'i
Step 3H. In the center section of the Journal, locate the House Committee report	House Journal
Step 4H. Using the Journal Index, check the journal pages for debate or commentary on this legislation	House Journal

Step 3S. In the center section of the Journal, locate the Senate Committee report	Senate Journal
Step 4S. Using the Journal Index, check the journal pages for debate or commentary on this legislation	Senate Journal

Table: Roberta F. Woods

When a statute is ambiguous courts will look at the statute's legislative history to determine whether it applies to the set of facts under review. Not all members of the Judiciary think the legislative history of a statute should be examined when deciding a case. And, very often you will not get a clear statement of intent from your research, but the process of research can lead to a better understanding of the statute and what the legislature considered when passing it.

The Hawai'i State Legislature is made up of the Senate and House of Representatives. The Legislature convenes annually in regular session at 10:00 a.m. on the third Wednesday in January. Regular sessions are limited to sixty legislative days, and state law requires a recess of at least five days between the twentieth and fortieth days of the regular session. A special session may be convened by the Governor or at the written request of two-thirds of the members of both houses. The Senate may also convene in special session at the written request of two-thirds of its members to consider judicial appointments.[1]

The Legislature operates over a biennium, which is the two-year term that begins in an odd-numbered year and ends in an even-numbered year. This means that bills introduced but not passed in the odd-numbered year can continue and pass in the even-numbered years.

Legislators introduce bills to be decided upon first by standing committees in their chamber and if passed there, the bills go to the other chamber where standing committees examine it and if passed in that chamber, the bill goes to the Governor for a signature or veto. If the Governor signs it, it becomes an Act, which is also a session law. All of this activity is recorded in each chamber's journal by bill number. You must research the journal of each chamber to compile a legislative history.

---

1. Haw. Const. art. III, §10 *Sessions*.

A. Legislative Journals

Hawai'i's legislative journals comprise one regular session of the legislature and could also include a special session, but they are not compiled together. Each session is its own publication and operates separately even if they are found in the same print volume. Generally, think of the journals as being organized in thirds. First, the daily journals by date, followed by committee reports roughly in the middle, and then the history of bills at the end that functions as an index to the journal section. Committee reports begin with conference committees followed by standing committee reports. The reports are numerically ordered; therefore, the page number is not listed with the history of bills. There is not a general index.

Understanding the legislative process should help when researching legislative history. For example, knowing that a legislator introduces a bill that could become a statute should remind you that knowing the bill number is important since everything in the legislative process prior to enactment is filed by the bill number. If the bill begins with the letter H it started in the House; accordingly, if it starts with the letter S it started in the Senate. The bill number never changes even when it goes to the other chamber for approval. Thus, H.B. (House Bill) 123 remains H.B. 123 even when the Senate takes it up.

There are many other numbers that are important to collect along the way so be prepared to keep track of your research. Some details of a legislative history require specific information for a proper citation, so make sure you know what citation information you will need before starting. It will save you lots of time in the long run. Also, collect information such as the name of the committees and the date the committee issued its report to take with you to the Hawai'i State Archives to search for committee testimony or bill drafts if needed.

II. The Four Steps to Determine Legislative Intent

1. Get the statute's history in the Hawai'i Revised Statutes.
2. Find the bill number and committee report numbers in the session laws.
3. Locate committee reports in journals. (Repeat for the other chamber.)
4. Check for debate or additional information in chamber journals. (Repeat for the other chamber.)

Keep track of your research and significant findings. An examination of the Aloha Spirit Law found in *Hawai'i Revised Statutes* section 5-7.5 will be used to illustrate the process. Through this process you will find Senate and House Committee Reports, a reference in the Journals to a Conference Committee that never materialized, and significant floor debate on this law. The freely available website offered by the Hawai'i State Legislature is robust and most modern-day legislative histories can be done online from this website.[2]

A. Step 1 — Get the statute's history in the *Hawai'i Revised Statutes*.

Begin in the *Hawai'i Revised Statutes* and find the law you want to research. For example, the Aloha Spirit Law is codified at section 5-7.5. From the text of the statute in the *Hawai'i Revised Statutes*, locate the history or credits at the end of the text. Each time something happened to the statute, whether it was placed in a different part of the code (recodification), amended, or repealed, it is noted in the history. The changes are separated by semicolons (;).

You will probably have to research each year's history if there is more than one year.[3] However, sometimes the Revisor's notes at the end of the statute or from a different tab in an online platform will indicate the substance of the changes so that you can focus on the most important ones for what you need to research. Without such guidance, you will most likely need to search each one.

In the official statutes, the last line of the text is abbreviated and followed by a bracketed clause. [L. 1986, ch. 202 §1]. The information will be the same in the unofficial codes (Michie's and West's) but it will be characterized differently. LexisNexis publications place the information at the end of the statute under the heading "History." West publications place the information at the end of the statute under the heading "Credits." Regardless, it is the statute's history. To interpret the abbreviations, look to an abbreviations table somewhere in the resource you are using or use this list. Table 9-2 lists some source note abbreviations you may encounter.

---

2. http://www.capitol.hawaii.gov.
3. Using your word processor's ability to convert horizontal lines to vertical lines, simply copy the history line; paste it into a document; search for a ; and replace it with a paragraph mark ^p in Microsoft Word. Then, with the text highlighted, number the lines.

Table 9-2. Source Note Abbreviations

L	Year of enactment in Session Laws of Hawai'i
c or ch	Act #
s or §	Section
am	Amended
rep	Repealed
gen ch	Gender Change
CC	Civil Code (Kingdom Era code)
PC	Penal Code (Kingdom Era code)
RL	Revised Laws of Hawai'i (Territorial Era code)

Table: Roberta F. Woods

The citation "L. 1986, ch. 202 §1" tells us that the Aloha Spirit Law began as the 1986 Session Laws of Hawai'i, act 202, section 1. But none of this tells us the bill number, a key fact in obtaining a statute's legislative history.

B. Step 2 — Find the bill number and committee report numbers in the session laws

Images for step two in the Session Laws are Figures 9-1 to 9-5.

Locate the Session Laws for the year your law was passed. All session laws since 1959 for the state of Hawai'i are online.[4] For example, Figure 9-1 shows the Hawai'i State Legislature website showing the location of the links for the 1986 Session Laws.[5] Earlier session laws are available on HeinOnline or LLMC, both proprietary resources. Check your law library for access.

If the session law you need is for 1984 or later, find the Table of Committee Reports on Measures Enacted and Vetoed from the online link to Index and Effect of Acts. See Figure 9-2 that shows the link to finding the Committee Reports Table. The table headers are shown in Figure 9-3. This is a feature found in the Session Laws beginning in 1984.

The table gives us much of the information needed to continue our research in the House and Senate Journals. Reading the line for Act 202, we get the bill number, HB 2569, Senate Committee Rept. No. 833-86, House Committee Rept. No. 399-86. There is not an entry under Conference Committee Report.

---

4. https://www.capitol.hawaii.gov/.
5. *Id.*

9 · HAWAI'I LEGISLATIVE HISTORY

Figure 9-1. Hawai'i State Legislature Website (capitol.hawaii.gov)

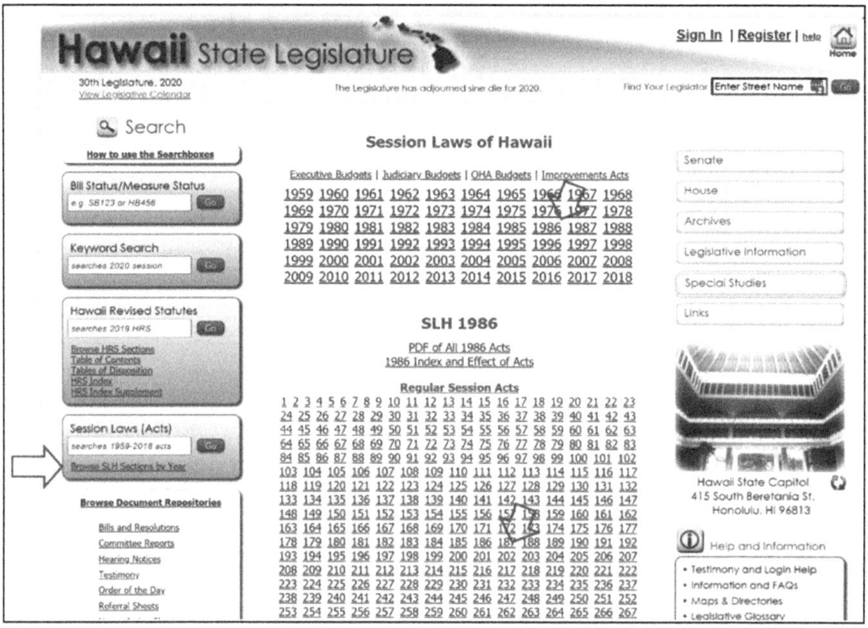

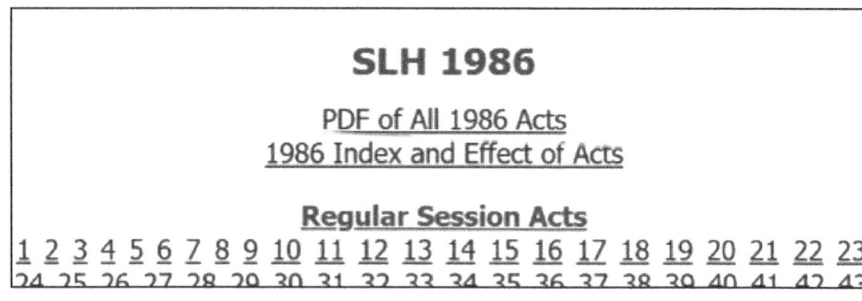

Source: State Legislature website, https://www.capitol.hawaii.gov.

Figure 9-2. Link to Finding the Committee Reports Table

Source: State Legislature website, https://www.capitol.hawaii.gov.

Figure 9-3. Committee Reports Table Headers

		Senate Committee Rept. No.	House Committee Rept. No.	Conference Committee Rept. No.
COMMITTEE REPORTS ON MEASURES ENACTED AND VETOED					
Compilation of Acts and Vetoed Measures, Together with the Pertinent Committee Report References, Listed by Act Numbers					
Act No.	Bill No.	Senate Committee Rept. No.	House Committee Rept. No.	Conference Committee Rept. No.

Source: State Legislature website, https://www.capitol.hawaii.gov.

That means that the House and Senate agreed on the language of the Bill and did not need to meet to settle their disagreements. If there is a Conference Committee Report, it is usually regarded as the most important report because it represents a statement of legislative agreement in both chambers rather than a single chamber. See Figure 9-4 showing Act 202 Committee Reports.

Figure 9-4. Act 202 Committee Reports

Act No.	Bill No.	Senate Committee Rept. No.	House Committee Rept. No.	Conference Committee Rept. No.
170	HB 122	518-86 812-86	407	HC 44-86 SC 33-86
171	HB 1727	629-86	286-86	
172	HB 1959	793-86	336-86	
173	HB 1993	802-86	389-86	
174	HB 1995	541-86	292-86	
175	HB 1998	329-86	761-86	HC 21-86 43-86 SC 13-86 34-86
176	HB 1999	707-86	398-86	
177	HB 2001	763-86	413-86	
178	HB 2002	764-86	412-86	
179	HB 2003	563-86	291-86	
180	HB 2011	698-86	226-86 523-86	
181	HB 2048	642-86	351-86	
182	HB 2111	647-86	476-86	
183	HB 2116	683-86	352-86	
184	HB 2129	740-86	541-86	
185	HB 2166	624-86	197-86 598-86	HC 12-86 SC 7-86
186	HB 2168	741-86	334-86	
187	HB 2202	703-86	477-86	HC 14-86 SC 12-86
188	HB 2444	760-86	402-86	HC 6-86 SC 6-86
189	HB 2596	637-86	327-86	HC 22-86 SC 15-86
190	SB 1855	106-86 288-86	726-86 865-86	
191	SB 909	644	320-86	SC 40-86 HC 49-86
192	HB 326	809-86	392	HC 37-86 SC 27-86
193	HB 2069	765-86	415-86	HC 11-86 SC 16-86
194	HB 2117	791-86	375-86	HC 31-86 SC 23-86
195	HB 2158	821-86	489-86	
196	HB 2170	601-86 807-86	397-86	HC 5-86 SC 9-86
197	HB 2284	730-86	189-86 577-86	
198	HB 2337	598-86 805-86	272-86 514-86	
199	HB 2358	803-86	376-86	
200	HB 2362	808-86	436-86	
201	HB 2363	800-86	437-86	
202	HB 2569	833-86	399-86	

Source: State Legislature website, https://www.capitol.hawaii.gov.

HB means House Bill, so this legislation originated in the House of Representatives. If it had originated in the Senate, the bill would begin with the letter S. While you are in the Session Laws, look at the act itself. Very often the act will include a section stating the purpose of the legislation that does not get reproduced in the *Hawai'i Revised Statutes*. (More on this in the chapter on Hawai'i State Statutes, Tables of Disposition.) The purpose could lead to an understanding of legislative intent.

Act 202 of the Session Laws of 1986 indicates a bill number with dash 86 appended to it. See Figure 9-5 showing Act 202 of the 1986 Session Laws of Hawai'i. The dash 86 means that you will find it in the 1986 Journals of the House and Senate. Remember that the Hawai'i Legislature sits in a biennium beginning with the odd-numbered year and ending with the even-numbered year. Not all session laws append the year to them.

Figure 9-5. Showing Act 202 of the 1986 Session Laws of Hawai'i

---

ACT 202

ACT 202   H.B. NO. 2569-86

A Bill for an Act Relating to "Aloha Spirit".

Be It Enacted by the Legislature of the State of Hawaii:

SECTION 1. Chapter 5, Hawaii Revised Statutes, is amended by adding a new section to be appropriately designated and to read as follows:

"§5- **"Aloha Spirit"**. (a) "Aloha Spirit" is the coordination of mind and heart within each person. It brings each person to the self. Each person must think and emote good feelings to others. In the contemplation and presence of the life force, "Aloha", the following unuhi laula loa may be used:

"Akahai", meaning kindness to be expressed with tenderness;
"Lokahi", meaning unity, to be expressed with harmony;
"Oluolu", meaning agreeable, to be expressed with pleasantness;
"Haahaa", meaning humility, to be expressed with modesty;
"Ahonui", meaning patience, to be expressed with perseverance.

These are traits of character that express the charm, warmth and sincerity of Hawaii's people. It was the working philosophy of native Hawaiians and was presented as a gift to the people of Hawaii. "Aloha" is more than a word of greeting or farewell or a salutation. "Aloha" means mutual regard and affection and extends warmth in caring with no obligation in return. "Aloha" is the essence of relationships in which each person is important to every other person for collective existence. "Aloha" means to hear what is not said, to see what cannot be seen and to know the unknowable.

(b) In exercising their power on behalf of the people and in fulfillment of their responsibilities, obligations and service to the people, the legislature, governor, lieutenant governor, executive officers of each department, the chief justice, associate justices, and judges of the appellate, circuit, and district courts may contemplate and reside with the life force and give consideration to the "Aloha Spirit"."

SECTION 2. New statutory material is underscored.[1]

SECTION 3. This Act shall take effect on July 1, 1986.

(Approved May 19, 1986.)

Note
1. Edited pursuant to HRS §23G-16.5.

Source: State Legislature website, https://www.capitol.hawaii.gov.

C. Step 3 H & S — Locate Committee Reports (House and Senate Journals)

Images for step three in the Senate Journals are Figures 9-6 to 9-9. The images for step three in the House Journals are Figures 9-16 to 9-19.

Figure 9-6. Link to Senate Pages

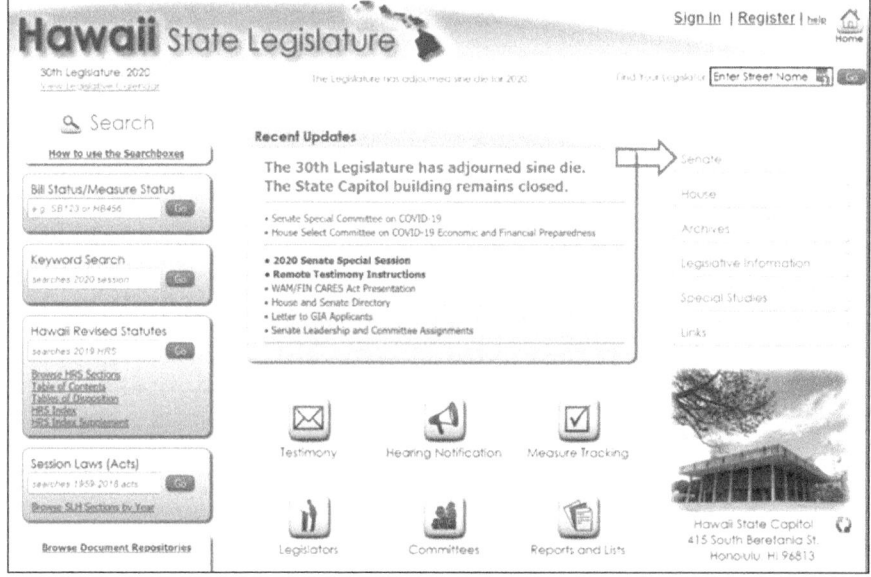

Source: State Legislature website, https://www.capitol.hawaii.gov.

Committee Reports are found in the journals for each chamber. The House and Senate Journals for 1986 are linked from the House and Senate site. It is necessary to examine the journal for each chamber. You should complete your research in one journal before moving on to the next. The process will be the same for both journals, but their online links will be worded slightly differently. Get used to looking for information displayed in different ways and noting information you may not know is needed until you begin to create the citation. For example, the actual date is often used in a citation for legislative materials. The Senate displays the legislative days individually with the actual date shown on the link. See Figure 9-8 toward the bottom indicating legislative day as well as the actual date. The House displays the page numbers for the legislative days.

Figure 9-7. Link to Senate Journals by Year

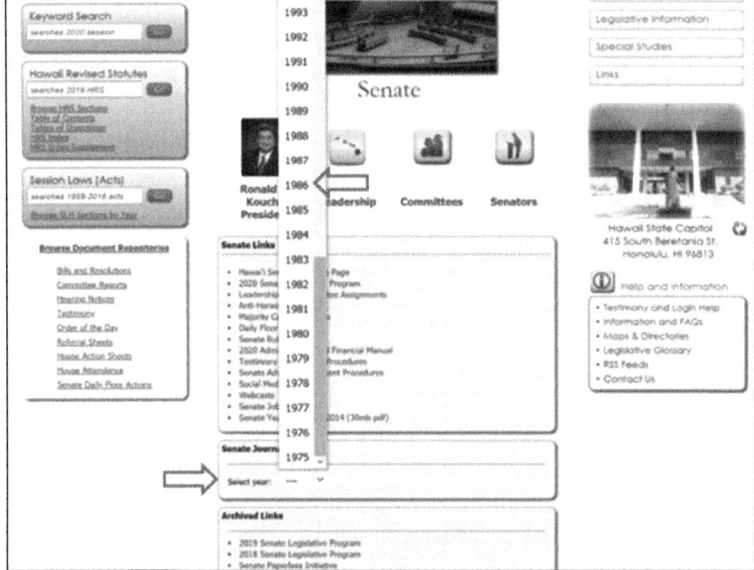

Source: State Legislature website, https://www.capitol.hawaii.gov.

Figure 9-8. Link to Committee Reports (Senate Journal) & Showing Legislative Day and Date

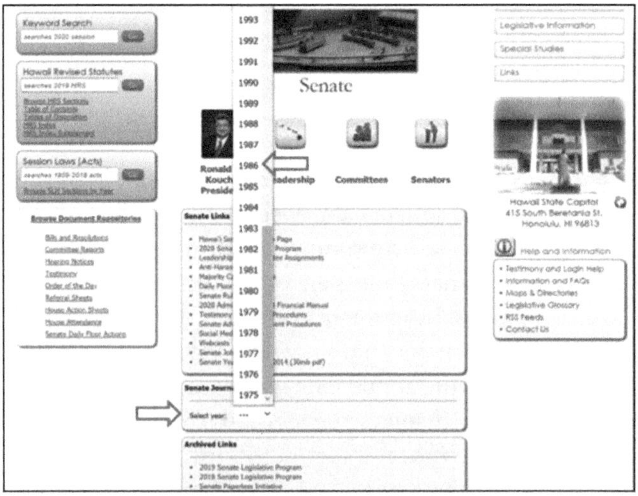

Source: State Legislature website, https://www.capitol.hawaii.gov.

To find the date from the legislative day in the House Journals, open the Front Section file. See Figures 9-18 showing the link to the Front Section of the House Journal and Figures 9-22 and 9-23 showing the legislative day and date. Capture the information when you are going through the first time.

Generally, think of the journals as being in thirds. First, the daily journals by date. The history of bills at the back of the book functions as an index to the journal section. There is not a general index. Committee Reports are arranged by report number in the middle of the books. The page numbers for reports are not included in the history of bills. If there was a conference committee report, it would come at the beginning of the committee reports followed by the standing committee reports. Report numbers are for standing committee reports.

Open the file with 1986 Committee Reports. See Figure 9-8 (Senate) and Figure 9-18 for Committee Report links. The files are searchable pdfs. Search for the Senate report number 833 or the bill number 2569.

This report gives the purpose of the bill. It also indicates that the Senate amended it so there are now two versions of the bill, the original, H.D. 1 or House Draft 1, and S.D. 1 or Senate Draft 1.[6] See Figure 9-9 showing the text of Senate Standing Committee Report 833-86.

After you have collected the committee report(s), open the Indices file (Figure 9-10) and search for HB 2569. See Figure 9-12. Except for the last column, these are page numbers to the Journal section. The bill was introduced on page 218; referred to committee(s) on page 222. Pay particular attention to the Second and Third Readings. Usually, the Second Reading introduces a Committee Report.

Open the Senate Journal 1986 Regular Session file and search for page 377 or "Aloha Spirit" or 2569-86. See Figure 9-11. The information conveyed here indicates that the committee report was adopted and the Senate changed the bill as mentioned in the Judiciary Committee report. Given that the House initiated the bill, everything that happened in the House happened prior to it coming to the Senate. Disagreements late in the legislative process typically trigger a conference committee to iron out the differences, but this bill did

---

6. The drafts of legislative bills prior to 1999 are found in the Hawai'i State Archives. Beginning in 1999, the text of bills introduced and subsequent drafts are found from the Archives link on the Legislative website.

Figure 9-9. Senate Standing Committee Report 833-86

```
            SENATE JOURNAL - STANDING COMMITTEE REPORTS            1183

    that such reforms have a significant effect on insurance rates, your Committee finds that
    immediate reduction and stabilization of insurance rates is warranted. Therefore, your
    Committee included a provision in the bill that makes its enactment effective only if H.B. No.
    2525-86 dealing with the issue of insurance rates becomes law.
        Your Committee on Ways and Means is in accord with the intent and purpose of H.B. No.
    1692-86, H.D. 2, S.D. 1, as amended herein, and recommends that it pass Third Reading in the
    form attached hereto as H.B. No. 1692-86, H.D. 2, S.D. 2.
            Signed by all members of the Committee.

    SCRep. 833-86       Judiciary on H.B. No. 2569-86
        The purpose of this bill is to express Aloha as the essence of the law in the State of Hawaii.
        The bill defines the Aloha Spirit in a way that conveys its relevance and importance to the
    State and its people. The bill also invites those who govern Hawaii to be guided by the Aloha
    Spirit.
        Your Committee finds that the bill renews and strengthens the State's commitment to the
    Aloha Spirit as the spirit that infuses Hawaii and lives in its people.
        Your Committee on Judiciary is in accord with the intent and purpose of H.B. No. 2569-86, as
    amended herein, and recommends that it pass Second Reading in the form attached hereto as
    H.B. No. 2569-86, S.D. 1, and be placed on the calendar for Third Reading.
        Signed by all members of the Committee except Senators Abercrombie, Aki, Cobb,
    Kuroda and George.
```

Source: State Legislature website, https://www.capitol.hawaii.gov.

not have a conference committee report. However, there are journal pages listed under the Conference Committee column in the history index.

D. Step 4 H & S — Check for debate or additional information spoken in chamber in the journals

Images for step four in the Senate Journal are Figures 9-10 to 9-15. Images for step four in the House Journal are Figures 9-20 to 9-24. Frequently the page number will be off by one. If you don't see your Bill on the page look at the page before or the page after.

From the Bill History you find Senate Journal pages 377, 392, 433, 520, 545, 582, and 461 could have relevant information to aid in our pursuit of legislative intent. Next, we examine some of those pages to gain some insight into the disagreement between the chambers. Many of the pages reveal little new information. Page 433 does not mention H.B. 2569-86; it does on page 434 in a list of bills state that the House disagreed with the Senate. The nature of the disagreement isn't given. On page 520 H.B. 2569-86 is again listed but the reason is on page 519. See Figure 9-14. The House decided to reconsider its disagreement with S.D. 1. Page 545 lists H.B. 2569-86 because the House agreed to the Senate's amendments on the bill and S.D. 1 became the final bill draft. See Figure 9-15.

Figure 9-10. Link to History of Bills (Senate Journal)

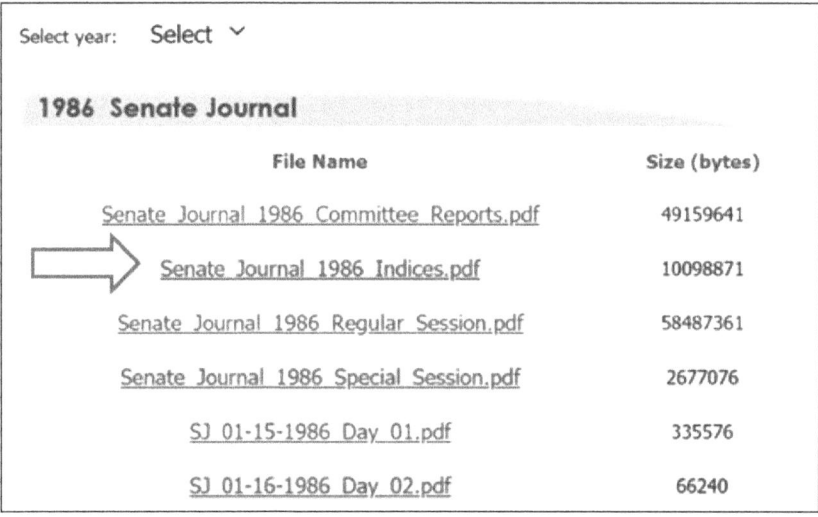

Source: State Legislature website, https://www.capitol.hawaii.gov.

Figure 9-11. 1986 Senate Journal, Page 377

```
              SENATE JOURNAL - 45th DAY                         377
```

Senate authorized the adoption of standing committee reports received by the Senate Clerk prior to midnight. In consequence thereof, and subsequent to its recessing at 11:36 o'clock p.m., the Senate took the following actions on the following bills and standing committee reports:

Stand. Com. Rep. No. 829-86 was adopted and House Bill No. 1940-86, H.D. 1, S.D. 1, entitled: "A BILL FOR AN ACT RELATING TO INTEREST AND USURY," passed Second Reading and was placed on the calendar for Third Reading on Monday, March 31, 1986.

Stand. Com. Rep. No. 830-86 was adopted and House Bill No. 2312-86, H.D. 1, S.D. 1, entitled: "A BILL FOR AN ACT RELATING TO ENVIRONMENTAL QUALITY IN HARBORS," passed Second Reading and was placed on the calendar for Third Reading on Monday, March 31, 1986.

Stand. Com. Rep. No. 831-86 was adopted and House Bill No. 2525-86, H.D. 1, S.D.

1, entitled: "A BILL FOR AN ACT RELATING TO THE HAWAII INSURANCE LAW," passed Second Reading and was placed on the calendar for Third Reading on Monday, March 31, 1986.

Stand. Com. Rep. No. 832-86 and House Bill No. 1692-86, H.D. 2, S.D. 2, entitled: "A BILL FOR AN ACT RELATING TO TORTS," were placed on the calendar for further consideration on Monday, March 31, 1986.

Stand. Com. Rep. No. 833-86 was adopted and House Bill No. 2569-86, S.D. 1, entitled: "A BILL FOR AN ACT RELATING TO 'ALOHA SPIRIT,'" passed Second Reading and was placed on the calendar for Third Reading on Monday, March 31, 1986.

ADJOURNMENT

At 12:00 o'clock midnight, on motion by Senator Cobb, seconded by Senator Soares and carried, the Senate adjourned until 11:00 o'clock a.m., Monday, March 31, 1986.

Source: State Legislature website, https://www.capitol.hawaii.gov.

Figure 9-12. History of HB 2569-86 Also Called the Index

Number and Title	Received Referred	First Reading	Second Reading	Third Reading	Action of House	Conference Committee	Final Action	Action of Governor	Further Action	Act No.	Vetoed
HB 2532-86. A BILL FOR AN ACT MAKING AN APPROPRIATION FOR PRESENTING THE PLAY "HEAR ME, O MY PEOPLE" IN WASHINGTON, D.C.	283 289	283	333								
HB 2536-86. A BILL FOR AN ACT RELATING TO THE ISSUANCE OF SPECIAL PURPOSE REVENUE BONDS TO ASSIST INDUSTRIAL ENTERPRISES.	283 289	283	315	565 571 604 648				680		227	
HB 2540-86. A BILL FOR AN ACT MAKING AN APPROPRIATION TO THE HAWAII CRIMINAL JUSTICE COMMISSION.	283 289	283	310								
HB 2549-86. A BILL FOR AN ACT RELATING TO WORKERS' COMPENSATION.	283 289	283	313	357 382 383	433 696	461 486 598 603	643 696	682		304	
HB 2561-86. A BILL FOR AN ACT RELATING TO ELECTIONS.	218 219	218	373	389 397	433	461 486 559 600	630 643	682		305	
HB 2569-86. A BILL FOR AN ACT RELATING TO "ALOHA SPIRIT".	218 222	218	377	392	433 520 545 582	461	582	679		202	

Source: State Legislature website, https://www.capitol.hawaii.gov.

Figure 9-13. 1986 Senate Journal, Page 392

392   SENATE JOURNAL - 46th DAY

Ayes, 25. Noes, none.

Stand. Com. Rep. No. 827-86 (H.B. No. 2468-86, H.D. 2, S.D. 2):

Senator Chang moved that Stand. Com. Rep. No. 827-86 be adopted and H.B. No. 2468-86, H.D. 2, S.D. 2, having been read throughout, pass Third Reading, seconded by Senator Cayetano.

At this time, Senator Cayetano asked for a ruling of the Chair as follows:

"Mr. President, may I have a conflict ruling? My law firm represents the organizations which want to sue the state."

The Chair ruled that Senator Cayetano was not in conflict.

The motion was put by the Chair and carried, Stand. Com. Rep. No. 827-86 was

1692-86, H.D. 2, S.D. 2):

By unanimous consent, action on Stand. Com. Rep. No. 832-86 and H.B. No. 1692-86, H.D. 2, S.D. 2, was deferred to the end of the calendar.

House Bill No. 2569-86, S.D. 1:

On motion by Senator Chang, seconded by Senator Cayetano and carried, H.B. No. 2569-86, S.D. 1, entitled: "A BILL FOR AN ACT RELATING TO 'ALOHA SPIRIT,'" having been read throughout, passed Third Reading on the following showing of Ayes and Noes:

Ayes, 22. Noes, 3 (Abercrombie, Henderson and McMurdo).

At 12:11 o'clock p.m., the Senate stood in recess subject to the call of the Chair.

Source: State Legislature website, https://www.capitol.hawaii.gov.

Figure 9-14. 1986 Senate Journal, Page 519

```
                SENATE JOURNAL - 57th DAY                         519

Senate Bill No. 1912-86 as Act 14,      House Bill No. 2113-86 as Act 26,
entitled:   "RELATING    TO    MOTOR    entitled: "RELATING TO DENTISTRY,"
VEHICLE ACCIDENT REPARATIONS,"
                                        House Bill No. 2115-86 as Act 27,
Senate Bill No. 2130-86 as Act 15,      entitled: "RELATING TO NURSING," and
entitled: "RELATING TO THE AGED,"
                                        House Bill No. 2516-86 as Act 28,
Senate Bill No. 2358-86 as Act 16,      entitled: "RELATING TO MORTGAGES,"
entitled: "RELATING TO HAWAIIAN
HOME LANDS,"                            was placed on file.

House Bill No. 1973-86 as Act 17,           HOUSE COMMUNICATIONS
entitled: "RELATING TO FORM OF
SUMMONS AND CITATION,"                  The following communications from the
                                        House (Hse. Com. Nos. 656 and 657) were
House Bill No. 1975-86 as Act 18,       read by the Clerk and were disposed of as
entitled:        "RELATING        TO    follows:
ADMINISTRATION OF OATH," and
                                        Hse. Com. No. 656, informing the Senate
House Bill No. 2028-86 as Act 19,       that the House on April 14, 1986
entitled: "RELATING TO BONDING OF       reconsidered its actions taken on April 3,
SOLAR ENERGY DEVICE DEALERS,"           1986 in disagreeing to the amendments
                                        made by the Senate to the following House
was placed on file.                     Bills:
```

Source: State Legislature website, https://www.capitol.hawaii.gov.

Figure 9-15. Senate Journal, Page 545

```
                SENATE JOURNAL - 58th DAY                         545

 Hse. Com. No. 675, informing the Senate    No. 2103-86, H.D. 1 (S.D. 1);
 that the House on April 15, 1986 agreed to No. 2105-86, H.D. 1 (S.D. 1);
 the amendments proposed by the Senate to   No. 2108-86, H.D. 1 (S.D. 1);
 the following House bills:                 No. 2109-86, H.D. 1 (S.D. 1);
                                            No. 2111-86 (S.D. 1);
No. 82, H.D. 1 (S.D. 2);                    No. 2112-86 (S.D. 1);
No. 526, H.D. 1 (S.D. 1);                   No. 2114-86 (S.D. 1);
No. 692, H.D. 1 (S.D. 1);                   No. 2116-86 (S.D. 1);
No. 1316, H.D. 1 (S.D. 1);                  No. 2119-86, H.D. 1 (S.D. 1);
No. 1322 (S.D. 1);                          No. 2123-86 (S.D. 1);
No. 1488 (S.D. 1);                          No. 2129-86, H.D. 1 (S.D. 1);
No. 1672-86, H.D. 1 (S.D. 1);               No. 2138-86, H.D. 1 (S.D. 1);
No. 1727-86, H.D. 1 (S.D. 1);               No. 2142-86, H.D. 1 (S.D. 1);
No. 1729-86 (S.D. 1);                       No. 2158-86 (S.D. 1);
No. 1815-86, H.D. 2 (S.D. 1);               No. 2168-86, H.D. 1 (S.D. 1);
No. 1826-86, H.D. 1 (S.D. 1);               No. 2173-86, H.D. 1 (S.D. 1);
No. 1829-86 (S.D. 1);                       No. 2189-86, H.D. 1 (S.D. 1);
No. 1855-86, H.D. 1 (S.D. 1);               No. 2191-86, H.D. 1 (S.D. 1);
No. 1869-86, H.D. 1 (S.D. 1);               No. 2192-86, H.D. 1 (S.D. 1);
No. 1870-86, H.D. 1 (S.D. 1);               No. 2193-86 (S.D. 1);
No. 1878-86, H.D. 1 (S.D. 2);               No. 2194-86 (S.D. 1);
No. 1898-86, H.D. 2 (S.D. 1);               No. 2201-86, H.D. 1 (S.D. 1);
No. 1905-86, H.D. 1 (S.D. 1);               No. 2216-86 (S.D. 1);
No. 1906-86, H.D. 1 (S.D. 1);               No. 2217-86 (S.D. 1);
No. 1907-86, H.D. 1 (S.D. 1);               No. 2238-86, H.D. 2 (S.D. 1);
No. 1908-86, H.D. 1 (S.D. 1);               No. 2273-86, H.D. 1 (S.D. 2);
No. 1913-86, H.D. 1;                        No. 2337-86, H.D. 2 (S.D. 1);
No. 1940-86, H.D. 1 (S.D. 1);               No. 2358-86 (S.D. 1);
No. 1945-86, H.D. 1 (S.D. 1);               No. 2362-86 (S.D. 1);
No. 1946-86, H.D. 1 (S.D. 1);               No. 2363-86 (S.D. 1);
No. 1951-86, H.D. 1 (S.D. 1);               No. 2374-86 (S.D. 1);
No. 1959-86, H.D. 1 (S.D. 1);               No. 2424-86 (S.D. 1);
No. 1967-86, H.D. 1 (S.D. 1);               No. 2425-86, H.D. 1 (S.D. 1);
No. 1969-86, H.D. 1 (S.D. 1);               No. 2427-86 (S.D. 1);
No. 1970-86, H.D. 2 (S.D. 1);               No. 2465-86 (S.D. 1);
No. 1971-86, H.D. 1 (S.D. 1);               No. 2479-86, H.D. 1 (S.D. 1);
No. 1974-86 (S.D. 1);                       No. 2483-86 (S.D. 1);
No. 1976-86 (S.D. 1);                       No. 2513-86, H.D. 2 (S.D. 1);
No. 1983-86 (S.D. 1);                       No. 2526-86, H.D. 1 (S.D. 1);
No. 1984-86 (S.D. 1);                       No. 2569-86 (S.D. 1);
No. 1993-86, H.D. 1 (S.D. 1);         ⇨     No. 2586-86 (S.D. 1);
No. 1995-86, H.D. 1 (S.D. 1);               No. 2599-86, H.D. 1 (S.D. 1);
No. 1999-86, H.D. 1 (S.D. 1);               No. 2605-86, H.D. 1 (S.D. 1);
```

Source: State Legislature website, https://www.capitol.hawaii.gov.

Figure 9-16. Link to House of Representatives Site

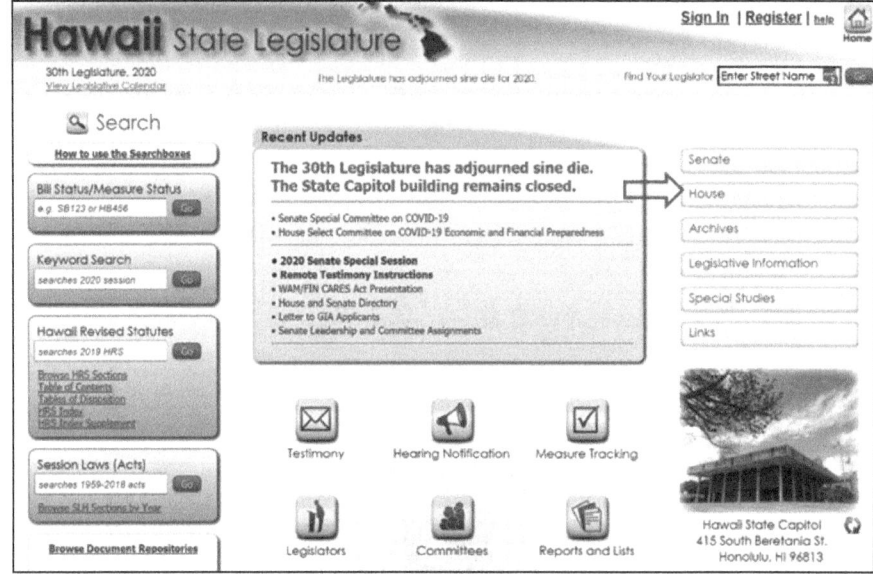

Source: State Legislature website, https://www.capitol.hawaii.gov.

Figure 9-17. Link to House Journals by Year

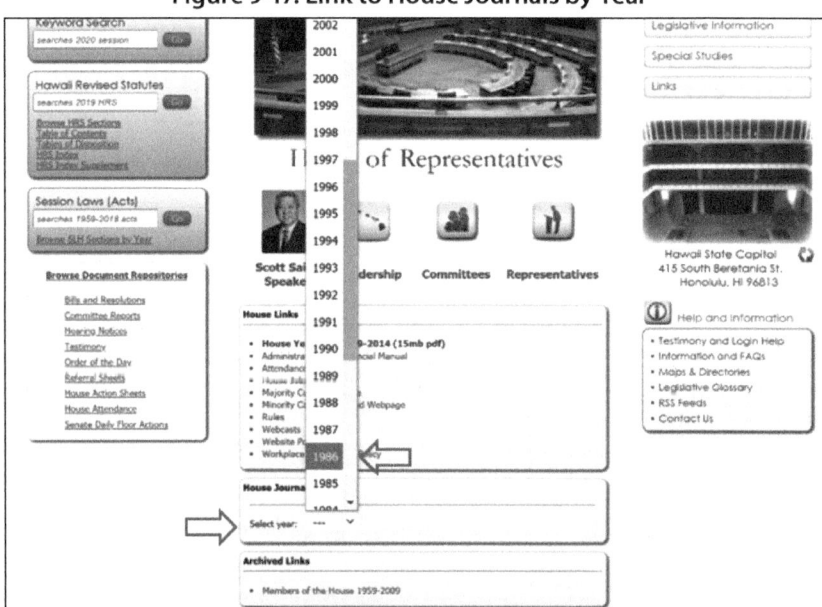

Source: State Legislature website, https://www.capitol.hawaii.gov.

Figure 9-18. Link to House Journal Committee Reports & Front Section

File Name	Size (bytes)
1986 HJournal 01 Front Section.pdf	4773424
1986 HJournal 02 Days 01-23 p001-232.pdf	24802401
1986 HJournal 03 Days 24-32 p234-433.pdf	24211768
1986 HJournal 04 Days 33-53 p434-652.pdf	25436222
1986 HJournal 05 Days 54-63 p653-873.pdf	25146942
1986 HJournal 06 Rules of the House.pdf	3033690
1986 HJournal 07 Conference and Special Committee Reports.pdf	6739540
1986 HJournal 08 Standing Committee Reports 1.pdf	20806173
1986 HJournal 09 Standing Committee Reports 2.pdf	20294595
1986 HJournal 10 Standing Committee Reports 3.pdf	19628897
1986 HJournal 11 Index.pdf	19512355
1986 HJournal 12 Special Session.pdf	6064509

Source: State Legislature website, https://www.capitol.hawaii.gov.

Figure 9-19. House Standing Committee Report 399-86

HOUSE JOURNAL - STANDING COMMITTEE REPORTS 1169

SCRep. 399-86 ⇒ Public Employment and Government Operations on H.B. No. 2569-86

The purpose of this bill is to provide that the legislative, executive and judicial branches of government may give consideration to the "Aloha Spirit" in exercising their respective powers.

Your Committee received testimony from the Judiciary, Alu Like, Incorporated and several individuals in support of this measure. The testimony indicated that the "Aloha Spirit" is the coordination of mind and heart within the individual and embodies kindness, unity, agreeableness, humility and patience. These character traits express the charm, warmth and sincerity of Hawaii's people and their working philosophy. Moreover, the "Aloha Spirit" is the essence of Hawaii and is what makes the "Aloha State" and its people so unique.

Although the Hawaiian Political Action Council of Hawaii testified in opposition to this bill claiming its enactment would constitute an infringement upon religious freedom, your Committee believes it is important that the "Aloha Spirit" be enacted as public policy. Its guiding principles are especially relevant to decision-making by all three branches of government. Hopefully, this legislation will help improve decisions made by government as well as perpetuate the "Aloha Spirit" so that future generations will not lose sight of the cultural bonds which hold the "Aloha State" together.

Your Committee on Public Employment and Government Operations is accord with the intent and purpose of H.B. No. 2569-86 and recommends that it pass Second Reading and be placed on the calendar for Third Reading.

Signed by all members of the Committee except Representative Nakasato.

Source: State Legislature website, https://www.capitol.hawaii.gov.

Repeat the process of examining the pages for mention of the bill in the House Journal. Refer to Figures 9-20 to 9-24 for guidance. From the House Journal history, pages 293 and 334 are likely places to find floor debate. An interesting chamber debate in the House Journal begins on page 334 with many of the members who introduced the bill indicating why they no longer back it.

Figure 9-20. Link to History of House Bills

File Name	Size (bytes)
1986 HJournal 01 Front Section.pdf	4773424
1986 HJournal 02 Days 01-23 p001-232.pdf	24802401
1986 HJournal 03 Days 24-32 p234-433.pdf	24211768
1986 HJournal 04 Days 33-53 p434-652.pdf	25436222
1986 HJournal 05 Days 54-63 p653-873.pdf	25146942
1986 HJournal 06 Rules of the House.pdf	3033690
1986 HJournal 07 Conference and Special Committee Reports.pdf	6739540
1986 HJournal 08 Standing Committee Reports 1.pdf	20806173
1986 HJournal 09 Standing Committee Reports 2.pdf	20294595
1986 HJournal 10 Standing Committee Reports 3.pdf	19628897
⇒ 1986 HJournal 11 Index.pdf	19512355
1986 HJournal 12 Special Session.pdf	6064509

Select year: Select ∨
1986 House Journal

Source: State Legislature website, https://www.capitol.hawaii.gov.

Figure 9-21. History of HB 2569-86 in House Journal — These Are Page Numbers in the Journal Section

NUMBER AND TITLE	Introduced Referred	First Reading	Second Reading	Third Reading	Action of Senate	Conference Committee	Final Action Governor	Further Action	Act No.	Vetoed
2569-86. "A Bill for an Act relating to 'Aloha Spirit'."	120 148	120	293	334	579	600 641	686 693 730	853	202	

Source: State Legislature website, https://www.capitol.hawaii.gov.

9 · HAWAI'I LEGISLATIVE HISTORY   177

Figure 9-22. House Journal, Page 293 with Report and Legislative Day

```
                    HOUSE JOURNAL - 2 7 t h DAY  ⇐                    293
```

to Representative Shon's announcement about the Ocean and Marine Resources hearing on Monday, we will be adding an item to the agenda, posting an addendum today; and also we'll be taking up the re-referred H.C.R. No. 52."

Representative Okamura made the following motion:

"I move that we keep the Journal open until midnight, and that all bills received by the Clerk up till midnight pass Second Reading and be placed on the calendar for Third Reading, and that all committee reports thereto be adopted, except those bills recommending passage on Third Reading shall be deferred until Monday, March 3, 1986."

The motion was seconded by Representative Ikeda and carried.

At 11:47 o'clock a.m. the Chair declared the House in recess for the purpose of receiving committee re-

calendar for Third Reading.

Representatives Bunda and Tom, for the Committees on Health and Judiciary, presented a joint report (Stand. Com. Rep. No. 398-86) recommending that H.B. No. 1999-86, as amended in HD1, pass Second Reading and be placed on the calendar for Third Reading.

Representative Tungpalan, for the Committee on Public Employment and Government Operations, presented a report (Stand. Com. Rep. No. 399-86) recommending that H.B. No. 2569-86 pass Second Reading and be placed on the calendar for Third Reading.

Representative Taniguchi, for the Committee on Transportation, presented a report (Stand. Com. Rep. No. 400-86) recommending that H.B. No. 2374-86 pass Second Reading and be placed on the calendar for Third Reading.

Source: State Legislature website, https://www.capitol.hawaii.gov.

Figure 9-23. Finding the Date for the Legislative Day

TABLE OF CONTENTS	Page
First Day, Wednesday, January 15, 1986	1
Second Day, Thursday, January 16, 1986	8
Third Day, Friday, January 17, 1986	22
Fourth Day, Monday, January 20, 1986	27
Fifth Day, Tuesday, January 21, 1986	33
Sixth Day, Wednesday, January 22, 1986	45
Seventh Day, Thursday, January 23, 1986	52
Eighth Day, Friday, January 24 1986	61
Ninth Day, Monday, January 27, 1986	70
Tenth Day, Tuesday, January 28, 1986	80
Eleventh Day, Wednesday, January 29, 1986	91
Twelfth Day, Thursday, January 30, 1986	98
Thirteenth Day, Friday, January 31, 1986	108
Fourteenth Day, Monday, February 3, 1986	137
Fifteenth Day, Tuesday, February 4, 1986	141
Sixteenth Day, Wednesday, February 5, 1986	155
Seventeenth Day, Thursday, February 6, 1986	159
Eighteenth Day, Friday, February 7, 1986	164
Nineteenth Day, Monday, February 10, 1986	174
Twentieth Day, Tuesday, February 11, 1986	179
Twenty-First Day, Thursday, February 20, 1986	188
Twenty-Second Day, Friday, February 21, 1986	202
Twenty-Third Day, Monday, February 24, 1986	225
Twenty-Fourth Day, Tuesday, February 25, 1986	233
Twenty-Fifth Day, Wednesday, February 26, 1986	249
Twenty-Sixth Day, Thursday, February 27, 1986	265
Twenty-Seventh Day, Friday, February 28, 1986	289
Twenty-Eighth Day, Monday, March 3, 1986	301
Twenty-Ninth Day, Tuesday, March 4, 1986	350

Source: State Legislature website, https://www.capitol.hawaii.gov.

Figure 9-24. House Journal, Page 334 — Beginning of Discussion and Debate

334   HOUSE JOURNAL - 2 8 t h DAY

seconded by Representative Metcalf and carried, H.B. No. 2373-86, HD 1, entitled: "A BILL FOR AN ACT RELATING TO THE DEFENSE OF INTOXICATION", passed Third Reading by a vote of 50 ayes, with Representative Leong being excused.

H.B. No. 1728-86, HD 1:

On motion by Representative Tom, seconded by Representative Metcalf and carried, H.B. No. 1728-86, HD 1, entitled: "A BILL FOR AN ACT RELATING TO CREDIT CARD OFFENSES", passed Third Reading by a vote of 50 ayes, with Representative Leong being excused.

The Chair directed the Clerk to note that H.B. Nos. 2375-86 and 1728-86 had passed Third Reading at 3:21 o'clock p.m.

MATTERS DEFERRED FROM EARLIER ON THE CALENDAR

H.B. No. 2569-86: ⬅

Representative Yoshimura moved that H.B. No. 2569-86, having been read throughout, pass Third Reading, seconded by Representative Manegdeg.

Representative Kamali'i rose and stated:

"Mr. Speaker, I rise to speak against this bill. I am sure my colleagues are surprised that I am doing this.

"Mr. Speaker, I was among those who signed this bill at introduction. Virtually every member of the House added their signature to this measure which would include Aunty Pilahi Paki's now well-known expression of what she felt the 'Aloha Spirit' meant to her. A coordination of mind and heart where a person must think and emote good feelings to others.

"However, Mr. Speaker, I have now had some time to reflect on this proposal, and feel compelled to vote 'no'.

"My hesitation, Mr. Speaker, is, first, in codifying such sentiments in law and further asserting them as legislative, executive, and judicial guides in decision-making. The Legislature has already adopted 'The Aloha State' as our popular name -- do we really need to go beyond that?

"It seems to me that if we have to statutory 'define' and remind ourselves and others to act with aloha -- then, we are implicitly acknowledging that we are losing that spirit.

"Mr. Speaker, I won't make that admission.

"Further, I am made uneasy by the potential commercialization of the sentiment. What have we come to when the 'Aloha Spirit' -- whether as a poster or a beach towel -- may literally be bought and sold?

"This possible denigration of so central a thought and feeling of Hawai'i deeply disturbs me.

"Further, if we are to decide that, legally, there is but one interpretation to 'Aloha' -- then I believe that we are also doing damage to the native Hawaiian culture.

"I wonder if the strength and variety of meanings to the 'Aloha Spirit' isn't derived from its elusiveness, its inability to be captured in words.

"Isn't the Aloha Spirit better held in the heart in wordless personal expressions of kindness, caring, and mutual respect?

"It is from a profound sense of Aloha, that I must vote 'no' on this bill.

"Thank you."

Representative Onouye rose and requested that his remarks, in favor of the bill with reservations, be inserted into the Journal and the Chair, noting that there were no objections, "so ordered."

Representative Onouye's remarks are as follows:

"Mr. Speaker, I rise this morning to speak in favor of this bill with certain reservations.

"Mr. Speaker, the Aloha Spirit is one of the beautiful and unique things about our island state. All residents of Hawaii, regardless of ethnic origin, feel the spirit and joy of Aloha. In our everyday actions we conduct ourselves here with both a conscious and unconscious application of the Aloha Spirit. Mr. Speaker, my reservations stem from my belief that the feeling of Aloha is a personal internalized feeling unique to each person. The manifestation of the spirit of Aloha is not contingent upon a legal mandate. It is not something

Source: State Legislature website, https://www.capitol.hawaii.gov.

III. Keeping Track of Your Research

It is important to keep track of each step when researching legislative history. Table 9-3 shows the brief legislative history research notes of the Aloha Spirit Law with pertinent information for making citations or being able to quickly return to the original source.

Table 9-3. 1986 Hawai'i Legislative History *Aloha Spirit Law* HRS 5-7.5

Step	Document	Resource	Page	Date
1	L. 1986, c. 202, §1	HRS 5-7.5	n/a	2020
2	Act 202 (HB 2569-86) (Fig.9-2)	1986 SLH	n/a	May 19, 1986 approved
				Effective: July 1, 1986
3S	SSCR 833-86 (Jud); SD 1 (Fig. 9-9)	Senate/1986 Senate Journal	1183	n/a
3S	JUD Com. Rpt. (Fig. 9-11)	1986 Senate Journal	377	45th day — Mar. 27, 1986
4S	Conf. Com.? No. (Fig. 9-15)	1986 Senate Journal	545	58th day — Apr. 16, 1986
3H	HSCR 399-86 (Fig. 9-19)	House/1986 House Journal	1169	n/a
3H	PE/GO Com. Rpt. (Fig. 9-22)	1986 House Journal	293	27th day — Feb. 28, 1986 (Fig. 23)
4H	Chamber Debate (Fig. 9-24)	1986 House Journal	334–36	28th day — Mar. 3, 1986

Table: Roberta F. Woods.

IV. Conducting Earlier Legislative History Research (Pre-1984)

Prior to 1984, the bill number will be shown on the Act either at the top or at the end of the text.[7] From 1959 to 1983 go directly to the Act in the Session Laws to get the bill number because the link to Index and Effect of Acts takes you to a table that indicates the impact of the legislative session on existing laws. Following this table is a general index. Only the act will reveal the bill number when researching in this time period.

Once you have the bill number go to the House and Senate Journals and find the History of Bills Index. Then, go to the page for the Second Reading and repeat the process of getting the committee reports.

V. Directory of Images for Hawai'i Legislative History

Table 9-4. Directory of Figures 9-1 to 9-24 with Steps and Resource

Figure Number	Step	Resource	Caption
9-1	2	Session Laws	Locate Session Laws. Hawai'i State Legislature Website (capitol.hawaii.gov)
9-2	2	Session Laws	Link for Committee Reports Table
9-3	2	Session Laws	Committee Reports Table Headers
9-4	2	Session Laws	Act 202 Committee Reports
9-5	2	Session Laws	Showing Bill # and Act 202 of the 1986 Session Laws of Hawai'i
9-6	3S	Senate Journal	Link to Senate Pages to Find Senate Journals

---

7. Between 1969 and 1984, a separate publication, *Digest and Index of Laws Enacted*, contained a similar table showing the committee report numbers; however, this publication may only be available in print or on LLMC Digital, a proprietary resource. It is not necessary to use this publication since you can discover the report numbers in the House and Senate Journals. However, if the publication is conveniently available referring to it will save some research time.

9-7	3S	Senate Journal	Link to Senate Journals by Year
9-8	3S	Senate Journal	Link to Committee Reports (Senate Journal) & showing legislative day and date.
9-9	3S	Senate Journal	Senate Standing Committee Report 833–86
9-10	4S	Senate Journal	Link to History of Bills (Senate Journal)
9-11	4S	Senate Journal	History of HB 2569-86 Also Called the Index.
9-12	4S	Senate Journal	1986 Senate Journal page 377
9-13	4S	Senate Journal	1986 Senate Journal page 392
9-14	4S	Senate Journal	1986 Senate Journal page 519
9-15	4S	Senate Journal	1986 Senate Journal page 545
9-16	3H	House Journal	Link to House of Representatives Site
9-17	3H	House Journal	Link to House Journals by Year
9-18	3H	House Journal	Link to House Journal Committee Reports & Front Section
9-19	3H	House Journal	House Standing Committee Report 399-86
9-20	4H	House Journal	Link to History of House Bills
9-21	4H	House Journal	History of HB 2569-86 in House Journal — these are page numbers in the Journal section
9-22	4H	House Journal	House Journal page 293 with report and legislative day
9-23	4H	House Journal	Finding the Date for the Legislative Day
9-24	4H	House Journal	House Journal page 334 — beginning of discussion and debate

Table: Roberta F. Woods.

Chapter 10

Administrative Law

I. Introduction

Administrative agencies reside within the executive branch of the federal and state governments. Each agency promulgates and enforces those rules that satisfy the broader mandates of the relevant legislation authorizing each specific regulation. To satisfy the intentions of the legislation, the agency often crafts rules and regulations that provide more details than the authorizing legislation, specifically as to its day-to-day, real-world application and enforcement. For this reason, regulations are the laws that most affect a person's life and an organization's operations.

Statutes and regulations are primary authorities often used in tandem to support an attorney's argument or a judge's opinion. Statutes, however, are still the higher authority because only an enabling statute of the federal or state congress or a constitutional provision may grant federal and state agencies quasi-legislative, -judicial, and -executive powers. Through its quasi-legislative power, the agency adopts final rules and regulations to extrapolate upon the broader language of the relevant legislation (e.g., public utility rates, licensing fees). The internal policies, guidelines, and procedures that help each agency enforce its regulations fulfill its quasi-executive power. Finally, the quasi-judicial power allows the agency, through hearing officers or administrative law judges (A.L.J.'s), to adjudicate rule violations and issue written opinions resolving those disputes. Some agency decisions are appealable to a higher authority within the agency. Any final agency decision can then be appealed to the appropriate court as determined by the relevant federal or state statute or constitutional provision.

II. Hawai'i Administrative Law Research

Researching administrative law in Hawai'i, from enabling act to applicable administrative decisions, requires the following steps: 1) identify the Hawai'i statute or the article within the Hawai'i Constitution enabling the agency's powers or the specific regulation at-issue; 2) locate the final published administrative rules for each agency at the Lt. Governor for the State of Hawai'i's website;[1] 3) from the Lt. Governor's site, link to each agency's webpage to locate any proposed rules that could impact the issue; and 4) locate administrative decisions and guidance to see how hearing officers and state judges have interpreted and applied the specific regulation.

A. Identify the Enabling Act and Implicating Acts

The enabling act determines the scope of an agency's powers and the implicating acts are those whose requirements the regulations seek to implement. Using the best practices discussed in the earlier chapters about searching topically within Hawai'i's constitutions and statutes on Westlaw and Lexis will lead a researcher to the enabling act and implicating acts. For instance, suppose your client was fired from her employment at a restaurant in Waikiki because, while at work, she called the police feeling unsafe after a co-worker allegedly threatened her life. Your client now wants to know what complaint might be filed against the employer. In Westlaw and Lexis, a simple search string, such as *employ! /p (discharg! OR fir!) & unsafe*, yields several statutory results but within the first few, only two would lead to relevant regulations applicable to an employer. One of the two is Hawai'i's Whistleblowers' Protection Act, which would not be relevant here since the conduct is attributable to a co-worker and not the employer, leaving only Hawai'i Revised Statute section 396-8, Employee Responsibility and Rights. On Westlaw, though not on Lexis or in any print annotated code, the relevant regulations citing the statute are located under the *Citing References* tab (see Figure 10-1). You would note the enabling and implicating statutes and relevant regulations in your research plan.

---

1. https://ltgov.hawaii.gov.

Figure 10-1. Regulations Citing the Relevant Enabling and Implicating Statutes

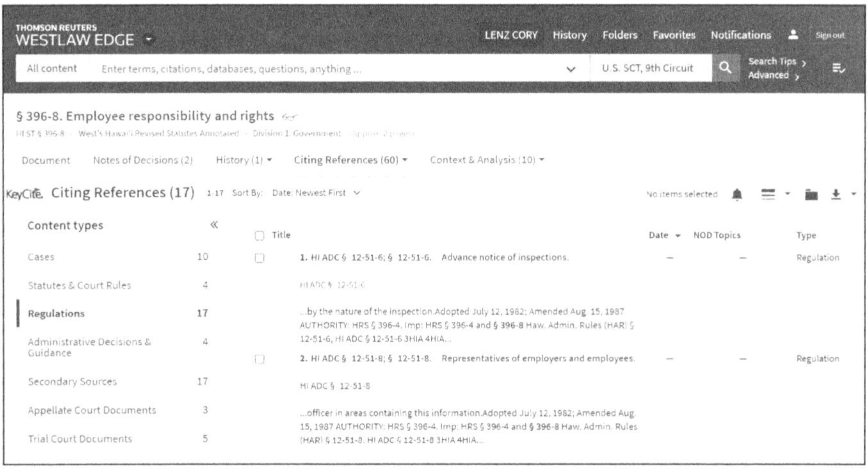

Source: Westlaw, reprinted with permission from Thomson Reuters.

Locating the relevant administrative regulation by way of the Lt. Governor's website also leads to the enabling act and implicating statutes.[2] Regulations and the statutory laws they implement can also be found in the annual publication *Hawaiʻi Administrative Rules [Year] Table of Statutory Sections Implemented and Directory* on the *publications* webpage of the Legislative Reference Bureau, a legislative services agency.[3]

B. Finding Hawaiʻi Agency Rules

The Constitution of the State of Hawaiʻi establishes the offices and qualifications of the executive branch's principal department heads.[4] The powers of the Hawaiʻi administrative agencies are described in the Administrative Procedure Act (HAPA). HAPA requires each agency to publish the following on the Lt. Governor's website and ensure it contains current and accurate: 1) descriptions as to how the public may obtain information, make submittals or requests, or attend public hearings about the proposed rules; 2) explanations

---

2. *Administrative Rules*, Lt. Governor of the State of Hawaiʻi, https://ltgov.Hawaii.gov/the-office/administrative-rules/ (last visited Oct. 29, 2020).

3. *Publications*, Legislative Reference Bureau, https://lrb.Hawaii.gov/publications (last visited Oct. 29, 2020).

4. Haw. Const. art. V, § 6.

of formal and informal procedures, including all forms and instructions used by the agency; and 3) rules and written statements of policy or interpretation formulated, adopted, or used by the agency in the discharge of its functions, and all final opinions and orders.[5] Each adopted, amended, or repealed rule becomes effective ten days after the agency files a permanent register of the rule for the public's inspection with the Lt. Governor's Office (or with the respective county clerks in the case of the administrative rules of the various city and county departments).[6] In addition to adopted rules, proposed rules, and notice of the public's opportunity to participate in and comment on those rules, the Lt. Governor's website gives the public access to emergency rules, proclamations, appointments, executive orders by the governor, and summaries of attorney general opinions.

Because Hawai'i does not have an official state administrative register, the same information provided by the Lt. Governor's website is available commercially on Lexis via the Hawai'i Government Register. Final rules of Hawai'i's administrative code are codified and updated on the Lt. Governor's website. Unofficial compilations are available electronically on Lexis as the Hawai'i Administrative Rules and on Westlaw, as the Hawai'i Administrative Code.[7]

1. Access the Lt. Governor's Website and Review the Agency Website

The Lt. Governor's website, under the banner *Office Services > Administrative Rules*, hyperlinks each state department and agency across the rules' 23 titles. At the end of this list of titles, a convenient hyperlink easily navigates the researcher to the proposed changes to each agency's rules. Linking within each title leads to an agency's website and a hyperlinked list of its relevant

---

5. Administrative Procedure Act, Haw. Rev. Stat. §§ 91-1 to -18 (2012), https://www.capitol.Hawaii.gov/hrscurrent/Vol02_Ch0046-0115/HRS0091/. Each government agency is also required to publish notice of the public hearings about the proposed rules in a daily or weekly publication with state-wide circulation. Haw. Rev. Stat. § 1-28.5 (2009), https://www.capitol.hawaii.gov/hrscurrent/Vol01_Ch0001-0042F/HRS0001/HRS_0001-0028_0005.htm.

6. § 91-4, https://www.capitol.hawaii.gov/hrscurrent/Vol02_Ch0046-0115/HRS0091/HRS_0091-0004.htm. The Lt. Governor's Office posts these filings of the permanent register of each adopted, amended, or repealed rule under the title *Hawai'i Administrative Rules Listing of Filings*.

7. Lexis through its subsidiary Matthew Bender & Co. acquired and rebranded the unofficial print publication *Weil's Code of Hawai'i Rules*, and since 2017 has fallen back on an irregular print schedule.

chapters and codified rules. Selecting a specific chapter opens a PDF with the exact language of the relevant sections. The parentheticals at the end of each section provide the following information about that specific rule: 1) its effective date and, as denoted by a semi-colon, any subsequent amendments and other treatments;[8] 2) the authorizing or enabling statute or statutes; and 3) other statutes whose conditions and requirements the rule implements.

For instance, browsing the relevant administrative agency's website would help locate the governing administrative law for your client who was fired from her restaurant job for calling the police on a co-worker who made her feel unsafe. The search capability of the Lt. Governor's and each agency's website is archaic and unhelpful; however, in some instances relevancy can sometimes be determined by the titles of the departments, rule chapters, and rule sections. Since your client's issue is an occupational one related to safety, you might navigate accordingly were you to consider and select the most relevant titles:

> Lt. Governor of the State of Hawai'i > Administrative Rules > Department of Labor and Industrial Relations > Hawai'i Occupational Safety & Health (HIOSH) > General, Legal and Administrative Provisions for Occupational Safety & Health > 12-57 Discrimination Against Employees Exercising Rights under Chapter 396, Hawai'i Revised Statutes.

Upon opening the relevant title and chapter, you can then consider the relevant sections for your client's issue and identify the relevant authorizing and implicating statutes and any amendments to the rule (see Figure 10-2). The relevant rule from Figure 10-2 perfectly illustrates how regulations fill-in the necessary details to implement the conditions and requirements of the authorizing and implicating statutes. The implicating statute, Hawai'i Revised Statute section 396-8, prohibits employers from discharging an employee for exercising her protected rights, but it does not provide the parameters or test to be used. The relevant rule, however, Hawai'i Administrative Rule section 12-57-3, fills in these important details, requiring that discharges after protected activity be evaluated under a substantial reason

---

8. Key for the credit history of the Hawai'i Administrative Rules: A = Rule has been amended in month of issue; A/C = Rule has been amended and compiled in month of issue; E = Rule subject to an emergency rule; N = New final rule has been added in month of issue; P = Proposal pending; R = Rule has been repealed in month of issue; Rn = Rule has been renumbered in month of issue; Comp = Compiled; and Am and Ren = Amended and Renumbered.

Figure 10-2. Locating the Enabling and Implicating Statutes via the Relevant Rule

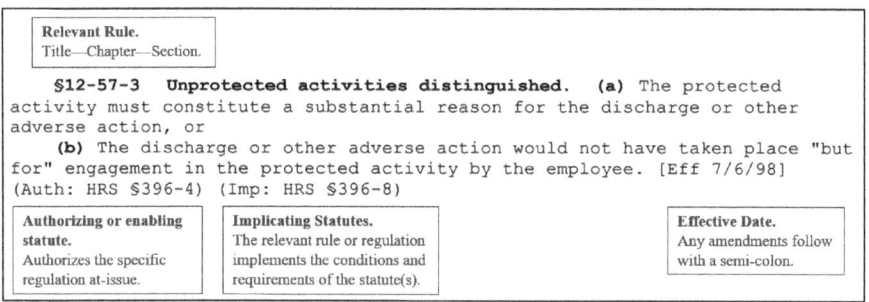

Source: Cory Lenz, reprinted with permission from author.

standard or but-for test. It is important that you note the relevant regulation in your research plan.

Since 2000, state law requires executive agencies to post the full text of proposed rule changes and new rules on the Lt. Governor's website.[9] Proposed rule changes are collected and explained in a PDF with some variance of the name *Proposed Rulemaking*, located as a hyperlink on each agency's *Administrative Rules* page, *Meeting & Reports* page, or under the *Statutes & Rules* dropdown. Proposed additions to the rules are underlined, while proposed deletions are crossed out. The *Statutes & Rules* dropdown also includes links to only those statutes that authorize and implicate that agency's rules.

Each agency's homepage offers links to relevant, but different, resources within the website. Most prominently featured are a director's message explaining the agency's mission and functions; links to the webpage of each division within the agency and its specific resources; agency minutes, public notices, instructions and forms for an open records request or complaint; annual, legislative, and special reports; and links to helpful non-profit or federal resources. The agency website often includes links to news releases about the agency's functions, frequently-asked-questions, a job board, and quick links to additional educational resources. For instance, the Department of Labor and Industrial Relations homepage provides additional videos, graphics, publications, and other resources to educate employees and employers about unemployment insurance, disability compensation, workplace safety,

---

9. § 91-2.6, https://www.capitol.hawaii.gov/hrscurrent/Vol02_Ch0046-0115/HRS0091/HRS_0091-0002_0006.htm.

workers' rights, and workplace readiness at popular businesses on the islands. The department's many divisions provide additional resources, such as HIOSH's directives and the *Discrimination (Whistleblower) Investigation Manual*. Reflecting Hawai'i's multiculturalism, each agency's services are offered in several languages.

2. Search in the Hawai'i Administrative Code with Lexis and Westlaw

Hawai'i, as the youngest state, has far fewer state-specific secondary sources than other states, so it is less likely a researcher would locate an annotation to a regulation in a secondary source. The state, however, does have its own bar and scholarly journals, probate and estate planning form books, and treatises relevant to divorce, evidence, business associations, and Native Hawaiian law, for instance, so annotations to a relevant regulation may be found there.

Browsing the rules' 23 titles functions close to the same on Lexis and Westlaw as it does on the Lt. Governor's website. Clicking the (+) icon next to the relevant title, drops the chapters down. On Lexis, selecting a specific chapter opens a list of all subchapters and sections within the chapter. Each section includes the parenthetical information as to credit history and the enabling and implicating statutes. Conversely, on Westlaw, the chapters further divide into subchapters and then each relevant section can be selected individually. Neither Lexis nor Westlaw hyperlink the rule's older versions in its credit history; however, both hyperlink the statutory references. The table of contents tab and the navigation string at the top of each chapter allow the researcher to quickly move among the rules. Each chapter also provides a link to the archived code versions: on Lexis, these go back to 2004, and on Westlaw, to 2009.

When searching the rules on Lexis, a researcher can search topically with key terms in the universal search box either within all Hawai'i resources, which would then require filtering the rules from the results, or specifically within the Hawai'i Administrative Rules (HAR). Using the latter approach, a sample search to locate the relevant regulations for your client's issue, for example, might use the following search string: *employee /p discharg! & unsafe*. The results include rules from several different agencies, but the Lexis algorithm based on the recurrence of the search terms lists, as the top three results, sections from the Department of Health and the Department of Labor and Industrial Relations. Selecting the *graphical view* and using the search term location bar within each result to navigate through the most relevant sections, where the color-coded key terms appear in context, reveals that title 12 (Department of Labor and Industrial Relations), chapter 57 (Discrimination Against Employees Exercising Rights Under Chapter 396, Hawaiʻi Revised Statutes) is the most relevant. After selecting this result, the search term location bar appears again at the top of the chapter page. Sliding the bar to the most relevant location of the key terms, which Lexis denotes with a blue star, or clicking on a color-coded term simultaneously scrolls the page down to that specific section. Here, the Lexis algorithm correctly identi-

Figure 10-3. Searching the Hawaiʻi Administrative Rules on Lexis

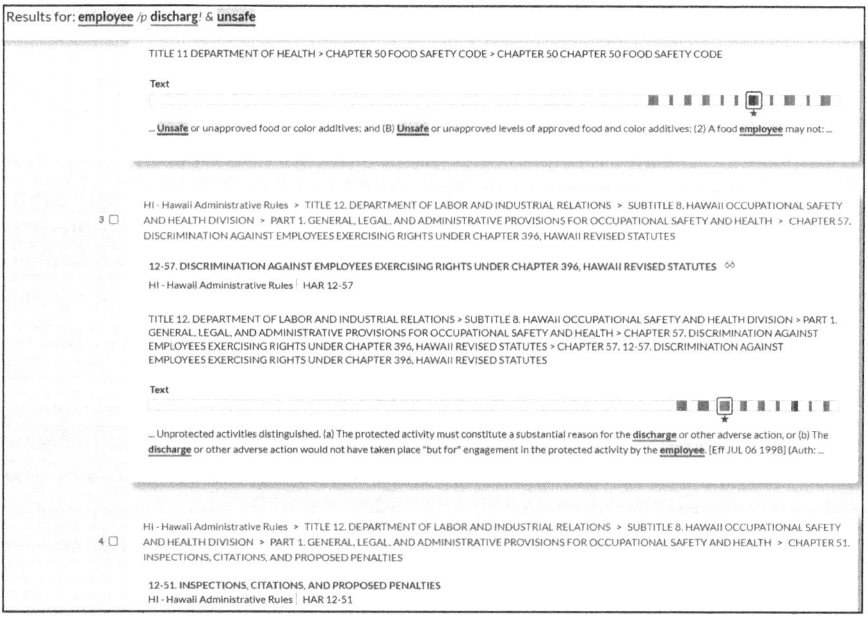

Source: Lexis, reprinted with permission from LexisNexis.

fies the blue-starred section (§ 12-57-3. Unprotected activities distinguished) as the most relevant (Figure 10-3).

Searching the rules on Lexis closely follows that on Westlaw. The biggest difference is keyword searches on Lexis cannot be conducted in the universal search box within each individual chapter or subchapter since the individual rule sections are grouped together. To gather background information about a relevant rule or find cases applying or interpreting the rule, citing references for all sections within the chapter on Lexis are accessed via the *find references to this administrative code* hyperlink. Proposed rules and recently adopted regulations are also available there. Conversely, in Westlaw, citing references to secondary sources and cases are available in a separate *Citing References* tab, and Westlaw makes the proposed rules and recently adopted regulations available on the chapter page via the *Hawaiʻi Proposed & Adopted Regulations — Current* hyperlink. Searching within on behalf of your client, for instance, with the search string *employee & discharg! & unsafe* shows a couple of proposed and final rules within the last two years related to the workplace safety of boiler inspectors, but nothing relevant to your client. Additionally, you would note in your research plan that there were no citing references giving treatment to or discussing the relevant rule sections within title 12, chapter 57 of HAR that might have helped you expand your research.

Another significant difference involves the relevant chapter's currency: even though both Lexis and Westlaw receive updates to the rules irregularly from the state of Hawaiʻi, at the time of the above search, the relevant chapter was more current on Lexis by several months (October 2020, compared to May 2020 on Westlaw). Finally, an additional access point to the Hawaiʻi Administrative Rules exists only on Westlaw and not Lexis or the State's resources. The citing references to the Hawaiʻi statutory code on Westlaw include the relevant administrative rules that the specific statute authorizes, implicates, and references (Figure 10-1). Placing the statute in close research proximity to the relevant regulations makes sense since the research process sometimes starts with an annotated statutory code and statutes and regulations often appear together in support of a legal argument.

3. Use the Hawaiʻi Government Register

Hawaiʻi does not have an official state administrative register. In 2017, Lexis stopped updating the unofficial print version of the *Hawaiʻi Government Register*. Up until then, a researcher could search in the *Hawaiʻi Government Register* to update results from searches in the Hawaiʻi Administrative Code for rules promulgated after the most recent publication of the code. Now the most recent publication of the code online can be updated by tracking the rulemaking process (e.g., emergency rules, proposed rules, public notice and comments, withdrawn rules) on the relevant agency's website or commercially via searches only in Lexis (Westlaw does not provide access to the Hawaiʻi Government Register). For instance, on behalf of your client who was discharged for engaging in a protected activity as per title 12, chapter 57,

Figure 10-4. Searching Proposed and Final Rules

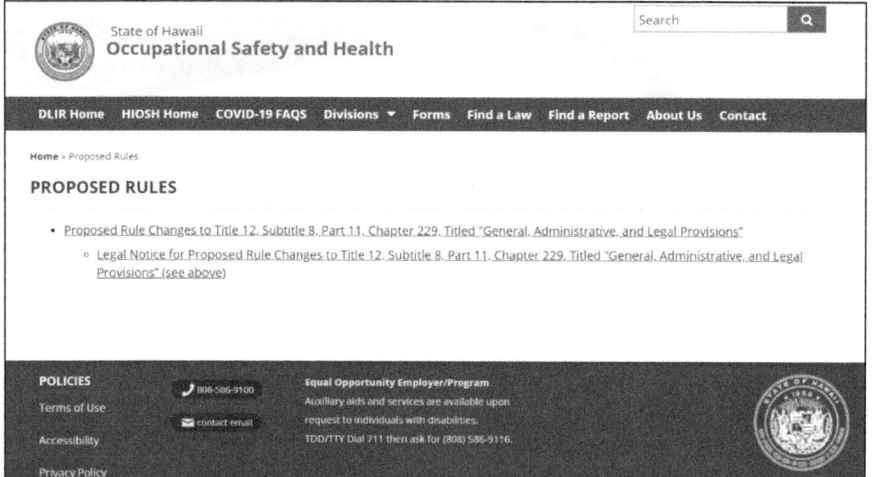

Source: HIOSH, a division of the Department of Labor and Industrial Relations, https://labor.hawaii.gov/hiosh.

you find no new proposed or final rules relevant to her issue (Figure 10-4). Closely tracking a new proposed rule on behalf of a client is an important best practice since clients' interests are very often impacted by administrative rules, and doing so helps you advise a client about an agency's policies and initiatives since they are often reflected in its proposed rules.

Electronic coverage to the Hawai'i Government Register on Lexis begins in 1998. The register chronicles developments in Hawai'i administrative law, including appointments and media releases from the Governor's Office; attorney general opinions and Ethics Commission advisory opinions; proposed, adopted, withdrawn, and emergency regulations; list of legislative bills enacted and proposed; administrative hearings, decisions and orders; as well as agency minutes, announcements, media releases, and notices. A specific document can be located by browsing and drilling down within the relevant year > month > and finally resource type. The cumulative index is also available within each month's dropdown. Finally, the universal search box can be used to search within all years of the register or selected years or months. Unfortunately, Lexis does not hyperlink cited authorities within the register's documents, so upon finding a new or amended rule in the register, there will be no links to the codified rules or authorizing statutes.

C. Finding Hawai'i Agency Decisions and Attorney General Opinions

Though Hawai'i has studied adopting a central panel system for administrative hearings, it currently has a decentralized administrative hearing system.[10] Thus, each agency can conduct its own hearings (often called contested case hearings) to adjudicate disputes related to its rules.[11] A unique challenge to conducting case hearings in Hawai'i is its geography: hearing officers (also known as Administrative Law Judges or A.L.J.s in other jurisdictions) whose agencies do not have offices on the other islands outside O'ahu travel at least once every other year, if not more often, to the other islands to conduct contested case hearings.

As with other powers, an agency's quasi-judicial power to adjudicate disputes must stem from a specific enabling statute.[12] The subject matter of contested case hearings varies considerably among, and even within, the agencies. For instance, the Department of Commerce and Consumer Affairs presides over hearings related to public utilities, retirement, professional licenses, insurance, education, and business mark infringement.[13] Depending on the agency, a hearing officer, chairperson or member of a board or commission, or an adjudicator contracted by the agency presides over the hearings.[14] Also depending on the agency, a hearing officer can issue final agency decisions or

---

10. Christina Zahara Noh, et al., *Legis. Reference Bur., Rep. No. 1, Hear Here or Hear There? A Review of Centralizing Administrative Hearing Functions* 86–89 tbls. 3.16–.17 (2020), https://lrb.hawaii.gov/wp-content/uploads/2020_HearHereOrHearThere.pdf (listing the following 27 states and the District of Columbia as having established a centralized administrative hearings agency: Alaska, Arizona, California, Colorado, Florida, Georgia, Illinois, Indiana, Iowa, Kansas, Louisiana, Maryland, Massachusetts, Michigan, Minnesota, Missouri, New Jersey, North Carolina, North Dakota, Oregon, South Carolina, South Dakota, Tennessee, Texas, Washington, Wisconsin, Wyoming, and the District of Columbia).

11. An agency hearing is a contested case, subject to judicial review under chapter 91, when the hearing is an agency hearing required by law (e.g., rule, statute, or due process) and the hearing determines the rights, duties, or privileges of specific parties. *E & J Lounge Operating Co. v. Liquor Comm'n of Honolulu*, 118 Hawai'i 320, 330–31, 189 P.3d 432, 442–43 (2008).

12. *Noh*, *supra* note 10, at 8–12 tbl. 2.1 (containing enabling statutes and other statutes and administrative rules relevant to the agencies' handling of contested cases).

13. *Id.* at 14–16 tbl. 2.2.

14. *Id.* at 21–26 tbl. 2.4.

only recommend decisions that another decision maker accepts or denies.[15] A party may appeal directly to a court after an agency's decision, whether it is a preliminary ruling or final decision.[16] These appeals occur infrequently, less than 100 total appeals a year.[17]

The total number of contested cases filed with an agency varies considerably, from a few dozen contested cases (e.g., Department of Education) to a few thousand (e.g., Department of the Attorney General).[18] However, a significant portion of an agency's contested cases never reach final decisions and are closed for reasons unrelated to the merits of the cases (e.g., parties withdraw their complaints or do not show at a hearing).[19] The contested case hearings can be either trial-type or non-trial-type; a majority in Hawai'i are trial-type.[20] Trial-type hearings function similarly to trials in state court: the adjudication operates under the same procedural and evidentiary rules; parties have a right to counsel and to present relevant facts, evidence, and arguments; and the agency issues a final, though appealable, decision on the merits. An agency, however, may issue a final decision without a trial-type hearing if the parties agree the agency can proceed without one. In non-trial-type hearings, the agency does not issue a final decision, considering only tangential matters like motion hearings or pre-trial conferences.

Select agencies post their decisions on their website or each division's website in PDF format. The depth of an agency's archive varies. For instance, the final decisions of the Department of Commerce and Consumer Affairs go back to 2000, the Office of the Attorney General opinions go back to 1993, while the final decisions of the Hawai'i Labor Relations Board, a division of the Labor and Industrial Relations department, go back to 1971. A researcher

---

15. *Id.*

16. Haw. Rev. Stat. § 91-14 (2012), https://www.capitol.hawaii.gov/hrscurrent/Vol02_Ch0046-0115/HRS0091/HRS_0091-0014.htm (providing that proceedings for review shall be instituted in circuit court or, if applicable, the environmental court "except where a statute provides for a direct appeal to the supreme court or the intermediate appellate court, subject to chapter 602."); *see also Kilakila 'O Haleakala v. Bd. of Land & Nat. Res.*, 131 Hawai'i 193, 200, 317 P.3d 27, 34 (2013) (stating the requirements used "to determine whether a circuit court can exercise jurisdiction over an appeal brought pursuant to HRS § 91–14").

17. *Noh, supra* note 10, at 60–61 tbl. 2.12.

18. *Id.* at 28–30 tbl. 2.5.

19. *Id.* at 32–35 tbl. 2.6.

20. *Id.* at 37–39 tbl. 2.7, 41–43 tbl. 2.8.

who has identified a relevant decision from an agency that does not make its decisions electronically accessible can call or visit and query the agency about its document delivery policies, including the fees, or electronically research the relevant index of the agency records at the Hawaiʻi State Archives.[21]

Lexis and Westlaw have minimal agency content and only from select divisions within the Hawaiʻi agencies (see Table 10-1). This content cannot be browsed on the research platforms but can be searched with key terms. Judicial decisions interpreting state regulations are located in the print case reporters and on Lexis and Westlaw using the citators and other best practices discussed in the earlier chapters.

Table 10-1. Coverage of Hawaiʻi Administrative Decisions on Westlaw and Lexis

Hawaiʻi Agency Materials		Subscription-Based Research Platforms	
		Lexis	Westlaw
Attorney General Opinions*		1970–	1959–
Dep't of Commerce & Consumer Affairs (DCCA)	DCCA Opinions	1985–2000	2004–06
	Insurance Bulletins & Advisory Material	1949–	1992–
	Public Utilities Commission Decisions**	1958–	1958–

---

21. *Archives Research*, Dep't of Acct. & Gen. Servs., Haw. State Archives, https://ags.hawaii.gov/archives/about-us/archives-research/ (last visited Oct. 23, 2020).

Dep't of Labor & Industrial Relations (DLIR)	Labor Relations Board (LRB) Decisions	2000–	2002–
	Occupational Safety & Health Administration (OSHA) Decisions		1994–
	Labor-Related Office of Information Practices (OIP) Decisions	1989–	1989–
	Workers' Compensation Decisions	1978–	1994–
Dep't of Taxation Rules		1988–	-
Ethics Commission Opinions^		1968–	1968–
Commission on Judicial Conduct^^		1993–	-

Table: Cory Lenz
*Office of the Attorney General opinions from 1904–94 are also available on LLMC Digital and from 1985 to current, on the Legislative Reference Bureau's website.
**The Public Utilities Commission is considered an *attached agency* of the DCCA.
^The State Ethics Commission is a *legislative services* agency, not an executive agency.
^^ The Commission on Judicial Conduct is a *judicial services* agency, not an executive agency.

Earlier in the research for your client, you located her issue's implicating statute. On Westlaw, the citing references to the statute led you to the relevant regulations (see Figure 10-1). There, you can also find administrative decisions citing the statute. One is on-point and should be added to your research plan, *Kay Miura v. Pacific Ohana Hostel*,[22] where a worker at a hostel was fired after she had called the police on a fellow employee who threatened her. Though the Hawai'i Labor Relations Board found for the employer because the employee's protected activity was not the cause of her discharge, this becomes an important decision to distinguish in arguing for your client because unlike the *Kay Miura* employer who could point to other legitimate, non-retaliatory reasons for the employee's termination, here the Waikiki restaurant where your client worked cannot. This decision and others that may

---

22. *Kay Miura v. Pac. Ohana Hostel*, 2002 WL 35630360 (Haw. Lab. Rel. Bd. Oct. 4, 2002); *see also Decisions*—HIOSH, Hawai'i Labor Relations Board, https://labor.hawaii.gov/hlrb/files/2018/10/Decision-No.-2-Kay-Miura-v.-Pacific-Ohana-Hostel.pdf.

be relevant to your client's issue can also be located on Lexis and Westlaw by searching within Hawaiʻi's administrative decisions with the following search string: *employ! /p (discharg! OR fire) /p saf! /p threat!* Unfortunately, there are no citators available on Westlaw or Lexis to update Hawaiʻi's administrative decisions.

III. Federal Administrative Law Research

Federal administrative agencies, often having served as models for their state counterparts, are similarly established and delegated their quasi-legislative, -executive, and -judicial powers and responsibilities by specific enabling acts. The Administrative Procedure Act (A.P.A.) provides the rulemaking requirements, hearing procedures, and adjudicatory standards and procedures for all federal agencies.[23] The enabling act of each agency further governs the scope of the agency's authority, internal organizations and procedures, and rights of judicial review. As with state regulations, federal agency regulations fill in the details missing from the broad conditions and requirements put into law by the authorizing statutes. Agencies are given broad discretion to expand the details of the controlling statute and apply the law so that the legislative program can function in the real world, for all persons similarly situated, on a day-to-day basis. More information about each federal agency can be found at its website or in the *United States Government Manual*, the official handbook of the federal government, available at govinfo.gov.

A. Finding Federal Agency Regulations

Federal rules and regulations are first published in the official government register, the *Federal Register*, then codified and published in the official publication, the *Code of Federal Regulations* (C.F.R.). The Office of the Federal Register publishes the *Federal Register* every federal workday. It is paginated consecutively through the entire year. The register contains current presidential proclamations and executive orders, federal agency regulations having general applicability and legal effect, notice of proposed agency rules, changes to previously published proposed rule documents, and documents required by statute to be published. The notice of the proposed rules announces possible changes to the C.F.R. and the statutory authority for those changes; provides the proposed regulatory text, amendatory language, or regulatory

---

23. 5 U.S.C. §§ 551–559 (2018).

analysis of the proposal's issues and objectives; solicits public comment on the proposal; and initiates the notice and comment rulemaking process under the A.P.A.

Barring a "good cause" exception if the proposed rule is "impracticable, unnecessary, or contrary to the public interest," the agencies must consider the public comments and justify decisions to finalize, change, or withdraw the proposed rules.[24] After considering the comments, if an agency promulgates a final rule, it is published in the *Federal Register*. The Final Rule describes the subject, need for, and intended regulatory and economic effects of the rule; shows the effective date and compliance date; and discusses the preceding Proposed Rule and responds to comments about it. The *Federal Register* can be browsed and searched free online at govinfo.gov, archived to 1936.

All federal regulations in force are codified annually in the *Code of Federal Regulations*. The C.F.R. is divided into 50 subject matter titles with each title containing one or more individual volumes. Each title is divided into chapters with the name of the issuing agency, then further subdivided into parts (and in some instances, subparts) covering specific regulatory areas. All parts are composed of specific sections (see Figure 10-7). The print titles are updated once each calendar year in four cycles: titles 1–16 are revised as of January 1; titles 17–27, as of April 1; titles 28–41, as of July 1; and titles 42–50, as of October 1. The C.F.R. can be browsed and searched at govinfo.gov, archived to 1996 (see Figure 10-5). However, the federal government's unofficial electronic C.F.R. is updated daily and includes more recently updated titles and Federal Register amendments. This e-C.F.R. (https://www.ecfr.gov/) can be browsed or searched with Boolean connectors, or for proximity.

Researching federal regulations in print or electronically often starts in secondary sources to help understand the agency's powers and responsibilities or the subject and effect of a specific regulation. The annotated federal statutory codes then help locate the specific regulation's authorizing statute. Upon locating the authorizing statute via an annotation in a secondary source, an indices, or a Lexis and Westlaw keyword search, the citing references section of the relevant statute can be narrowed to the C.F.R. sections interpreting or applying the statute, and browsed or further narrowed by searching within the filtered results with additional keywords. Additionally,

---

24. *Id.* § 553.

Figure 10-5. Searching and Browsing the CFR Online

Source: Code of Federal Regulations, http://govinfo.gov.

the C.F.R. and Federal Register (from 1936 to current) are accessible on the Lexis and Westlaw homepages under the *Federal* tab. The C.F.R. is browsable and searchable with keywords on both research platforms; the Federal Register, however, can only be searched on Westlaw, whereas on Lexis it can be browsed and even searched selectively by date.

The Parallel Table of Authorities and Rules in the print index volume of the C.F.R. also helps locate the rulemaking authority for regulations, including statutory citations interpreted or applied by those regulations.[25] The table is divided into the following four rows, each arranged in numerical order in the left column, with the corresponding C.F.R. sections in the right column: (1) United States Code citations, by title and section; (2) United States Statutes at Large citations, by volume and page number; (3) public law citations, by number; and (4) presidential document citations (e.g., to proclamations, executive orders, and reorganization plans), by document number (see Figure 10-6).

---

25. The C.F.R. Index and Finding Aids is free online at govinfo.gov, beginning in 2017. The Parallel Table of Authorities and Rules is free online at govinfo.gov, for years 2009 and 2011, and from 2013–current.

Figure 10-6. Parallel Table of Authorities

Authorities

49 U.S.C.—Continued	CFR
41101	14 Parts 380, 385
41102	14 Parts 217, 248, 250, 298
41103	14 Parts 291, 380
41301 et seq	14 Parts 200, 201, 203, 205, 211, 213, 215, 216, 217, 218, 221, 249, 295, 250, 300, 302, 303, 372
41301	14 Parts 222, 380, 385
41313	14 Part 243
41501 et seq	14 Parts 200, 201, 203, 206, 211, 213, 221, 300, 302, 374a
41501	14 Part 253
41504	14 Parts 212, 214, 253, 254, 292, 293, 380
41506	14 Part 253
41509	14 Part 253
41510	14 Parts 253, 254
41511	14 Part 253
41701 et seq	14 Parts 200, 201, 203, 204, 205, 206, 211, 213, 215, 216, 221, 249, 250, 271, 294, 295, 296, 297, 298, 300, 302, 303, 305, 323, 325, 372, 374a, 398
41701	14 Parts 252, 292, 293, 385
41702	14 Parts 212, 243, 244, 252, 253, 254, 259, 380
41703	14 Parts 48, 375, 382
41706	14 Parts 5, 120, 121, 135, 252
41707—41709	14 Part 292
41707	14 Parts 254, 293
41708	14 Parts 212, 214, 217, 234, 240, 241, 243, 248, 250, 291, 293, 298, 380
41709	14 Parts 217, 234, 240, 241, 243, 248, 250, 291, 293, 298
41711	14 Parts 223, 240, 243, 252, 253
41712	14 Parts 212, 243, 244, 250, 255, 256, 258, 259, 292, 293, 380, 381, 399
41721	14 Parts 120, 235 19 Part 119
41724	14 Part 251
41901 et seq	14 Parts 206, 300, 302
42101 et seq	14 Part 300
42121	29 Part 1979
42301 preceding note	14 Part 121
44101—44108	14 Parts 47, 49
44101—44105	14 Part 45
44101—44103	14 Part 48
44101	14 Parts 5, 91, 117, 121, 129, 136, 142
44101 note	14 Parts 47, 49
44103—44106	14 Part 13
44105	14 Parts 48, 110, 119
44106	14 Parts 48, 110, 119, 120
44107—44111	14 Part 45
44110—44113	14 Parts 47, 48, 49
44110	14 Part 11
44111	14 Parts 91, 110, 119
44301—44310	14 Part 198
44501—44502	14 Part 169
44502	14 Parts 11, 16, 77, 93, 97, 99, 101, 157, 170, 171, 189 32 Part 855
44503	14 Part 189
44504	14 Part 45
44514	14 Parts 93, 97, 101
44701—44723	49 Part 821
44701—44717	14 Parts 110, 119
44701—44703	14 Parts 13, 61, 63, 65, 68
44701—44702	14 Parts 5, 11, 14, 121, 135

49 U.S.C.—Continued	CFR
44701	14 Parts 1, 3, 21, 23, 25, 26, 27, 29, 31, 33, 34, 35, 36, 39, 43, 45, 60, 67, 77, 91, 93, 97, 101, 103, 105, 117, 120, 125, 129, 133, 136, 137, 139, 141, 142, 145, 147, 153, 170, 171, 414 49 Parts 107, 171, 172, 173, 175
44701 note	14 Part 125
44702	14 Parts 21, 23, 25, 26, 27, 29, 31, 33, 34, 35, 36, 67, 101, 105, 117, 120, 125, 129, 133, 136, 137, 139, 141, 142, 145, 147, 170, 171, 183, 187
44703	14 Parts 43, 47, 67, 120, 139, 141, 142
44703 note	14 Parts 61, 68, 91
44704	14 Parts 3, 14, 21, 23, 25, 26, 27, 29, 31, 33, 34, 35, 36, 47, 49, 91, 139
44705	14 Parts 5, 43, 117, 121, 125, 129, 135, 136, 139, 142
44706	14 Part 139
44707	14 Parts 21, 43, 61, 63, 65, 67, 141, 142, 145, 147
44708	14 Parts 45, 147, 170, 171
44709—44711	14 Parts 5, 61, 63, 65, 117, 120, 121, 129, 136, 142, 147
44709	14 Parts 11, 13, 21, 45, 67, 91, 135, 139, 141, 145, 170, 171
44710—44711	14 Part 125
44710	14 Parts 13, 67
44711—44713	14 Part 135
44711	14 Parts 11, 21, 43, 45, 67, 91, 141, 171
44712	14 Parts 45, 91
44713	14 Parts 5, 13, 21, 43, 45, 47, 49, 117, 121, 125, 129, 136
44714	14 Part 34
44715—44717	14 Parts 91, 135
44715	14 Parts 21, 36, 93
44716—44717	14 Parts 5, 117, 121, 125, 129, 136
44717	14 Parts 43, 145
44718	14 Part 77
44719	14 Parts 93, 97, 139, 170, 171
44720	14 Part 171 15 Part 911
44721	14 Parts 15, 97, 99, 101, 105, 170, 171
44722	14 Parts 5, 91, 97, 110, 117, 119, 121, 125, 129, 135, 136, 170
44725	14 Parts 13, 43, 45
44729	14 Parts 61, 121
44730	14 Part 135
44732	14 Part 121
44732 note	14 Part 121
44901 et seq	14 Part 300
44901—44907	49 Parts 1500, 1502, 1503, 1520, 1540, 1550
44901—44905	49 Parts 1542, 1544, 1546, 1548, 1549
44901	14 Parts 110, 119, 136 49 Parts 1511, 1560
44902	49 Part 1560
44903-44904	14 Part 117
44903	14 Parts 61, 110, 119, 136 49 Parts 1554, 1560
44904	14 Parts 110, 119, 136
44906	14 Parts 110, 119, 129
44907	49 Parts 1542, 1544, 1546
44909	14 Part 243 19 Part 122

999

Source: *Code of Federal Regulations*, Government Printing Office.

Figure 10-7. Authority and Federal Register Source for CFR Title 14, Part 77 (showing various sections)

Federal Aviation Administration, DOT § 77.3

§ 73.83 Restrictions.

No person may operate an aircraft within a prohibited area unless authorization has been granted by the using agency.

§ 73.85 Using agency.

For the purpose of this subpart, the using agency is the agency, organization or military command that established the requirements for the prohibited area.

EDITORIAL NOTE: Sections 73.87 through 73.99 are reserved for descriptions of designated prohibited areas. For FEDERAL REGISTER citations affecting these prohibited areas, see the List of CFR Sections Affected, which appears in the Finding Aids section of the printed volume and at www.govinfo.gov.

PART 75 [RESERVED]

PART 77—SAFE, EFFICIENT USE, AND PRESERVATION OF THE NAVIGABLE AIRSPACE

Subpart A—General

Sec.
77.1 Purpose.
77.3 Definitions.

Subpart B—Notice Requirements

77.5 Applicability.
77.7 Form and time of notice.
77.9 Construction or alteration requiring notice.
77.11 Supplemental notice requirements.

Subpart C—Standards for Determining Obstructions to Air Navigation or Navigational Aids or Facilities

77.13 Applicability.
77.15 Scope.
77.17 Obstruction standards.
77.19 Civil airport imaginary surfaces.
77.21 Department of Defense (DOD) airport imaginary surfaces.
77.23 Heliport imaginary surfaces.

Subpart D—Aeronautical Studies and Determinations

77.25 Applicability.
77.27 Initiation of studies.
77.29 Evaluating aeronautical effect.
77.31 Determinations.
77.33 Effective period of determinations.
77.35 Extensions, terminations, revisions and corrections.

Subpart E—Petitions for Discretionary Review

77.37 General.
77.39 Contents of a petition.
77.41 Discretionary review results.

AUTHORITY: 49 U.S.C. 106 (g), 40103, 40113–40114, 44502, 44701, 44718, 46101–46102, 46104.

SOURCE: Docket No. FAA-2006-25002, 75 FR 42303, July 21, 2010, unless otherwise noted.

Subpart A—General

§ 77.1 Purpose.

This part establishes:

(a) The requirements to provide notice to the FAA of certain proposed construction, or the alteration of existing structures;

(b) The standards used to determine obstructions to air navigation, and navigational and communication facilities;

(c) The process for aeronautical studies of obstructions to air navigation or navigational facilities to determine the effect on the safe and efficient use of navigable airspace, air navigation facilities or equipment; and

(d) The process to petition the FAA for discretionary review of determinations, revisions, and extensions of determinations.

§ 77.3 Definitions.

For the purpose of this part:

Non-precision instrument runway means a runway having an existing instrument approach procedure utilizing air navigation facilities with only horizontal guidance, or area type navigation equipment, for which a straight-in non-precision instrument approach procedure has been approved, or planned, and for which no precision approach facilities are planned, or indicated on an FAA planning document or military service military airport planning document.

Planned or proposed airport is an airport that is the subject of at least one of the following documents received by the FAA:

(1) Airport proposals submitted under 14 CFR part 157.

(2) Airport Improvement Program requests for aid.

(3) Notices of existing airports where prior notice of the airport construction

693

Source: *Code of Federal Regulations,* Government Printing Office.

Because the federal agencies sometimes present the rulemaking authority citations in an inconsistent manner, the parallel tables should not be considered all-inclusive and a researcher should search the specific agency and relevant keywords in the C.F.R. Index to double-check the rulemaking authority. This authority, along with the Federal Register source, is located after each part within the C.F.R. titles (see Figure 10-7). Additionally, the C.F.R. Index is browsable and searchable on Lexis and Westlaw; however, while it is easily accessible on Westlaw via a link in the right column of the C.F.R. webpage, on Lexis the link populates in the word wheel once the C.F.R. Index is typed into the universal search box. Notably, neither Lexis nor Westlaw provides access to the Parallel Table of Authorities and Rules.

B. Updating with the Federal Register

The C.F.R. volumes are updated in cycles. To update the volumes, you must consult the List of CFR Sections Affected (L.S.A.). The L.S.A. is a stand-alone volume at the end of the C.F.R. main volumes. It lists proposed, new, and amended federal regulations that have been published in the *Federal Register* since the most recent revision date of a C.F.R. title. Each cumulative, monthly L.S.A. issue contains the C.F.R. part and section numbers, a description of its status (e.g., amended, confirmed, revised), and the Federal Register five-digit page number where the change(s) may be found (Figure 10-8). Look up the relevant agency first within the most recent L.S.A. issue to see if the relevant C.F.R. section and the corresponding Federal Register page number are listed.[26]

To finish updating, check the *Federal Register* for changes between the dates of the most recent L.S.A. and the current date by following these steps:

1. Locate the *C.F.R. Parts Affected During [Month]* table, a cumulative, monthly index published at the end of each *Federal Register* issue in the *Reader Aids* section;
2. Find the relevant C.F.R. title and part in the *C.F.R. Parts Affected During [Month]* table for each complete month since the most recent L.S.A. (Figure 10-9);

---

26. For years before 1986, use the seven separate volumes of the List of CFR Sections Affected.

3. Determine whether the documents published during the current month that affect the relevant C.F.R. titles and parts are rules or proposed rules; and
4. Check the most current *Federal Register* issues online at govinfo.gov since the shelved print issues are likely behind by several days; or
5. Consult the relevant agency's website or call to see if any additional changes have occurred or are about to occur.

The L.S.A. can be browsed and searched free online at govinfo.gov, archived to 1997. Notably, neither Lexis nor Westlaw provides access to the L.S.A. HeinOnline provides access from 1949 to current. All the research

Figure 10-8. List of CFR Sections Affected

DECEMBER 2020 57

CHANGES JANUARY 2, 2020 THROUGH DECEMBER 31, 2020

134.1201—134.1217 (Subpart L) Added; interim 52887
142.1 (b) amended 13727
146.400 Nomenclature change 13727

Chapter III—Economic Development Administration, Department of Commerce (Parts 300—399)

302.4 Removed 8379
302.5 Removed 8379
302.11 Removed 8379
302.14 Removed 8379
315 Authority citation revised 8379
315.1 Revised 8379
315.2 Introductory text revised; section amended 8379
315.4—315.5 (Subpart B) Revised 8380
315.4 Removed 8380
315.5 Removed 8380
315.6—315.10 (Subpart C) Revised 8380
315.6 Removed 8380
315.11—315.12 (Subpart D) Revised 8380
315.13—315.14 (Subpart E) Revised 8380
315.15 (Subpart F) Added 8380

Proposed Rules:

107..61654
109..12875
119..7254
120 ....1783, 80676, 83837
121 ....1289, 62239, 62372, 72584, 76390
123..80676
124..................................1289, 3273, 23487
125..........................1289, 3273, 6106, 23487
126..1289, 23487
127 1289
129 3273
134 ....1289, 7893

TITLE 14—AERONAUTICS AND SPACE

Chapter I—Federal Aviation Administration, Department of Transportation (Parts 1—199)

1.1 Amended 79825
21 Amended 26344
21 Amended; interim; eff. through 4-21-21 62968
21 Special FAA conditions 38777
21 Policy statement.........................58251
23 Special FAA conditions 59400
25 Special FAA conditions........642, 6026, 6027, 6029, 11838, 12864, 16892, 18110, 41333, 41336, 43423, 43425, 48646, 67435, 67436, 67438
25 Special FAA conditions; eff. 1-19-21 81785
25 Correction: Special FAA conditions 14559, 67439
21 Technical correction 47295
27 Special FAA conditions 9364
27 Special FAA conditions; eff. 1-11-21 79828
27 Regulation at 85 FR 79826 comment period extended to 1-11-21 83415
29 Special FAA conditions 34494, 48648
33 Special FAA conditions 52041
39.13.....436, 438, 441, 445, 450, 453, 456, 459, 2288, 2628, 2868, 3256, 4198, 4200, 4203, 5306, 5310, 5312, 5315, 6740, 6743, 6745, 6748, 6751, 6753, 6756, 6759, 7192, 7654, 7660, 7858, 7861, 7865, 7867, 7871, 8147, 8149, 8152, 8155, 8385, 8387, 8719, 10041, 10045, 10049, 10969, 10973, 10976, 10979, 11276, 11279, 11281, 11283, 11285, 11288, 11291, 11293, 13477, 13479, 13729, 14145, 14410, 14412, 14415, 14561, 14564, 14786, 14789, 14791, 14793, 15054, 15056, 15058, 15921, 15923, 15926, 15929, 15932, 15935, 15937, 15939, 15942, 15945, 15947, 16239, 16532, 17475, 17480, 17482, 17486, 17489, 17493, 17740, 17744, 18430, 18433, 18437, 18863, 19079, 19081, 19383, 19658, 19877, 20152, 20396, 20398, 20401, 20404, 20407, 20410, 20412, 20588, 20591, 21074, 21319, 21754, 21756, 21758, 21761, 21763, 21765, 22585, 22954, 22957, 23454, 26843, 27111, 27113, 27666, 27669, 27672, 27911, 29597, 29600, 29602, 30591, 30594, 30596, 30600, 30603, 30839, 30842, 31044, 31048, 31361, 31362, 34090, 34092, 34958, 34961, 35176, 35179, 35554, 35556, 36144, 36147, 36315, 36319, 37002, 37334, 37548, 37550, 37554, 38054, 38059, 38314, 39830, 40586, 40587, 40875, 41176, 41179, 41182, 41909, 41911, 42688, 42691, 43684, 43988, 44455, 44459, 44461, 44463, 44466, 44687, 45061, 45064, 45068, 45071,

Source: *Code of Federal Regulations*, Government Printing Office.

Figure 10-9. CFR Parts Affected in the *Federal Register*

Source: *Federal Register*, Office of the Federal Register.

platforms update the *Federal Register* daily. All the subscription platforms also update the C.F.R. to include recent regulations. However, these updates typically lag the most recent publication of the *Federal Register* by at least a week and in some instances more, so it is recommended that a researcher follow the updating steps described above. Finally, the C.F.R. archive of each subscription platform varies: HeinOnline's is comprehensive, dating back to inception (1938); Westlaw's goes back to 1984; and Lexis' goes back to 1981.

C. Finding Federal Agency Decisions and Attorney General Opinions

Similar to hearing officers in Hawai'i, federal administrative law judges conduct hearings and render decisions in proceedings between the specific agency and persons, businesses, government entities, and other organizations that are regulated under the agency's laws in accordance with its enabling statutes. Federal administrative law judges are certified by the Office of Personnel Management and appointed in accordance with 5 U.S.C. § 3105. They have decisional independence to ensure fair and impartial resolutions;[27] though, like their state agency counterparts, those decisions are either final or merely recommendations for another decision maker to accept or deny depending on the specific agency's governing laws. If the latter, an administrative law judge's decision does not become binding legal precedent in other agency cases unless it has been adopted by the agency board reviewing the decision.

Many agencies, like the National Oceanic and Atmospheric Administration, publish their decisions in an official print reporter (e.g., *Ocean Resources and Wildlife Reporter*). A list of such reporters is located in the T1.2 Table of the *Bluebook*. Most law and university libraries that are official depositories of the U.S. Government Printing Office include the official agency reporters in their collections, along with unofficial reporters from commercial publishers like C.C.H. (e.g., *Labor Law Reporter*) and B.N.A. (e.g., *Labor Relations Reporter*). Like the Hawai'i state agencies, many federal agencies also publish their decisions on the specific agency's or its division's website. For instance, the website of the Office of Legal Counsel, the division of the Department of Justice that writes opinions and offers legal advice for the president and the department heads of the executive branch under authority of the Attorney General, publishes select opinions, archived to 1934. A comprehensive list of links to federal agencies can be located at the usa.gov website. Additionally, federal administrative decisions and guidance from all the executive branch agencies and most of the independent agencies can be located on Lexis and Westlaw and updated with Shepard's or KeyCite. These decisions can only be searched with relevant keywords, and not browsed. Coverage of the decisions

---

27. 5 U.S.C. § 557 (2018).

varies by agency or division (e.g., Attorney General opinions begin in 1791 and EPA decisions, in 1972, on Westlaw), though notably Lexis does not provide the archival dates.

Depending on the specific statutes and regulations governing an agency and barring those instances where a district court has original jurisdiction over an agency matter,[28] some federal administrative agency decisions are reviewable in the district court and others are reviewable directly in the court of appeals.[29] Under the A.P.A., only *final* agency actions are subject to judicial review. Courts use the two-pronged *Bennett* test to determine the finality of an agency decision.[30] Common issues from final agency decisions that a court might be asked to review include abuse of agency discretion; arbitrary and capricious decisions; constitutional, due process, and separation of power violations; or questions related to the interpretation of the enabling statute or the regulation. These judicial decisions interpreting federal regulations are located in the print case reporters and on Lexis and Westlaw using the citators and other best practices discussed in the earlier chapters.

---

28. Federal district courts have original jurisdiction over an agency matter when: 1) the agency is the plaintiff, as per 28 U.S.C. 1345 (2018); 2) there is a federal question, as per 28 U.S.C. 1331 (2018); 3) there is a mandamus action to compel an agency to perform a duty owed to the plaintiff, as per *Kerr v. U.S. Dist. Ct. for the N. Dist. of Cal.*, 426 U.S. 394, 402 (1976); or 4) there is a specific statute authorizing original jurisdiction in the federal district court.

29. *See, e.g., Biotics Rsch. Corp. v. Heckler*, 710 F.2d 1375, 1377 (9th Cir. 1983); 28 U.S.C. § 2342 (2018).

30. *Bennett v. Spear*, 520 U.S. 154, 178 (1997); *see also Or. Nat. Desert Ass'n v. U.S. Forest Serv.*, 465 F.3d 977, 982 (9th Cir. 2006).

Chapter 11

Legal Citation

I. Introduction to the *Bluebook*

The *Bluebook* is a system of legal citation for practitioners and scholars to concisely provide the citing authority for each sentence in a legal document or scholarly work. These citations with their specific pincites help practitioners and scholars locate the authority for a closer consideration of its larger context. Citing accurately is a professional courtesy, a defense against plagiarism, and a requirement of all state codes of professional responsibility.

The *Bluebook* is divided into Bluepages for legal documents (around 60 pages), Whitepages for scholarship (around 170 pages), and Tables for the appropriate abbreviations (around 130 pages) (hereinafter T + [table number]). Legal practitioners rely most heavily on the Bluepages but often incorporate rules from the Whitepages when the local court rules or the Bluepages are silent about a citation. Navigating the *Bluebook* and locating a relevant rule for a specific resource is easy because the index is so comprehensive and granular. The *Bluebook* includes these additional finding aids: 1) a *Quick Reference* guide inside the front cover for academic citations; 2) a *Quick Reference* guide inside the back cover for legal documents; 3) a comprehensive table of contents; 4) a quick table of contents, printed on the back cover; and 5) *Basic Citation Forms* at the beginning of every rule governing a legal authority.

A legal practitioner or scholar should use the following steps to ensure an accurate citation:

1. Discern the source material (e.g., primary law or secondary authority, letter, e-book, translation, tweet, interview, website).
2. Locate the relevant *Bluebook* rule or rules with the index and other finding aids.
3. Cite to the official rather than unofficial source, if available.

4. Follow the relevant rule's listed requirements closely. Look out for expressions of strong determination (e.g., shall, will, should), language that includes the phrase *if any*, and optional requirements like URL's.
5. Abbreviate according to the Tables.
6. Double-check the typeface (e.g., ordinary roman, italicizing or underscoring, small and large cap) and capitalization requirements, as illustrated in Table 11-1.
7. Locate the short form rules for the relevant authority at the end of the section.

Table 11-1. Typeface and Capitalization Requirements for Non-Academic and Academic Citations

Italicize or underscore the following in a non-academic citation	Italicize the following in an academic citation	Large and Small Cap the following in an academic citation
BLUEPAGES	WHITEPAGES	
Full and short case names	Short form case names	• Constitutions • Statutes • Regulations • Rules of Evidence and Procedure • Ordinances (political subdivision + state + code name)
Introductory signals	Introductory signals	• Model codes, Restatements, and Uniform acts
Procedural and explanatory phrases in case citations	Procedural and explanatory phrases in case citations	• Legislative and administrative reports, documents, and debates • Authors (including institutional authors) and Titles of books and other non-periodic materials (e.g., treatises, reports, white papers, manuals, primers) • Titles of periodicals
Id. or Id. *supra* or supra	*Id.* / *supra*	
Titles of books, articles, and essays	Titles of articles in periodicals	

Titles of some legislative materials	Titles of congressional committee hearings
Punctuation within italicized or under-scored material	Punctuation within italicized material
Introductory phrases for related authority	Introductory phrases for related authority
Internal cross-references	Internal cross-references

Table: Cory Lenz.

The *Bluebook* also offers an electronic subscription at https://www.legal-bluebook.com/, though with the twenty-first edition, the *Foreign Jurisdiction Table* is available free online. Most of the legal research platforms, like Westlaw, Lexis, and HeinOnline, offer citation generators; unfortunately, their accuracy is hit-or-miss. But there are several free online tutorials that can help with *Bluebook* citations for legal documents and scholarship, such as *The Introduction to Basic Legal Citation* by Peter W. Martin at the Legal Information Institute.

II. *Bluebook* and Local Rules for Citing Hawai'i Legal Authority in Legal Documents

Practitioners in most jurisdictions follow the form prescribed in the *Bluebook* for citations in legal documents. Many require the citations to conform to sources in addition to the *Bluebook*, like Texas' *The Greenbook* or the specific rules of the court where the filing is being made.[1] Hawai'i does not specify a citation form in its court rules. Local citation rules, however, do exist. In 2008, a committee of law clerks published *A Handbook of Citation Form for*

---

1. Tex. R. Ann., App. 4th R. 8 note (West, Westlaw through July 15, 2020) (stating that citations "should conform to the most recent editions of *Harvard L. Rev., A Uniform System of Citation* (the *Bluebook*), and *Tex. L. Rev., Texas Rules of Form* (the *Greenbook*)").

Law Clerks at the Appellate Courts of the State of Hawai'i to supplement the *Bluebook*. This handbook continues to be followed and is readily available online. Its distinctions will be noted alongside the *Bluebook* where relevant.

In legal documents, the citation may be written as a citation sentence, citation clause, or an embedded citation, as illustrated in Table 11-2. The citation sentence comes at the end of the text sentence (or at the end of the footnote text in scholarship) because it supports the entire idea of the sentence. This is the most preferred method of citation among practitioners. The citation clause might be used when the ideas of the sentence are supported by two or more authorities. In a citation clause, it is common for one citation to drop in the middle of the sentence, set-off by commas, in support of the ideas from the front end, and another citation to finish in support of the ideas expressed in the tail end of the sentence, also set off by a comma.

Finally, the embedded citation (sometimes called a textual citation) incorporates the full citation in the main text (or footnote text in scholarship). A comma always follows the case citation in the text, though not other authorities unless grammatical rules require a comma. When embedded, case citations follow Bluebook Rule (hereinafter BB R.) 10.2.1(c), which allows only widely known acronyms and abbreviations for the following eight words, unless the word begins the party's name: &, Ass'n, Bros., Co., Corp., Inc., Ltd., and No. Embedded federal statutes and regulations can also be abbreviated. Every other embedded authority, however, cannot be abbreviated. Thus, constitutions (federal and state) (BB R. 11), legislative materials (federal and state) (BB R. 13.8), and state statutes and regulations (BB R. 12.10) are spelled out when embedded in the main text and footnote text, even the section and paragraph symbols.

Table 11-2. Types of Citations

Citation Type	Case and Statutory Law Examples
Citation Sentences support the entire preceding sentence.	A contractual duty of performance is discharged where a party's performance is made impracticable, without his fault, by the occurrence of an event the non-occurrence of which was a basic assumption on which the contract was made. *Aiea Lani Corp. v. Haw. Escrow & Title, Inc.*, 64 Haw. 638, 639–40 (1982). Even if performance is discharged, both parties may be entitled to restitution for any benefit they have conferred on the other party by part performance or reliance. Restatement (Second) of Conts. §§ 272, 377 (Am. Law. Inst. 1981).
	Employees are protected against discriminatory practices of employers because of sex. Haw. Rev. Stat. § 378-2(a)(1) (2015). Discriminating because of sex includes "because of pregnancy, childbirth, or related medical conditions." *Id.* § 378-1.
Citation Clauses support only the part of the sentence that immediately precedes.	A contractual duty of performance is discharged where a party's performance is made impracticable, without his fault, by the occurrence of an event the non-occurrence of which was a basic assumption on which the contract was made, *Aiea Lani Corp. v. Haw. Escrow & Title, Inc.*, 64 Haw. 638, 639–40 (1982), though even if performance is discharged, both parties may be entitled to restitution for any benefit they have conferred on the other party by part performance or reliance, Restatement (Second) of Conts. §§ 272, 377 (Am. Law. Inst. 1981).
	Employees are protected against discriminatory practices of employers because of sex, Haw. Rev. Stat. § 378-2(a)(1) (2015), which includes "because of pregnancy, childbirth, or related medical conditions." *Id.* § 378-1.

Embedded Citations are integrated into the sentence with limited abbreviations.	According to *Aiea Lani Corp. v. Hawai'i Escrow & Title, Inc.*, 64 Haw. 638, 639–40 (1982), a contractual duty of performance is discharged where a party's performance is made impracticable, without his fault, by the occurrence of an event the non-occurrence of which was a basic assumption on which the contract was made. However, the Restatement (Second) of Contracts sections 272 and 377 (American Law Institute 1981) note that even if performance is discharged, both parties may be entitled to restitution for any benefit they have conferred on the other party by part performance or reliance.
	According to Hawai'i Revised Statutes section 378-2(a)(1) (2015), employees are protected against discriminatory practices of employers because of sex. Discriminating *because of sex* is defined in section 378-1 to include "because of pregnancy, childbirth, or related medical conditions."

Table: Cory Lenz.

Every authority in a legal document is usually cited only once in full. Every subsequent citation to the same authority uses a condensed form called a short form when not interrupted by an intervening authority or a modified short form (sometimes called an alternate short form) when interrupted by an intervening authority. An intervening authority is one that comes in between the citations to the same authority. When there is no intervening authority, the Latin word *idem*, meaning *the same*, is abbreviated and underlined or italicized to *id.* to indicate the immediately preceding citation is to the same authority. Any different subdivision (e.g., page, section, paragraph, article, amendment, clause) within the same authority is identified after the *id*. *Id.* can only be used with citation sentences and citation clauses, not with embedded citations; it can also be used only to refer back to a citation with a single source. When an intervening authority comes between citations to the same authority, *id.* also cannot be used, and a modified short form must be used in its place. The modified short forms differ for each authority, so those will be discussed in separate sections.

Signals are often placed in front of a citation to indicate how the cited authority treats the proposition stated in the preceding text. Bluebook Rules 1.2–.4 describe each signal, explain the different types, and list their appropriate rank order when more than one type of signal follows in a string citation. Table 11-3 below synthesizes that explanation. According to the twenty-first edition of the *Bluebook*, multiple authorities sharing the same signal should be ordered within the string in a logical manner, placing those more helpful or authoritative first. Multiple authorities of the same type are separated with semicolons, while each different type of signal closes with a period. All signals are either underlined or italicized.

Table 11-3. Signal Order

Signal Order	Type of Signal	Rank Within Signal Type
1st	Supportive	1. No signal... [;] 2. *e.g.,*... [;] 3. *accord*... [;] 4. *see*... [;] 5. *see also*... [;] 6. *cf*.... [.]
2nd	Comparative	7. *Compare...with*.... [.]
3rd	Contradictory	8. *Contra*... [;] 9. *but see*... [;] 10. *but cf*.... [.]
4th	Background	11. *See generally*... [.]

Table: Cory Lenz.

For assistance crafting citations to legal documents, there are a host of fantastic resources available. A Creative-Commons implementation of the *Bluebook's* Bluepages called *The Indigo Book: A Manual of Legal Citation* (also known as *Baby Blue's Manual of Legal Citation*) is available free online. Another free, comprehensive resource is a popular YouTube series by law professor Allison Ortlieb. Finally, Linda J. Barris's *Understanding and Mastering the Bluebook* (Carolina Academic Press 4th ed. 2020) is a phenomenal resource.

Figure 11-1. Anatomy of a Full Citation to the Hawai'i Constitution

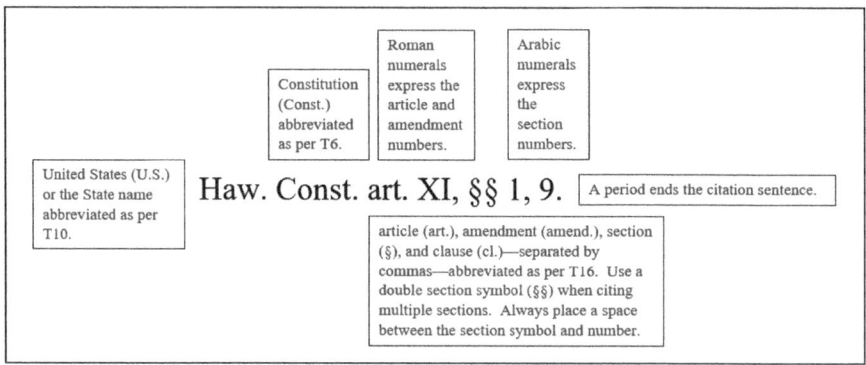

Source: Cory Lenz, reprinted with permission from author.

A. Constitutional Law

According to BB R. 11, the components of a full citation to the U.S. Constitution and a state's constitution, as illustrated in Figure 11-1, are written in ordinary roman type. Constitutions are the only authority that do not incorporate the modified short form, so when there is an intervening authority between the same constitutional article or amendment, the citation must be restated in full. The *id.* short form, however, is used (see Table 11-4).

Table 11-4. Short Citation Form, Constitutions

	Full Citation	U.S. Const. art. I, § 3, cl. 2.	
Id. Short Form	No Intervening Authority	Exact same subdivisions from the preceding citation.	*Id.*
		Same article or amendment but different section.	*Id.* § 2.
		Same article or amendment but different clause.	*Id.* § 2, cl. 5.
		Different article or amendment.	*Id.* art. II.

Table: Cory Lenz.

The local rules do not provide a Hawaiʻi distinction as it relates to the pre-statehood constitutions. Bluebook Rule 11 recommends citing constitutions that are no longer in effect by the year of adoption. Thus, the citation to article 72 of the Constitution of 1840 of the Kingdom of Hawaiʻi would look like this: Kingdom of Haw. Const. of 1840, art. LXXII.

Figure 11-2. Anatomy of a Full Citation to Hawaiʻi Statutory Law

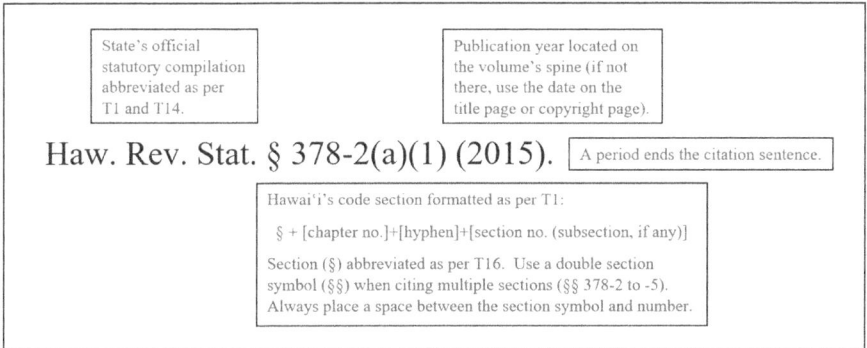

Source: Cory Lenz, reprinted with permission from author.

B. Statutory Law

1. Print Statutory Compilations

According to BB R. 12, the components of a full citation to Hawaiʻi's official code, as illustrated in Figure 11-2, are written in ordinary roman type. The official code set for each jurisdiction is found in T1 under *Statutory compilations* and identified by the *cite to* [OFFICIAL STATUTORY COMPILATION] *if therein* language.[2] The official code sets are published either by the state government printing office like Hawaiʻi's or a commercial publisher (e.g., West, LexisNexis, Deering, McKinney). If citing the official code, do not include the publisher information in the parenthetical with the publication year. The unofficial code set of one or more commercial publishers is listed in T1 below

---

2. T1 in the *Bluebook* uses small/large caps in the citation form, which is appropriate for academic citations but not for citations in legal documents, so practitioners will need to change the typeface to ordinary roman type.

the official set. Citations to the unofficial code usually include the abbreviation of the word *Annotated* (Ann.) in the title and the commercial publisher in the parenthetical with the publication year. For instance, citations to the unofficial Hawai'i statutory compilations look like this:

Haw. Rev. Stat. Ann. § 378-2(a)(1) (West 2008).

Haw. Rev. Stat. Ann. § 378-2(a)(1) (LexisNexis 2016).

Each state adopts a slightly different citation form for its codes. Some like Illinois and Pennsylvania include the title or chapter number before the statutory compilation and the section number after. However, most include the title and/or chapter number and the section number after the statutory compilation, separated by a unique mark of punctuation (e.g., hyphen, colon, period, slash). Finally, the statutory compilations of California, Maryland, New York, and Texas include subject matter codes before the section symbol and number, abbreviated as per T1.

When citing multiple sections of a statute that uses internal punctuation, use double section symbols (§§) and drop the repetitious digits preceding the punctuation, but keep the punctuation and the section number. If the multiple cited sections are non-consecutive within the same chapter, carry the internal punctuation forward with the non-repetitious digits and separate them with a comma. Do the same if the multiple cited sections are consecutive within the same chapter unless the state uses hyphens as internal punctuation. In that instance, carry the internal punctuation forward but separate the consecutive sections with the preposition "to" (see examples below).

<u>Citing Non-Consecutive Sections in a Full Citation</u>

Haw. Rev. Stat. §§ 378-2, -5 (2015).

<u>Citing Consecutive Sections in a Full Citation</u>

Haw. Rev. Stat. §§ 378-2 to -5 (2015).

If cited material only appears in the supplement or pocket part of the official statutory compilation, include the abbreviation "Supp." as per T16 and the year the supplement was published. Additionally, include the publisher if the cited material appears in the supplement of an unofficial statutory compilation. Moreover, if cited material appears in both the main volume and the supplement or pocket part, indicate as such with an ampersand (&) and include the publication years (see Table 11-5).

Table 11-5. Statutory Supplements in a Full Citation

Statutory Supplements	
Citing the Supplement to Hawai'i's Official Code	Haw. Rev. Stat. § 378-2 (Supp. 2019).
Citing the Supplement to Hawai'i's Unofficial Codes	Haw. Rev. Stat. Ann. § 378-2 (LexisNexis Supp. 2019).
	Haw. Rev. Stat. Ann. § 378-2 (West Supp. 2020).
Citing the Replacement Volume of and the Supplement to Hawai'i's Official Code	Haw. Rev. Stat. § 378-2 (2015 & Supp. 2019).
Citing the Replacement Volume[3] of and the Supplement to Hawai'i's Unofficial Codes	Haw. Rev. Stat. Ann. § 378-2 (LexisNexis 2016 & Supp. 2019).
	Haw. Rev. Stat. Ann. § 378-2 (West 2008 & Supp. 2020).

Table: Cory Lenz.

2. *Id.* and Modified Short Forms

Statutory compilations use the *id.* short form when there has been no intervening authority between code sections cited within the same title. When the immediately preceding citation is a different section or subsection, the *id.* short form includes the abbreviation *id.* + § + [title and/or chapter + section (subsection, if any)]. Unlike with case law citations, the *id.* short form with statutory compilations does not use the preposition "at." However, if there has been an intervening citation to a different authority, statutory compilations use a modified short form that clearly identifies the statute being cited, accounting for the recentness of the citation and potential for confusion. The *id.* short form and the modified short form for statutes located within the official and unofficial statutory compilations and on the electronic databases look very similar to each other, but for the "Ann." abbreviation of the unofficial code. Finally, the subject matter codes of California, Maryland, New York, and Texas are included in the modified short form (see Table 11-6).

---

3. After statehood, the *Hawai'i Revised Statutes* was first published in 1968, followed by replacement volumes in 1976, 1985, and 1993 and then on a volume-by-volume basis after 1993.

Table 11-6. Short Citation Forms, Hawai'i Statutory Law

	Id. Short Form and Modified Short Form	
Full Citation	Haw. Rev. Stat. § 378-2(a)(1) (2015).	
No Intervening Authority	Immediately preceding citation is the same section and subsection.	*Id.*
	Immediately preceding citation is the same section but different subsection (No "at" and include the chapter and section number).	*Id.* § 378-2(b).
	Immediately preceding citation is the same title but different section (No "at" and include the chapter number).	*Id.* § 378-5.
	Immediately preceding citation is to a different title.	Use a full citation.
Intervening Authority, e.g., Haw. Rev. Stat. § 560:2-101(b) (2016) or a case citation.		
After an intervening citation to a different title within the code or to a different authority, use the modified short form.	If the statute has been cited recently AND there will be no confusion (e.g., to another cited statutory or regulatory section) include: § + [title and/or chapter no. + section no. + (subsection, if any)].	§ 378-2(a)(1).
	If the statute has not been cited recently OR there will be confusion, include: [Statutory compilation] + § + [title and/or chapter no. + section no. + (subsection, if any)].	Haw. Rev. Stat. § 378-2(a)(1).
	California, Maryland, New York, and Texas statutory compilations include a subject matter code in the full and modified short forms.	Crim. Law § 2-210.

Table: Cory Lenz.

3. Online and Electronic Statutory Compilations

Figure 11-3. Anatomy of a Full Citation to Hawai'i Statutory Law from an Electronic Database

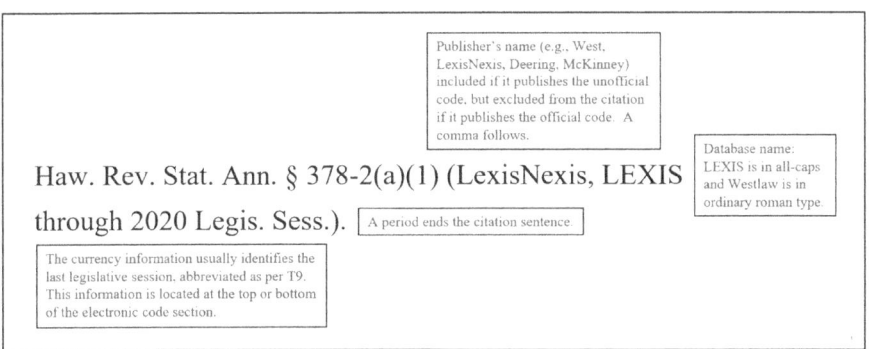

Source: Cory Lenz, reprinted with permission from author.

The twenty-first edition of the *Bluebook* further facilitates citations to official and unofficial codes in online databases. For instance, BB R. 12.3 requires citation to the official federal code *only if available*, and BB R. 12.5(b) allows citations to online sources for official state and municipal codes *whenever* available (emphasis added). Some states like Connecticut and Nevada publish their official codes in print and online by way of their government printing offices.[4] Hawai'i's online statutory compilation on the State Legislature's website, however, is considered unofficial. Regardless of whether official or unofficial, citations to a state's online statutory authority follow the same full citation rules already discussed for the print authority, plus the addition of the URL. For instance, the citation to the Hawai'i code published on the State Legislature's website might look like this:

Haw. Rev. Stat. § 378-2(a)(1) (2015), http://www.capitol.hawaii.gov/hrscurrent/Vol07_Ch0346-0398/HRS0378/HRS_0378-0002.htm.

Other states rely on a commercial publisher to make their official codes available in print and online. Likewise, the only distinction for a citation to a statutory authority located in an electronic database, as opposed to one pulled from the print source, is the parenthetical information: as per BB R.

---

4. *Official Version of the State Statutes/Code*, National Conference of State Legislatures, https://www.ncsl.org/documents/lsss/Official_Version_Statutes.pdf (last updated July 2011).

12.5, when citing an official code by way of a commercial database, the parenthetical includes the following:

> (Name of the database + currency information).

When citing an unofficial code, the parenthetical includes the following (Figure 11-3):

> (Publisher, + Name of the database + currency information).

The *id.* and modified short forms for citations to electronic statutory compilations follow the same rules as those for the print.

4. Hawai'i Distinctions

The local citation rules mirror many of the *Bluebook* rules already discussed. One important distinction, however, is that under the local rules, in the first full citation, Hawai'i's statutory compilation is spelled out, with the Hawaiian diacritics,[5] followed by its acronym in parentheses (HRS), for instance:

> Hawai'i Revised Statutes (HRS) § 378-2(a)(1) (2015).

The acronym then continues to be used for the modified short form if the statute has not been cited recently or there will be confusion, for instance:

> HRS § 378-2(a)(1).

As with citing the Kingdom of Hawai'i constitutions, the *Bluebook* is also silent as to citing the statutory laws before the 1968 publication of the *Hawai'i Revised Statutes*. Those earlier laws governing the Territory of Hawai'i and the first few years after statehood were published in a statutory compilation called the *Revised Laws of Hawai'i*.[6] In the first full citation, the local rules recommend spelling out the revised laws, with the Hawaiian diacritics, followed by the acronym RLH in parentheses, for instance:

> Revised Laws of Hawai'i (RLH) § 2141-42 (1925).

The acronym then continues to be used for the modified short form if the statute has not been cited recently or there will be confusion, for instance:

> RLH § 2141-42.

---

5. Lilinoe Andrews, *Hawaiian Diacritical Marks*, Historic Hawai'i Foundation (Dec. 21, 2018), https://historichawaii.org/2018/12/21/hawaiian-diacritical-marks/.

6. *The Revised Laws of Hawai'i* were published in 1905, 1915, 1925, 1935, 1945, and 1955. *The Revised Laws of 1955* were supplemented in the following years: 1957, 1960, 1961, 1963, 1965.

C. Administrative Law

Under BB R. 14 and in T1, the *Bluebook* lists LexisNexis as the official publisher of Hawai'i's administrative rules and regulations. Since 2017, LexisNexis has fallen back on an irregular print schedule for the administrative rules, so the online and commercial sources are often the best ones to cite. The citation format of Hawai'i's rules mirrors that of its statutes in commercial databases:

[Regulatory compilation] + § + [title-chapter-section of rule] + (Name of the database + currency information).

The citation to administrative rules additionally follows the *id.* and modified short forms for statutes.

Table 11-7 compares the *Bluebook* and local rules. Notably, the local rules defer to the Hawai'i Administrative Rules on the Lt. Governor's website. Though not required, adding the relevant URL to the end of the citation could be helpful to a researcher. Additionally, while the *Bluebook* calls for the currency information in the parenthetical, the local rules provide the effective date.

Table 11-7. Full Citation and Modified Short Forms, Hawai'i Administrative Rules

Type of Citation		Full Citation Form	Modified Short Form	
Bluebook	Electronic Database	HAR § 13-167-2 (LEXIS through Oct. 5, 2020).	Cited recently AND no confusion.	§ 13-167-2.
			Not cited recently OR there will be confusion.	HAR § 13-167-2.
	Print (irregular print schedule)	Haw. Code R. § 13-167-2 (LexisNexis 2018).	Cited recently AND no confusion.	§ 13-167-2.
			Not cited recently OR there will be confusion.	Haw. Code R. § 13-167-2.

Local	Lt. Governor's Office Online	Hawaiʻi Administrative Rules (HAR) § 13-167-2 (effective May 27, 1988).	Cited recently AND no confusion.	§ 13-167-2.
			Not cited recently OR there will be confusion.	HAR § 13-167-2.

Table: Cory Lenz.

D. Case Law

There are minor citation differences between the *Bluebook* and local rules for the authorities already discussed. However, there are vast differences for case law citations, which the *Bluebook* acknowledges in BB R. B1 and R. 10.3.1(a), recommending practitioners defer to their respective local rules governing citations. Thus, the Hawaiʻi local rules will be illustrated along with their comparable *Bluebook* rules.

Local rules require a parallel citation to the state reporter, followed by the regional reporter. When citing Hawaiʻi Supreme Court opinions from 1847–1994, use the abbreviation "Haw." in the citation to indicate the state publication of volumes 1 to 75 of the *Official Hawaiʻi Reports*. The Hawaiʻi Intermediate Court of Appeals was established in 1979.[7] From 1980–1994, its court opinions were published separately by the State in volumes 1 to 10 of the *Official Hawaiʻi Appellate Reports*. Use "Haw. App." to indicate the appellate reporter in the citation. However, in 1994, West replaced the State as the publisher of the official reporters and brought the appellate and supreme court decisions together in *West's Hawaiʻi Reports*, starting with volume 76. The local citation rules reflect this change. When citing appellate or supreme court decisions from volume 76 to the current volume in *West's Hawaiʻi Reports*, indicate the reporter in the citation by spelling out "Hawaiʻi" with the ʻokina. Follow the citation to the state reporter with a citation to the *Pacific Reporter* (P.2d or P.3d), the starting page and pincite, and then a parenthetical at the end of the citation indicating the court level and/or location and the date of the decision. Pincites to consecutive pages within the court opinion are separated by a hyphen, while those that are

---

7. 1979 Haw. Sess. L. 111, https://www.capitol.hawaii.gov/slh/Years/SLH1979/SLH1979_Act111.pdf.

nonconsecutive are separated by a comma. Exclude the court level and/or the court location from the parenthetical if either or both are clear from the name of the reporter (Figure 11-4).

The local rules follow BB R. 10.2 for constructing the case names and T6 and T10 for their proper abbreviations. The caption of a case often includes multiple plaintiffs or appellants on the left side of the "v." and multiple defendants or appellees on the right side. The case name becomes the sum of the first party listed on either side of the "v," omitting all other parties. The party name is then modified and abbreviated depending on whether it is an individual, business, government agency, or geographic location as the named party. Each will be discussed separately here.

Figure 11-4. Anatomy of a Full Citation to Hawai'i Case Law

First Party Name. If an individual, provide the last name and exclude any descriptors. Follow BB R. 10.2. v. for "versus" follows the first party name.	Second Party Name. If a business, drop the double business designation, follow BB R. 10.2, and abbreviate as per T6 and T10. A comma follows the second party name. Only the full case name is underlined or *italicized*, not the comma.	Volume + Reporter + Starting Page. Vol. 1-75, abbreviate the reporter "Haw." Vol. 76-Current, spell out "Hawai'i". Starting page of the case, then a comma, follow the reporter.	Parallel Citation: Volume + Reporter + Starting Page. Pacific Reporter, Second Series abbreviated as per T1. Starting page of the case, then a comma, follow the reporter.

<u>Kalipi v. Hawaiian Tr. Co.</u>, 66 Haw. 1, 11-12, 656 P.2d 745, 751-52 (1982).

Pincite. If consecutive pages, keep at least two digits and drop the other repeating digits.	Court Level/Location + Year of Decision. Follow BB R. 10.4 and 10.5 and abbreviate as per T1. Exclude the court level and/or the court location if either or both are clear from the reporter name.	A period ends the citation sentence.	Pincite. A comma follows the pincite.

Source: Cory Lenz, reprinted with permission from author.

1. Individuals

Keep the last name and omit first and middle names and initials. However, retain the full name if in a language where the surname is given first (e.g., many Asian names), and retain initials or a first name and last initial if those are the only parts of the name provided by the caption (e.g., common in family law cases to protect the parties' privacy). Moreover, omit titles, descriptive words (e.g., plaintiff, defendant), lineage identifiers, and Latin phrases (e.g., *et al.*).

2. Businesses

Omit the article "the" from the beginning of the business name and any *doing business as* (d/b/a) information. If the name includes a double business designation—Ass'n, Bros., Co., Corp., F.S.B., Inc., Ins., L.L.C., Ltd., N.A., R.R., Sons, Daughters, or similar—keep the first and drop the second business designation. The remaining business name is then abbreviated as per T6 and T10, for instance:

Hawaiian Trust Company, Ltd.	*AIG Hawai'i Insurance Company, Inc.*
BECOMES	BECOMES
Hawaiian Tr. Co.	*AIG Haw. Ins.*

Moreover, widely known acronyms, without the periods, may be used in place of the full business name (e.g., UPS, CBS, NCR Corp.).

3. Government Agencies

Federal agencies, departments, or divisions are abbreviated as per T6 and T10. Well-known acronyms may also be used, for instance:

City of Berkeley v. United States Postal Serv.,

BECOMES

City of Berkeley v. U.S. Postal Serv.,

OR

City of Berkeley v. USPS,

State agencies, departments, or divisions in the case names are modified and abbreviated depending on whether a federal court or a court in the *same* state decided the case. If the case was decided in a federal court, retain the state's name and abbreviate it as per T10, omit the phrases "State of," "People of," or "Commonwealth of," and abbreviate the state agency, department, or division as per T6, for instance:

Sherez v. State of Hawai'i Department of Education, 396 F. Supp. 2d 1138 (D. Haw. 2005).

BECOMES

Sherez v. Haw. Dep't of Educ., 396 F. Supp. 2d 1138 (D. Haw. 2005).

However, if the case was decided by a court in the *same* state as the agency, department, or division that is the named party, omit and substitute the name of the state with its official designation, "State," "People," or "Commonwealth," and abbreviate the state agency, department, or division as per T6, for instance:

Life of the Land, Incorporated v. Hawaiʻi Land Use Commission, 61 Haw. 3, 594 P.2d 1079 (1979).

BECOMES

Life of the Land, Inc. v. State Land Use Commʻn, 61 Haw. 3, 594 P.2d 1079 (1979).

4. Geographic Location as the Named Party

Always spell out "United States" when the country itself is the named party; however, abbreviate "United States" in business names and when an agency, department, or division within the U.S. government is the named party.

When the state itself is the named party (*not* an agency, department, or division within the state), the state's name is modified and abbreviated depending on whether a federal court or a court in the *same* state decided the case. If the case was decided in a federal court, retain the name of the state, without abbreviating it, and omit the phrases "State of," "People of," or "Commonwealth of." However, if the case was decided by a court in the *same* state as the state that is the named party, omit the name of the state and substitute with its official designation, "State," "People," or "Commonwealth," for instance:

Bailey v. State of Hawaiʻi, 57 Haw. 144, 552 P.2d 365 (1976).

BECOMES

Bailey v. State, 57 Haw. 144, 552 P.2d 365 (1976).

When a borough, city, county, township, village, or the equivalent is the named party and begins the party name with "Borough of," "City of," "County of," "Township of," "Village of," or the equivalent, retain the full party name without abbreviating it, for instance: *Pickard v. City & County of Honolulu*, 51 Haw. 134, 452 P.2d 445 (1969). However, omit the expressions entirely if they fall in the middle of the party name of a municipal government agency, department, or division, and keep any geographic designation that follows, for instance:

Sandy Beach Defense Fund v. City Council of the City and County of Honolulu, 70 Haw. 361, 773 P.2d 250 (1989).

BECOMES

Sandy Beach Def. Fund v. City Council of Honolulu, 70 Haw. 361, 773 P.2d 250 (1989).

5. Court Location and Year Parenthetical

If the cited reporter does not indicate the court level or location, that information then needs to appear in the parenthetical at the end of the full case citation, along with the year the case was decided. The court is abbreviated as per T1. When citing a Hawaiʻi Supreme Court opinion decided after statehood, from either the *Official Hawaiʻi Reports* or *West's Hawaiʻi Reports*, the parenthetical only requires the year the case was decided because its location is indicated by the name of the reporter and in accordance with BB R. 10.4(b), the level of court is never included when the court of decision is the highest court of the state.

However, when citing Hawaiʻi Supreme Court cases decided before statehood, the local rules include the court location in the parenthetical, indicating either the Kingdom of Hawaiʻi or the different government systems that replaced Hawaiʻi's sovereignty (see Table 11-8). The abbreviation for the "Provisional Government" setup after the Kingdom's overthrow uses T6 and BB R. 10, which allows words of eight letters or more to be abbreviated if substantial space is saved and the result is unambiguous. "Kingdom" is seven letters and, thus, cannot take advantage of the rule. "Republic" is abbreviated as per T10.3 and "Territory," as per T7.

Table 11-8. Court Location for Pre-Statehood Hawaiʻi Case Law Citations

Pre-Statehood	Relevant Dates	Abbreviation
Kingdom of Hawaiʻi	On and before January 16, 1893	Haw. Kinqdom
Provisional Government	January 17, 1893 to July 3, 1894	Haw. Prov. Gov't
Republic of Hawaiʻi	July 4, 1894 to July 6, 1898	Haw. Rep.
Territory of Hawaiʻi	July 7, 1898 to August 20, 1959	Haw. Terr.

Table: Cory Lenz.

When citing an appellate court decision from the *Official Hawai'i Appellate Reports*, the parenthetical only requires the year the case was decided because its location and court level are indicated by the name of the reporter. However, this is not so when citing appellate court decisions from *West's Hawai'i Reports*. To indicate court level, the T1 Table in the *Bluebook* requires the abbreviation "Ct. App." in the parenthetical, while the local rules use only the abbreviation "App." Finally, when the reporter is the *Pacific Reporter*, Hawai'i Supreme Court decisions are abbreviated "Haw." in the parenthetical and those from the Hawai'i Intermediate Court of Appeals are abbreviated "Haw. Ct. App."

6. *Id.* and Modified Short Forms

Case law uses the *id.* short form when no intervening authority comes between the citation of a case and its subsequent citations. Omit the party names, the first volume number, and the first reporter from the parallel citation and replace with "*id.* at" followed by the pincite, even if citing to the same page or a different page. In the second part of the parallel citation, omit the case location and year parenthetical, but retain the Volume Number + Reporter + at + Pincite, followed by a period, for instance:

Kalipi v. Hawaiian Tr. Co., 66 Haw. 1, 11–12, 656 P.2d 745, 751–52 (1982).

NO INTERVENING AUTHORITY

Id. at 5, 656 P.2d at 748.

However, when a different authority intervenes between the citation of a case and its subsequent citation, use the modified short form. Omit the case location and year parenthetical but retain the First Party Name, followed by a comma + Volume Number + 1st Reporter + at + Pincite, followed by a comma + Volume Number + 2nd Reporter + at + Pincite, followed by a period, for instance:

Kalipi v. Hawaiian Tr. Co., 66 Haw. 1, 11–12, 656 P.2d 745, 751–52 (1982).

AFTER INTERVENING AUTHORITY

Kalipi, 66 Haw. at 5, 656 P.2d at 748.

When using the modified short form, business names are shortened to two words, although one is acceptable if a well-known business (e.g., Walmart). There are also instances when the first party name is avoided in favor of the second party name. When the legal document includes two cases with the same first party name, revert to the second party name in the modified short form for one of the case citations to avoid confusion for the reader. Additionally, when the first party name is a frequent litigant, such as the United States, an individual state, city, or the equivalent, or a government agency, department, or division, use the second party name, for instance:

County of Kauai v. Pac. Standard Life Ins., 65 Haw. 318, 653 P.2d 766 (1982).

AFTER INTERVENING AUTHORITY

Pac. Standard, 65 Haw. at 338, 653 P.2d at 780.

7. Procedural Phrases

Bluebook Rule 10.2.1(b) governs procedural phrases in case citations. When the first party name on either side of the "v." includes the expressions *on the relation of, for the use of, on behalf of, as next friend of,* or similar, abbreviate the expression as *ex rel.* Likewise, when the first party name on either side of the "v." includes the expressions *in the matter of, petition of, application of,* or similar, abbreviate the expression as *In re.* Retain all procedural phrases in the full citation and modified short form when the case is non-adversarial (e.g., probate or bankruptcy proceedings where only one party is captioned), for instance:

Application of Clinton Rutledge Ashford, 50 Haw. 314, 440 P.2d 76 (1968).

BECOMES

In re Ashford, 50 Haw. 314, 440 P.2d 76 (1968).

However, when the case is adversarial, drop all procedural phrases from the full citation and modified short form, except *ex rel.* The relator's name comes first followed by the represented party's name, for instance:

Troy S. Leong, a minor, by his next friend, Gail M. Petagno v. Takasaki, 55 Haw. 398, 520 P.2d 758 (1974).

BECOMES

Petagno ex rel. Leong v. Takasaki, 55 Haw. 398, 520 P.2d 758 (1974).

NO INTERVENING AUTHORITY

Id. at 410, 520 P.2d at 766.

AFTER INTERVENING AUTHORITY

Petagno ex rel. Leong, 55 Haw. at 410, 520 P.2d at 766.

8. Parentheticals and Subsequent History

Bluebook Rules 1.5 and 10.6 govern the additional parenthetical information that may follow the year in a case citation. Such parenthetical information may include the following, in the listed order: hereinafter short name; en banc; dissents and concurrences (e.g., Richardson, J., concurring); weight of authority (e.g., plurality opinion, per curiam); alterations to quoted material (e.g., emphasis added, footnote or citations omitted); quoting or citing another source; URL; explanatory parenthetical; prior or subsequent history.

The subsequent history, as per BB R. 10.7, is provided if the case is relevant to the argument being made and was addressed by the same or a higher court. The explanatory phrase introducing the subsequent history is underlined or italicized. However, unless relevant, omit denials of certiorari more than two years old, history on remand to a lower court, and denials of rehearing.

9. Citing Other State Cases and Federal Cases

All the same full citation, *id.* short form and modified short form rules apply when citing federal case law or other states' cases (see Table 11-9). The only distinction is these authorities do not require a parallel citation, so cite only to the official or preferred reporter as listed in T1 of the *Bluebook* under the relevant jurisdiction. Select the official or preferred reporter in T1 by locating the appropriate court level, the "Cite to [Reporter Name], if therein" language, and in some instances the date coverage of the reporter. Typically, the regional reporter is the preferred reporter when citing an outside state case.

Table 11-9. Full Citation and Short Forms, Outside States and Federal Case Law

	Outside State Opinion	Federal Opinion
Full Citation	*Elden v. Sheldon*, 758 P.2d 582, 584 (Cal. 1988). *Rodriguez v. Kirchhoefel*, 26 Cal. Rptr. 3d 891, 893 (Ct. App. 2005). *Pino v. Campo*, 19 Cal. Rptr. 2d 483, 484 (App. Dep't Super. Ct. 1993).	*Burwell v. Hobby Lobby Stores, Inc.*, 573 U.S. 682, 690 (2014). *Cunha v. Ward Foods, Inc.*, 804 F.2d 1418, 1424 (9th Cir. 1986). *Sherez v. Haw. Dep't of Educ.*, 396 F. Supp. 2d 1138, 1142 (D. Haw. 2005).

No Intervening Authority—Same Page—*Id.* Short Form	*Id.*	*Id.*
No Intervening Authority—Different Page—*Id.* Short Form	*Id.* at 586. *Id.* at 895. *Id.* at 485.	*Id.* at 685. *Id.* at 1420. *Id.* at 1140.
After Intervening Authority—Modified Short Form	*Elden*, 758 P.2d at 586. *Rodriguez*, 26 Cal. Rptr. 3d at 895. *Pino*, 19 Cal. Rptr. 2d at 485.	*Burwell*, 573 U.S. at 685. *Cunha*, 804 F.2d at 1420. *Sherez*, 396 F. Supp. 2d at 1140.

Table: Cory Lenz.

E. Secondary Sources

The specific citation forms for secondary sources are listed in Table 11-10. Secondary sources are only moderately cited in legal documents as persuasive authority and never alone when a primary authority exists on the issue. The Restatement is the only secondary source that can become primary authority if a state's highest court adopts it; once adopted, the relevant rule from the Restatement is then applied to the instant facts as statutory law would be. Likewise, the citation format of the Restatement in full and short form parallels that of a statute: the title and subject and publisher are abbreviated as per T6 in the full citation and the modified short form depends on the recentness of the citation and the possibility of any confusion (see Table 11-10).

The most significant distinction between the Restatement and other secondary sources is the citation format in the modified short form. All secondary sources adopt the *id.* short form. However, all except the Restatement incorporate the Latin phrase *supra* in the modified short form to indicate the source has been cited earlier; for instance, consider the citation format for the modified short form below:

Single Author: Author's Last Name, + *supra*, + Pincite.
  (only use "at" with a new page)

Two Authors: 1st Last Name + & + 2nd Last Name, + *supra*, + Pincite.
  (only use "at" with a new page)

| Three or More Authors: | 1st Last Name + et al., + *supra*, + Pincite. (only use "at" with a new page) |

In the parenthetical of the full citation, books and treatises might include publication information abbreviated as per T6 along with the year, e.g., editors (ed., or eds.,), translators (trans.,), specific editions (ed.) or supplements (supp.). A comma follows only the editor and translator abbreviations in the parenthetical. Book titles, annotation titles in ALR, and article titles in law reviews and journals are not abbreviated. However, periodical titles are abbreviated as per T6, T10, and T13. If the word "University" exists in the periodical title, use the abbreviation in T13 (U.), not in T6 (Univ.). Additionally, periodical titles remove the following articles, prepositions, and conjunctions—a, at, in, of, the—but retain the preposition "on."

Table 11-10. Full Citation and Short Forms, Secondary Sources

	Secondary Sources — Citation Examples			
	Restatements	Treatises & Books	American Law Reports	Law Reviews & Journals
Full Citation	Restatement (Second) of Torts § 338 (Am. Law Inst. 1965).	Samuel P. King & Randall W. Roth, *Broken Trust* 129 (2006).	Kate D. Reynaga, Annotation, *Observation Through Binoculars as Constituting Unreasonable Search*, 59 A.L.R.5th 615, 623 (1998).	Lu'ukia Nakanelua, *Na Mo'o o Ko'olau: The Water Guardians of Ko'olau Weaving and Wielding Collective Memory in the War for East Maui Water*, 41 U. Haw. L. Rev. 189, 223 (2018).
No Intervening Authority— *Id.* Short Form —Same page, §, ¶, cmt., or illus.	*Id.*	*Id.*	*Id.*	*Id.*

No Intervening Authority—*Id.* Short Form—Different page, §, ¶, cmt., illus.	*Id.* § 314A. *Id.* § 314A cmt. a.	*Id.* at 189.	*Id.* at 625.	*Id.* at 220.
After Intervening Authority—Modified Short Form	§ 314A. —or to avoid confusion— Torts § 314A. —OR— Restatement (Second) of Torts § 314A.	King & Roth, *supra*, at 189.	Reynaga, *supra*, at 625.	Nakanelua, *supra*, at 220.

Table: Cory Lenz.

III. Citing Hawaiʻi Legal Authority in Scholarship

A citation in a non-academic source like a legal document and an academic source like a scholarly article have the same parts and are identical but for the typeface and the modified short form, in some instances. The chart at the beginning of this Chapter shows all the typeface distinctions, e.g., constitutional, statutory, and regulatory sources of law and book titles and authors are written in ordinary roman type in non-academic writing; whereas, in academic writing they are written in small/large caps. Both styles of writing use the *id.* short form in the same manner.

The use of *supra* in the modified short form takes on greater prominence in academic writing. Primary sources of law, legislative materials (other than hearings), restatements, and model codes follow the same modified short form rules in academic writing as they do in non-academic writing, but for the typeface. Conversely in academic writing, court filings, secondary sources (except restatements and model codes), legislative hearings, treaties, and international agreements use *supra* in the modified short form. As per BB R. 4.2, construct the modified short form using *supra* in an academic citation as follows (e.g., Williston, *supra* note 45, § 3.):

Last Name of the Author, Full Institutional Name, or (if neither is available) the Title of the Work + comma + *supra* + note where full citation can be found + comma + new volume, page number, ¶, or § being cited.

Academic writing also adheres to the Five-Footnote Rule, which allows the writer to continue to use the short form if the case, statute, legislative material, regulation, or foreign and international equivalents can be readily found, in either full or short form, *in one of the preceding five footnotes.*[8] If the above-mentioned sources of law cannot be found in either full or short form, in one of the preceding five footnotes, the writer then uses the full citation again.

Table 11-11 gives examples of citations to Hawai'i sources of law and to secondary authorities to illustrate the differences between non-academic and academic citations, notably with regards to typeface and the use of *supra*.

Table 11-11. Non-Academic Versus Academic Citations

Source of Law	Type	Non-Academic Citations	Academic Citations
Constitution	Full	Haw. Const. art. XI, §§ 1, 9.	Haw. Const. art. XI, §§ 1, 9.
	Mod. Short	Haw. Const. art. XI, §§ 1, 9.	Haw. Const. art. XI, §§ 1, 9.
Statutes	Full	Haw. Rev. Stat. § 378-2(a)(1) (2015).	Haw. Rev. Stat. § 378-2(a)(1) (2015).
	Mod. Short	If confusion or not cited recently: Haw. Rev. Stat. § 378-2(a)(1).	If confusion or not cited recently: Haw. Rev. Stat. § 378-2(a)(1).

---

8. The Five-Footnote Rule applies to the following authorities: cases (BB R. 10.9), statutes (BB R. 12.10), legislative materials (BB R. 13.8), regulations (BB R. 14.5), and the foreign (BB R. 20.7) and international (BB R. 21.17) equivalents.

Regulations	Full	Hawai'i Administrative Rules (HAR) § 13-167-2 (effective May 27, 1988).	Hawai'i Administrative Rules (HAR) § 13-167-2 (effective May 27, 1988).
	Mod. Short	If confusion or not cited recently: HAR § 13-167-2.	If confusion or not cited recently: HAR § 13-167-2.
Case Law	Full	*Kalipi v. Hawaiian Tr. Co.*, 66 Haw. 1, 11–12, 656 P.2d 745, 751–52 (1982).	Kalipi v. Hawaiian Tr. Co., 66 Haw. 1, 11–12, 656 P.2d 745, 751–52 (1982).
	Mod. Short	*Kalipi*, 66 Haw. at 11–12, 656 P.2d at 751–52.	*Kalipi*, 66 Haw. at 11–12, 656 P.2d at 751–52.
Legislative Reports	Full	Comm. on Agric. & Env't, S. Stand. Comm. Rep. No. 2072, 29th Leg., Reg. Sess. (Haw. 2018), *reprinted in* 2018 Haw. S. J. 829.	Comm. on Agric. & Env't, S. Stand. Comm. Rep. No. 2072, 29th Leg., Reg. Sess. (Haw. 2018), *reprinted in* 2018 Haw. S. J. 829.
	Mod. Short	S. Stand. Comm. Rep. No. 2072, at 829.	S. Stand. Comm. Rep. No. 2072, at 829.
Bills	Full	S.B. 2582, 30th Leg., Reg. Sess. (Haw. 2020).	S.B. 2582, 30th Leg., Reg. Sess. (Haw. 2020).
	Mod. Short	Haw. S.B. 2582.	Haw. S.B. 2582.
Restatements	Full	Restatement (Second) of Torts § 338 (Am. Law Inst. 1965).	Restatement (Second) of Torts § 338 (Am. Law Inst. 1965).
	Mod. Short	If confusion or not cited recently: Torts § 338. -OR- Restatement (Second) of Torts § 338.	If confusion or not cited recently: Torts § 338. -OR- Restatement (Second) of Torts § 338.

Treatises & Books	Full	Samuel P. King & Randall W. Roth, *Broken Trust* 129 (2006).	Samuel P. King & Randall W. Roth, Broken Trust 129 (2006).
	Mod. Short	King & Roth, *supra*, at 189.	King & Roth, *supra* note 10, at 189.
ALR	Full	Kate D. Reynaga, Annotation, *Observation Through Binoculars as Constituting Unreasonable Search*, 59 A.L.R.5th 615, 623 (1998).	Kate D. Reynaga, Annotation, *Observation Through Binoculars as Constituting Unreasonable Search*, 59 A.L.R.5th 615, 623 (1998).
	Mod. Short	Reynaga, *supra*, at 625.	Reynaga, *supra* note 10, at 625.
Law Reviews & Journals	Full	Lu'ukia Nakanelua, *Na Mo'o o Ko'olau: The Water Guardians of Ko'olau Weaving and Wielding Collective Memory in the War for East Maui Water*, 41 U. Haw. L. Rev. 189, 223 (2018).	Lu'ukia Nakanelua, *Na Mo'o o Ko'olau: The Water Guardians of Ko'olau Weaving and Wielding Collective Memory in the War for East Maui Water*, 41 U. Haw. L. Rev. 189, 223 (2018).
	Mod. Short	Nakanelua, *supra*, at 220.	Nakanelua, *supra* note 10, at 220.

Table: Cory Lenz.

Appendix 1

Sample Research Plan[1]

Cover Page

[You can use one cover page for each matter, but a separate tracking document must be created for each issue. You might start with one issue but realize over time you have more than one subissue which will require different tracking plans.]

Client Matter:

Client Status: Plaintiff   Defendant   Other: _____

Deliverable: Internal Memo   Client Memo   Motion   Brief
               Oral Presentation   Other:_____

Due Date:

Jurisdiction: Hawai'i   Federal   Other: _____

Law: Hawai'i   Federal   Tribal   Other: _____

Court: Administrative   Trial   IAC   Supreme   Fed. District Court
         Ninth Circuit   Other:_____

Legal Doctrine/Potential Issue(s): [initial issue statement which should identify the controlling law, relevant facts and the legal issue. Draft more than one if applicable.]

Relief Sought: [monetary, specific performance, etc.]

---

1. Compiled by Victoria Szymczak.

Key Fact Grid:

	Description of relevant facts should include synonyms and draw attention to any relationships that exist between the parties/facts.
WHEN—Date of event	
WHO—Plaintiff	
WHO—Defendant	
WHAT caused the event	
WHAT was the harm	
WHAT are potential claims and defenses	

Sample Research Plan

Tracking Document

Issue Statement:

Working keywords and search strings:

[base your search strings on the keywords you identify in your fact grid]

West Digest Topics and Key Numbers:

TOPIC	KEY NUMBER

Secondary Sources: Finding Aids

Source	Keywords or Index	Lexis+ or WL	Cite	Notes
American Jurisprudence (Encyclopedia)				
Corpus Juris Secundum (Encyclopedia)				
ALR				
Dictionary				
Jury Instructions				
Practice Aids				
Court Documents				
Background Information				
Other				

Secondary Sources: Citable Resources

Source	Keywords or Search String	Source	Cite	Notes
Restatement				
Treatises				
Journal Articles				
Other				

Primary Authority

Source	Digest topic and key numbers or Search String	Source	Cite	Notes
Cases				
Statutes				
Regulations				
Constitution				
Treaties				

Appendix 2

Common Boolean Search Connectors[1]

Bloomberg Boolean Search Connectors

Connector	Use	Example
OR	Include any of the search terms in a document	Ship or vessel or boat
AND	Include all of the search terms in a document	Hearsay and evidence
NOT	Excludes a search term in a document	Capital and not gains
""	Exact phrase	"intellectual property"
NP/x	Search terms within a certain number of words of each other	Retirement NP5 benefit
S/	Search terms within the same sentence as each other	Contract S/ breach
P/	Search terms within the same paragraph as each other	Charity P/ "tax credit"
ATLx	Mentions the search term a certain number of times in the document	ATL5 co-conspirator

Lexis Boolean Search Connectors

Connector	Use	Example
OR	Includes any of the search terms in a document	Ship or vessel or boat
AND	Include all of the search terms in a document	Hearsay and evidence
NOT	Excludes a search term in a document	Capital and not gains

---

1. Compiled by Victoria Szymczak.

APPENDIX 2 · COMMON BOOLEAN SEARCH CONNECTORS

""	Exact phrase	"intellectual property"
/x	Search terms within a certain number of words of each other	Retirement /5 benefit
/S	Search terms within the same sentence as each other	Contract /s breach
/p	Search terms within the same paragraph as each other	Charity /p "tax credit"
AtleastX( )	Mentions the search term a certain number of times in the document	ATL5(co-conspirator)
&, AND	Include all of the search terms in a document	Hearsay and Evidence
/S	Search terms within the same sentence as each other	Contract /s breach
OR	Includes any of the search terms in a document	Ship or vessel or boat
/P	Search terms within the same paragraph as each other	Charity /p "tax credit"
""	Exact phrase	"intellectual property"
%	The percent symbol stands for the 'NOT' operators on Westlaw	Capital % gains
/X	Search terms within a certain number of words of each other	Retirement /5 benefit

Westlaw Boolean Connectors

Operator	Bloomberg	LEXIS+	Westlaw
Exact match	*"search phrase"*	*"search phrase"*	*"search phrase"*
Includes both terms	AND (default)	and | &	and | &
Includes at least one term	OR	or	[space between search terms = or] (default)
Terms within the same sentence	S/ | /S | /SENT	/s | w/s | w/sent	/s

APPENDIX 2 · COMMON BOOLEAN SEARCH CONNECTORS

Terms within the same paragraph	P/ | /P | /PARA	/p | w/p | w/para	/p
Terms within *x* words of one another (*x* is a number)	n/x | /x | w/x	/x | w/x	/x
Exclude terms	NOT | AND NOT | BUT NOT	and not	but not

The vertical bar | means "or" in this table.

Appendix 3

Citator Symbols[1]

Bloomberg Law BCite Signals as of November 2019

Red square with horizontal line	There is strong negative analysis of your cases indicating it has been reversed, vacated or depublished in full or in part.
Orange square with circle	Your case was superseded, displaced or rendered obsolete by an intervening statute, rule, or regulation.
Yellow square with a triangle	This is a caution symbol indicating that the legal reasoning in your case has been criticized by another court, or, the opinion was modified, clarified or amended by a subsequent decision within the direct history of your case.
Blue square with a diagonal line	This symbol indicates that your case was distinguished by the law or facts by another court.
Grey square with a plus sign	No courts have cited to your case.
Green square with a plus sign	One or more courts cite to, discuss, or follow your case with approval.

Lexis Shepard's Signals as of November 2019

Red Stop Sign	There is strong negative analysis impacting your case such as overruled or Reversed.
Red circle with red exclamation point	There is strong negative analysis impacting your statute. (i.e., held unconstitutional.
Orange square with the letter Q	The precedential value of your case is being questioned.
Yellow triangle	Your case received treatment that may be considered negative (i.e., distinguished)

---

1. Compiled by Victoria Szymczak.

Green diamond with a plus sign	Your case was followed by other cases and treated positively (i.e., affirmed)
Blue circle with the letter A	Your case was cited by not treated either positively or negatively.
Blue circle with the letter I	There are citing references for your case but there is no analysis by the citing court.

Westlaw KeyCite Signals as of November 2019

Red flag	Your case or statute is no longer good law for at least one of the points of law it contains (i.e., overruled or held unconstitutional).
Yellow flag	Your case or statute has some negative treatment (i.e., your case has been distinguished, or a bill is pending that will change the statute)
Blue striped flag	Your case has been appealed to the U.S. Court of Appeals or the U.S. Supreme Court (excluding appeals originating from agencies).

Index

ABA Journal, 82
Administrative law research,
    Hawai'i, 183-97
    Agencies, 186-89, 193-96
    Agency decisions on Lexis and Westlaw, 195-96
    Archives, 189, 194-95
    Case hearings and decisions, 193-97
    Citing references, 190-91, 196
    Enabling and implicating statutes, 184-85, 187-88, 191
    Hawai'i's Administrative Procedures Act (H.A.P.A.), 185-86
    Hawai'i Government Register, 186, 191-92
    Proposed rules, 186, 188, 191-92
    Rules and regulations on the Lt. Governor's website, 184-89, 192
    Rules and regulations on Lexis and Westlaw, 189
    Sample search on Lexis, 184, 189-91, 196-97
    Sample search on the Lt. Governor's website, 187-88, 191-92, 196
    Sample search on Westlaw, 184, 191, 196-97
    Steps in the research process, 184
    Updating, 191-92
Administrative law research, federal, 197-98, 206
    Administrative Procedures Act (A.P.A.), 197, 206
    Agency decisions, 205-06
    Archives, 199, 203, 205-06
    Citing references, 198
    Code of Federal Regulations (C.F.R.), 197-205
    C.F.R. Index, 202
    Enabling and implicating statutes, 197-98, 205
    Federal Register, 197-99, 202-05
    List of CFR Sections Affected (L.S.A.), 202-03
    Parallel Table of Authorities and Rules, 199, 200, 202
    Proposed rules, 198, 202-04
    Updating, 202-05
Advance sheets, digests, 98
Alexander Liholiho (*See* Kamehameha IV)
Allodial titles (*See* Kuleana Act)
A.L.R., (See American Law Reports)
Am Jur Causes of Action, 80
Am Jur Proof of Facts, 79
Am Jur Trials, 80
Amendments, constitutional, 50-51
American Jurisprudence, 64, 66-69
American Law Reports (A.L.R.), 64-67, 69, 231-32, 235

Annotations, constitution, 37-38, 44-50
Annotations, statutes, 132-33, 135, 145, 149-50
Articles (See Legal periodicals*)*
Asia – Pacific Law & Policy Journal, 71
Atlantic Reporter, 96
Attorney General opinions, 186, 192-96, 205-06

Bar journals, 81-82
BCite, 13-15, 129
Bennett test, 206
Bills, federal, 148
Bills, Hawaiʻi, 132, 159-63, 165-66, 169-81, 192, 234
Binding authority, 3, 5-6, 13, 15, 46, 63, 91, 104-06, 115, 120, 157, 205
Black's Law Dictionary, 73
Bluebook citation, 207-35
    Acronyms, 210, 220, 224
    Administrative law, 221-22
    Bluepages, 207-09, 213
    Case law (pre-statehood, state & federal), 222-30
    Case names, businesses, 224, 227
    Case names, geographic location as named party, 225-26, 228
    Case names, government agencies, 224-25, 228
    Case names, individuals, 223
    Citation clause, 210-11
    Citation sentence, 210-11
    Consecutive sections, 216
    Constitutional law (pre-statehood, state & federal), 214-15
    Court location, 222-23, 226-27
    Embedded citation, 210, 212
    Five footnote rule, 233
    Handbook of Citation Form for Law Clerks at the Appellate Courts of the State of Hawaiʻi, 209-10
    Id. short form, 208, 212, 214, 217-18, 221, 227-32
    Indigo Book: A Manual of Legal Citation, 213
    Introduction to Basic Legal Citation, 209
    Local rules for citing Hawaiʻi legal authority, 209-10, 215, 220-23, 226-27
    Modified short form, 212, 214, 217-22, 227-35
    Non-consecutive sections, 216
    Online and electronic statutory codes, 219-20
    Parallel citations, 222-29
    Parentheticals, 215-17, 219-23, 226-27, 229, 231
    Pincites, 222-23, 227-28, 230-31
    Procedural phrases, 208, 228
    Quick reference, 207
    Quoted material, 229
    Replacement volumes, 217
    Reporters, 222-23, 226-27, 229
    Revised Laws of Hawaiʻi, 220
    Secondary sources, 230-32, 234-35
    Signals, 212-13
    Statutory law (pre-statehood, state code), 215-20
    String citations, 212-13,
    Subject matter codes, 216-18
    Subsequent history, 229
    Supplements, 216-17
    Supra short form, 208, 230-35
    Tables, 207-09, 215, 221-35

INDEX   249

Typeface, 208-09, 213-15, 229, 232-35
Understanding and Mastering the Bluebook, 213
Whitepages, 207-09, 232-35
YouTube citation series, 213
Boolean connectors, 6-11, 40, 42, 47, 49, 198, 241
Bureau of Conveyances, 88

Canons of construction, 7
Case analysis, 105-06
Case citation, 222-30
Case digests, 107-11
Case headnotes, 101-02
Case reporters, 90-92, 222-23, 226-27
Case research, 105-29
Case updating, 120-29
Case verification, 120-29
C.F.R. *(See Code of Federal Regulations)*
Checklists
   Checklist for Developing a Research Plan, 5-6
   Checklist for Researching Native Hawaiian Custom and Law, 55
   Checklist for Constitutional Law Research, 37-38
   Post 1984 Hawai'i Legislative History Checklist, 159
Citation form (See Bluebook citation)
Citators,
   Generally, 13-15, 37-38, 46-49, 120, 190-91, 196, 198
   BCite, 13-15, 129
   KeyCite, 13-15, 51, 127-28, 205
   Shepard's, 13-15, 51, 122-26, 205

Symbols, 245
Treatment, 46-48, 121-22, 196
C.J.S. *(See Corpus Juris Secundum)*
Code of Federal Regulations (C.F.R.), 197-205
Codified statutes,
   Federal, 148-57
   Hawai'i, 131-48, 215-20
Committee reports, legislative, 25, 159-65, 167-70, 175, 177, 179-81, 234
Concurring opinion, 229
Constitutional law research
   1968 Constitution, 35-36, 41-42
   1978 Constitution, 36, 41-42
   Annotations, 37-38, 44-50
   Checklist, 37-38
   Citing references or decisions, 37-38, 46-49
   Constitutional conventions, 35-36, 38, 41-42, 50
   Constitutional interpretation, 29, 39, 44-54
   Constitution of 1840, 30, 41-42
   Constitution of 1852, 30-32, 41-42
   Constitution of 1864, 32-33, 41-42
   Constitution of 1887 ("Bayonet Constitution"), 33-34, 41-42
   Fundamental Law of Hawai'i, 31-33, 42
   Hawai'i, 29-54
   Hawai'i Revised Statutes, 40, 43-44
   Hawai'i State Archives Digital Collections, 41-42
   Hawai'i's unofficial statutory codes, 37-38, 43-44
   History, 30-36
   Key numbers, 46-47
   Kingdom of Hawai'i, 30-34

LLMC Digital, 31-33, 37-38, 41-43
Notes of decisions, 37-38, 46-49
Overthrow & Republic of Hawai'i Constitution, 34, 41-42
Sample search on Lexis, 39-40, 48-51
Sample search on Westlaw, 39-40, 46-51
Statehood Constitution, 35, 41-42
Territory of Hawai'i Constitution ("Organic Act"), 34-35, 41-42
Updating by amendment, 50-51
Corpus Juris Secundum (C.J.S.), 64, 69
Current Awareness Resources, 81-82

Descriptive Word Index, 109-10
Dicta, 104
Dictionary, 72-74
Digests, 107
Digest Topics and Key Numbers, 15-16, 46-47, 107-11
Dissenting opinions, 104, 229
District courts, 87, 90
Docket number, 101-02

Enabling statutes, 184-85, 187-88, 191, 197-98, 205
Enacted law, 147, 159, 161, 163, 180, 192
En banc panel, 103 (f11), 229
Encyclopedias, 64-69
Environmental Courts, 87-88
Estee's Reports, 97
Ethics, 52, 192, 196
Executive orders, 186, 197, 199
Explanatory parentheticals, 215-17, 219-23, 226-27, 229, 231

Federal administrative law, 183, 197-206
Federal cases (*See* Federal research)
Federal constitution, 29, 51-52
Federal court system, 89-90
Federal digests (*See* Federal research)
Federal district courts, 90
Federal Practice and Procedure, 80
Federal Practice Digest (*See* Federal research)
Federal Register, 197-99, 202-05
Federal Reporter, 97
Federal reporters, 97
Federal research,
    Administrative law, 183, 197-206
    Cases, 97, 105-06
    Digests, 107-11
    Reporters, 97-98
    Statutes, 148-51
Federal Supplement, 97
Five footnote rule, 233

Generating search terms, 6-11
Good law, 120-29
Governor's statement, 186, 192
Great Mahele, 30-31

Hawai'i Administrative Rules, 55, 184-89, 192
Hawai'i Appellate Courts, 86, 222, 227
Hawai'i Appellate Reports, 95, 222, 227
Hawai'i Attorney General opinions, 186, 192-96
Hawai'i Bar Journal, 81
Hawai'i case law, 67, 93, 97, 99, 105-07, 112-14, 145, 157

INDEX

Hawaiʻi case law, citation, 222-29
Hawaiʻi case updating (*See* BCite, KeyCite, Shepard's or Citators generally)
Hawaiʻi committee reports, legislative, 25, 161-79, 234
Hawaiʻi Constitution, 35-36, 41-42
Hawaiʻi Constitutional Convention, 35-36, 38, 41-42, 50
Hawaiʻi courts, 85-89
Hawaiʻi Digest, 107
Hawaiʻi district courts, 87
Hawaiʻi Environmental Courts, 87-88
Hawaiʻi Government Register, 186, 191-92
Hawaiʻi Intermediate Court of Appeals, 36, 86-87, 222, 227
Hawaiʻi judiciary, 85-89
Hawaiʻi Land Court, 88
Hawaiʻi Law Review (See University of Hawaiʻi Law Review)
Hawaiʻi legislative history, 159-81
Hawaiʻi Legislature, 131-33, 139, 141, 146-47, 155, 159-78
Hawaiʻi practitioner aids, 77-78
Hawaiʻi reporters, 93-95, 222, 226-27
Hawaiʻi Reports, 93-95, 222, 226-27
Hawaiʻi research process, 3-17, 48, 61-62, 78, 157-58, 191
Hawaiʻi Revised Statutes,
   Citation, 215-20
   Constitutional law research, 40, 43-44
   Court rules research (*See* Rules, Court)
   Index volumes, 27-28, 40, 41 (fn), 144
   Interpretation, 14 (fn), 28, 43 (fn), 44, 52, 144, 206
   Legislative history research, 159-81
   Legislative journals, 147, 159-81
   Online research, 132-36, 141, 145
   Print research, 43, 112, 121, 132, 135, 143-44, 147
   Prior codifications, 20-21, 28
   Statutory research, 131-48
   Tables of Disposition, 147-48, 166
Hawaiʻi Revised Statutes Annotated, online, 136
Hawaiʻi Rules of Professional Conduct (*See* Ethics, and Rules, Ethics, and Rules of Professional Conduct)
Hawaiʻi Session Laws, 20, 28, 41, 50, 88, 132, 139, 146-47, 159-60, 163, 166, 180
Hawaiʻi State Archives, 24, 161, 169 (fn), 195
Hawaiʻi State Archives Digital Collections, 37-38, 41-42
Hawaiʻi Supreme Court, 86-87, 222, 226-27
Hawaiʻi Tax Appeal Court, 89
Hawaiʻi Trial Courts, 87
Hawaiian Dictionary: Hawaiian-English, English-Hawaiian, 74
Hawaiian Reports, 93-94, 226
Headnotes,
   Digests, 107
   Generally, 6, 13, 14 (fn), 15, 18, 46, 95, 99, 102-03, 106-07, 115-19, 121-25, 127-28
   KeyCite, 127-28
   Reporters, 101-02, 117
   Shepard's, 125

252   INDEX

Topic and Key Number Searching, 15-16, 46-47, 67, 73, 95, 107-13, 118
Hearings
    Administrative, 193-94
    Legislative (*See also* committee reports), 209, 232
HeinOnline, Generally, 4, 41 (fn), 71-72, 203, 205
Historical citations, case law, 226
Historical citations, legislative, 220
Historical statutory codes, 20-21, 28
House Journal, 159, 167, 169-70, 174-79, 181

Judicial opinions, parts of, 101-04
    Caption, 101-02
    Citation, 100, 222-30
    Concurring opinions, 104
    Date of opinion, 101-02
    Dicta, 104
    Dissenting opinions, 104
    Headnotes, 101-02
    Holding, 104
    Majority opinions, 104
    Names of attorneys, 101, 103
    Parallel citation, 100
    Plurality opinions, 104
    Procedural history, 104
    Title, 101-02
    Syllabus, 101-02
    Synopsis, 101-02
Jump cite (*See* Pinpoint citation)
Jury instructions, 78-79

Kalakaua, David (King), 21, 33-34
Kamaka'eha, Lydia (See Lili'uokalani)
Kamehameha
    III (Kauikeaouli), 20, 22 (fn), 30-31, 42 (fn)
    IV (Alexander Liholiho), 20, 32
    V (Lot), 21, 32-33, 42 (fn)
Kānaka Maoli (Native Hawaiian people), 55-59
Kauikeaouli (*See* Kamehameha III)
Ke Alakai o Ki Kanaka Hawai'i, 92-93
KeyCite, 13-15, 51, 83, 126-28, 152-58, 205, 246
Key Number system, 15, 46-47, 67-68, 73, 107-18
Keyword searching, 6-11, 38-41, 49, 112-15, 144, 190, 198-99, 202, 205, 241
Kuleana Act, 30-31, 57-59

Land Courts, 86-88
Law reviews and journals, 81-82, 231-32, 235
Lee, William Little, 20, 59 (fn)
Legal encyclopedias, 64-69
Legal periodicals, 71-72, 231-32, 235
Legislative history research, 159-81
Legislative process, 161, 169
Legislative Reference Bureau (LRB), 24, 41 (fn), 139, 185, 196
LexisNexis, Generally, 4, 15, 82
Library of Congress, 93 (fn)
Lieutenant Governor of Hawai'i's website, 184-89
Liholiho, Alexander (*See* Kamehameha IV)
Lili'uokalani (Queen), 34
List of CFR Sections Affected (L.S.A.), 202-03
LLMC Digital, 4, 31-33, 37-38, 41-43, 196

Loose-leaf services, 84
Lot (See Kamehameha V)
Lunalilo (King), 32-33

Māhele (*See* Great Māhele)
Majority opinion, 104
Mandatory authority, 3, 105-06 (*See also* Binding authority)
Martial law research, 26-27
Michie's Hawai'i Revised Statutes Annotated, 40, 43, 133, 136, 143-45, 162
Model acts or codes, 6, 12-13, 131, 208, 232
Moore's Federal Practice, 81

National Law Journal, 82
Native Hawaiian Custom and Law, (*See* Kānaka Maoli)
Native Hawaiian Law, a Treatise, 55-57
Natural language searching, 115
Ninth Circuit Court of Appeals, 229-30
North Eastern Reporter, 96
North Western Reporter, 96
Notes of decisions, 37-38, 44-49, 145

Office of the Attorney General, 194, 196, 205-06
Official Reporters, 92
Opinions (*See also* Judicial opinions, parts of)
   Strategies for research, 105-20
   Updating with citators, 120-29
   Verifying good law, 120-29
Organic Act, 34-35, 40-43

Pacific Reporter, 96, 222, 227

Parallel citations, 100, 222-29
Parties and procedural designations, 208, 222-30
Per curiam, 104, 229
Periodicals, 71-72
Persuasive authority, 41, 46, 48, 105-06, 230
Pinpoint citation, 222-23, 227-28, 230-31
Pocket parts, 50, 69, 83, 139, 216-17, 231
Polynesian, 93 (fn)
Practitioner Aids, 77-81
   Am Jur Proof of Facts, 79
   Am Jur Trials, 80
   Am Jur Causes of Action, 80
   Hawai'i specific, 77-79
   Federal Practice and Procedure, 80
   Moore's Federal Practice, 81
   Weinstein's Federal Evidence, 81
Primary authority, 3, 16, 18, 44, 55, 61, 64, 77, 82, 183, 230, 232, 240
Principles of the Law, 75, 77
Proposed rules, 186, 188, 191-92, 198, 202-04
Proximity connectors, 5, 8-9, 198
Public hearings, administrative, 185-86
Public law number, 148-49
Public Trust Doctrine, 54

Quoting authority, 229

Regional reporters, 95-96, 222, 229
Regulations (*See* Administrative law research)
Reported opinions, 90-91
Reporters, 90-92, 222-23
   Federal cases, 97-98, 229-30

Hawaiʻi cases, 92-97, 222-29
Updating, 98
Reports of Cases Determined in the District Court for the District of Hawaiʻi, 97
Research log, 5, 12-13, 57, 131, 150
Research notes (*See* Research log and Research plan)
Research plan, 46-48, 52, 64-65, 67-69, 131, 184, 188, 191, 196, 237-40
Research terms (*See* Search terms)
Research vocabulary (*See* Generating search terms)
Restatements, 75-76, 230-34
Revised Laws of Hawaiʻi, 21, 88 (fn), 163, 220
Ricord, John, 20, 22 (fn)
Rulemaking, 188, 191, 197-99, 202
Rules,
    Administrative, 184-89, 191-92
    Court, 40, 48, 89, 91, 149, 207, 209
    Ethics, 192, 196
Rules of Professional Conduct, 48, 52, 207

Search string, 38-40, 49, 114-15, 184, 189, 191, 197
Search terms, 5-11, 38, 40, 42, 114, 189
Secondary authority, 61, 233
Secondary sources, 29, 37-40, 43-46, 48, 51, 61-63, 189, 191, 198, 230-35
    Am Jur Causes of Action, 80
    Am Jur Proof of Facts, 79
    Am Jur Trials, 80
    American Jurisprudence, 2d, 64-67, 69

American Law Reports, 69-70
Articles,
Bar journals, 81-82
Citations, 230-35
Corpus Juris Secundum, 64, 69
Dictionaries, 72-74
Encyclopedias, 64-69
Federal Practice and Procedure, 80
Finding aids, 63-64
Highly persuasive secondary sources, 71-72
Jury instructions, 78-79
Loose-leaf services, 84
Moore's Federal Practice, 81
Periodicals, 71-72
Persuasive authority, 63, 71-77
Practitioner aids, 77-78
Principles of the Law, 75, 77
Restatements, 75-76
Topical, 82
Treatises, 74-75
Types, 63
Uniform laws and model codes, 131, 208
Updating, generally, 83-84
Use in research process, 61, 65, 68
Weinstein's Federal Evidence, 81
Senate Journal, 160, 163, 167-81
Session laws, 50, 88, 132, 146-49, 155, 161-66, 180
Shepard's, 13-15, 51, 120-126, 205
Shepardize (*See also* Shepard's), 120-26
Signals, citation, 212-13, 245
South Eastern Reporter, 96
South Western Reporter, 96
Southern Reporter, 96
Stare decisis, 105

State Constitutional Conventions, 30, 35-36, 38, 41-42, 50
Statement of purpose, 166, 169
Statutes,
   Canons of construction, 139
   Citation, 215-20
   Definitions, 138, 143, 150
   Enabling, 184-85, 187-88, 191, 197-98, 205
   Federal, 148-57
   Hawaiʻi research, 131-48
   Online, 136
   Pocket parts, 50, 139
   Research process, 131
   Updating (*See also* shepardize and validate), 6, 13-14, 152-56
Statutes at Large, 25, 148-49, 199
Statutory construction, 139
Statutory research, federal, 148-57
Statutory research, Hawaiʻi, 131-48
Supreme Court of the United States, 90
Supreme Court Reporter (S. Ct.), 98
Supreme Court Reporter, Lawyers' Edition (L. Ed. 2d), 98
Synopsis, 32

Tax Appeal Court, 89
Temporary Laws, 146-48
Terms-and-connectors searching, 10-11, 47, 49
Territory of Hawaiʻi research, 25-26
Topic searching, 82
Torrens, 88
Treatises, 74-75, 231-32, 235
Treatise Finders, 74
Trial courts, 87, 90

Uniform laws, 131, 208
Uniform Laws Annotated, 131
United States Code (U.S.C.), 44, 145, 149-51, 199
United States Code Annotated (U.S.C.A.), 149-50
United States Code Service (U.S.C.S.), 149-50
United States Constitution, 29, 51-52, 214
United States Courts of Appeals, 97, 103, 105, 156, 206
United States District Courts, 89-90, 97
United States Reports (U.S.), 229-30
United States Statutes at Large, 25, 148-49, 199
United States Supreme Court, 53, 54 (fn), 90, 103 (fn), 105, 156, 246
University of Hawaiʻi Law Review, 71, 231-32, 235
Unofficial codes, 37, 44, 133, 136, 149-51, 162, 215-17, 219-20
Unofficial reporters, 92, 95-96, 205
Unpublished opinions, 48, 91 (fn)
Unreported opinions, 90-91, 102, 115, 123
Updating (*See also* shepardize and validate),
   Cases, 120-29
   Federal regulations, 202-05
   Generally, 13-14
   Hawaiʻi administrative rules, 191-92
   Hawaiʻi state statutes, 139
   Secondary Sources, 75, 83-84

Validate, 6, 12-13, 99, 121, 131, 152, 155
Veto, 33, 132, 148, 159-60, 163

Weinstein's Federal Evidence, 81

West's Hawai'i Reports, 222, 226-27
West's Hawai'i Revised Statutes Annotated, 43, 133, 135, 145, 162